SOURCES FOR PATTERNS OF WORLD HISTORY

VOLUME TWO: SINCE 1400

SOURCES FOR PATTERNS OF WORLD HISTORY

VOLUME TWO: SINCE 1400

EDITED BY

Jonathan S. Perry
UNIVERSITY OF SOUTH FLORIDA, SARASOTA-MANATEE

NEW YORK   OXFORD
OXFORD UNIVERSITY PRESS

Oxford University Press is a department of the University of Oxford.
It furthers the University's objective of excellence in research,
scholarship, and education by publishing worldwide.

Oxford   New York
Auckland   Cape Town   Dar es Salaam   Hong Kong   Karachi
Kuala Lumpur   Madrid   Melbourne   Mexico City   Nairobi
New Delhi   Shanghai   Taipei   Toronto

With offices in
Argentina   Austria   Brazil   Chile   Czech Republic   France   Greece
Guatemala   Hungary   Italy   Japan   Poland   Portugal   Singapore
South Korea   Switzerland   Thailand   Turkey   Ukraine   Vietnam

For titles covered by Section 112 of the US Higher Education
Opportunity Act, please visit www.oup.com/us/he for the
latest information about pricing and alternate formats.

Published in the United States of America by
Oxford University Press
198 Madison Avenue, New York, NY 10016
http://www.oup.com

Library of Congress Cataloging-in-Publication Data
Sources in Patterns of world history / [edited by] Jonathan Perry. -- Second edition.
    volumes cm
    Summary: "A sourcebook of primary sources collected to complement OUP's
textbook Patterns of World History, 2nd edition"--Provided by publisher.
    Contents: Volume One. To 1600 -- Volume Two. Since 1400.
    ISBN 978-0-19-939972-7 (volume 1 : paperback : acid-free paper) --
ISBN 978-0-19-939973-4 (volume 2 : paperback : acid-free paper) 1. World history--Sources.
I. Perry, Jonathan Scott. II. Von Sivers, Peter. Patterns of world history.
    D21.S6755 2015
    909--dc23
                                                            2014020327

Printing number: 9 8 7 6 5 4 3 2 1

Printed in the United States of America
on acid-free paper

CONTENTS

HOW TO READ A PRIMARY SOURCE

This sourcebook is composed of eighty-five primary sources. A primary source is any text, image, or other source of information that gives us a first-hand account of the past by someone who witnessed or participated in the historical events in question. While such sources can provide significant and fascinating insight into the past, they must also be read carefully to limit modern assumptions about historical modes of thought. Here are a few elements to keep in mind when approaching a primary source.

AUTHORSHIP

Who produced this source of information? A male or a female? A member of the elite or of the lower class? An outsider looking *in* at an event or an insider looking *out*? What profession or lifestyle does the author pursue, which might influence how he is recording his information?

GENRE

What type of source are you examining? Different genres—categories of material—have different goals and stylistic elements. For example, a personal letter meant exclusively for the eyes of a distant cousin might include unveiled opinions and relatively trivial pieces of information, like the writer's vacation plans. On the other hand, a political speech intended to convince a nation of a leader's point of view might subdue personal opinions beneath artful rhetoric and focus on large issues like national welfare or war. Identifying genre can be useful for deducing how the source may have been received by an audience.

AUDIENCE

Who is reading, listening to, or observing the source? Is it a public or private audience? National or international? Religious or nonreligious? The source may be geared toward the expectations of a particular group; it may be recorded in a language that is specific to a particular group. Identifying audience can help us understand why the author chose a certain tone or why he included certain types of information.

HISTORICAL CONTEXT

When and why was this source produced? On what date? For what purposes? What historical moment does the source address? It is paramount that we approach primary sources in context to avoid anachronism (attributing an idea or habit to a past era where it does not belong) and faulty judgment. For example, when considering a medieval history, we must take account of the fact that in the Middle Ages, the widespread understanding was that God created the world and could still interfere in the activity of mankind—such as sending a terrible storm when a community had sinned. Knowing the context (Christian, medieval, views of the world) helps us to avoid importing modern assumptions—like the fact that storms are caused by atmospheric pressure—into historical texts. In this way we can read the source more faithfully, carefully, and generously.

BIAS AND FRAMING

Is there an overt argument being made by the source? Did the author have a particular agenda? Did any political or social motives underlie the reasons for writing the document? Does the document exhibit any qualities that offer clues about the author's intentions?

STYLISTIC ELEMENTS

Stylistic features such as tone, vocabulary, word choice, and the manner in which the material is organized and presented should also be considered when examining a source. They can provide insight into the writer's perspective and offer additional context for considering a source in its entirety.

SOURCES FOR PATTERNS OF WORLD HISTORY

VOLUME TWO: SINCE 1400

15. THE RISE OF EMPIRES IN THE AMERICAS, 600–1550 CE

15.1 The Temple of the Jaguars, Chichén Itzá, ca. 850–1000 CE

Chichén Itzá was founded during a period of renewed urbanization in the Mayan states around 650, and a remarkable state flourished in its vicinity between 850 and 1000. The population was composed of local Maya, as well as Maya-speaking peoples from the Gulf of Mexico coast. It owed its prosperity to long-distance trade, both overland and in boats along the coast. Around 1000, the ruling-class factions abandoned Chichén Itzá for unknown reasons, and the city-state dwindled in size to the level of a town.

Dreamstime/© Alexandre Fagundes De Fagundes (above); Shutterstock/Danilo Ascione (on next page)

WORKING WITH SOURCES

1. What does the construction of this monument suggest about the social structure of Chichén Itzá at its height?
2. What might have been the significance of the jaguars? Why would the temple have been decorated in such an elaborate fashion?

15.2   Skeletons in a Wari Royal Tomb Site, El Castillo de Huarmey, Peru, ca. 600–1000 CE

In 2013, 63 skeletons were discovered in a tomb at El Castillo de Huarmey, about 175 miles north of Lima, in what would seem to be the first imperial tomb of the Wari culture discovered in modern times. Most of the bodies were female, and wrapped in bundles in a seated position typical of Wari burials. Three of the women appear to have been Wari queens, as they were buried

---

Source: REUTERS/Enrique Castro-Mendivil.

with gold and silver jewelry and brilliantly painted ceramics. However, six of the skeletons were not wrapped in the textiles, but instead positioned on top of the burials. Archaeologists have concluded that these people may have been sacrificed for the benefit of the others.

WORKING WITH SOURCES

1. How do the burial practices of Wari culture compare with those of other civilizations in Mesoamerica and the Andes?
2. What might this tomb suggest about the roles and expectations of women in Wari culture?

15.3   Bernal Díaz, *The Conquest of New Spain*, ca. 1568

In the course of the fifteenth century, the Aztecs established an empire centered in the Valley of Mexico (surrounding present-day Mexico City, after the drainage of most of the valley) but encompassing Mesoamerica from the Pacific to the Gulf of Mexico. The resulting state, far more

Source: The Conquest of New Spain, translated with an introduction by J. M. Cohen (Penguin Classics, 1963), pp. 232–234. Copyright © J. M. Cohen, 1963. Reproduced by permission of Penguin Books Ltd.

centralized than the preceding Teotihuacán and Toltec city-states, commanded a large extent of territory and thrived on the trade in raw materials that were brought in from both coasts of their empire. Bernal Díaz, born in 1492 in Spain, would join the Spaniards in the "conquest" of Mexico, but he also left behind vivid eyewitness accounts of occupied Aztec society in the sixteenth century. Among them is this description of the market in Tlatelolco, one of the central cities at the heart of Aztec imperial power.

Our Captain and those of us who had horses went to Tlatelolco mounted, and the majority of our men were fully equipped. On reaching the market-place, escorted by the many *Caciques* whom Montezuma had assigned to us, we were astounded at the great number of people and the quantities of merchandise, and at the orderliness and good arrangements that prevailed, for we had never seen such a thing before. The chieftains who accompanied us pointed everything out. Every kind of merchandise was kept separate and had its fixed place marked for it.

Let us begin with the dealers in gold, silver, and precious stones, feathers, cloaks, and embroidered goods, and male and female slaves who are also sold there. They bring as many slaves to be sold in that market as the Portuguese bring Negroes from Guinea. Some are brought there attached to long poles by means of collars round their necks to prevent them from escaping, but others are left loose. Next there were those who sold coarser cloth, and cotton goods and fabrics made of twisted thread, and there were chocolate merchants with their chocolate. In this way you could see every kind of merchandise to be found anywhere in New Spain, laid out in the same way as goods are laid out in my own district of Medina del Campo, a centre for fairs, where each line of stalls has its own particular sort. So it was in this great market. There were those who sold sisal cloth and ropes and the sandals they wear on their feet, which are made from the same plant. All these were kept in one part of the market, in the place assigned to them, and in another part were skins of tigers and lions, otters, jackals, and deer, badgers, mountain cats, and other wild animals, some tanned and some untanned, and other classes of merchandise.

. . .

Then there were the sellers of pitch-pine for torches, and other things of that kind, and I must also mention, with all apologies, that they sold many canoe-loads of human excrement, which they keep in the creeks near the market. This was for the manufacture of salt and the curing of skins, which they say cannot be done without it. I know that many gentlemen will laugh at this, but I assure them it is true. I may add that on all the roads they have shelters made of reeds or straw or grass so that they can retire when they wish to do so, and purge their bowels unseen by passers-by, and also in order that their excrement shall not be lost.

But why waste so many words on the goods in their great market? If I describe everything in detail I shall never be done. Paper, which in Mexico they call *amal*, and some reeds that smell of liquidamber, and are full of tobacco, and yellow ointments and other such things, are sold in a separate part. Much cochineal is for sale too, under the arcades of that market, and there are many sellers of herbs and other such things. They have a building there also in which three judges sit, and there are officials like constables who examine the merchandise. I am forgetting the sellers of salt and the makers of flint knives, and how they split them off the stone itself, and the fisher-women and the men who sell small cakes made from a sort of weed which they get out of the great lake, which curdles and forms a kind of bread which tastes rather like cheese. They sell axes too, made of bronze and copper and tin, and gourds and brightly painted wooden jars.

We went on to the great *cue*, and as we approached its wide courts, before leaving the market-place itself, we saw many more merchants who, so I was told, brought gold to sell in grains, just as they extract it

---

Caciques: Nobles.

Cue: Temple.

from the mines. This gold is placed in the thin quills of the large geese of that country, which are so white as to be transparent. They used to reckon their accounts with one another by the length and thickness of these little quills, how much so many cloaks or so many gourds of chocolate or so many slaves were worth, or anything else they were bartering.

WORKING WITH SOURCES

1. How and why does Díaz use comparisons from other markets while describing the one in Tlatelolco?
2. What do the specific elements of this market suggest about the importance of trade and commerce in pre-Columbian Mexico?

15.4   Pedro Cieza de León on Incan Roads, 1541–1547

The Incas created an imperial communications and logistics infrastructure that was unparalleled in the Americas, with two highways extending to the north and south from Cuzco nearly the entire length of the empire. The roads, which were up to 12 feet wide, crossed the terrain as directly as possible, which clearly required a tremendous labor force to create. In many places, even today, the 25,000-mile road network still exists. Pedro Cieza de León was born in Spain in 1520 and undoubtedly traveled along the extensive, and still-functional, Roman road system of his native land as a child. When he arrived in the New World at the age of 13, he was captivated and impressed by the civilizations that the Spanish were supplanting. In 1541, he began writing his account of the Incas, tracing their heritage and government for the benefit of those who would never see the territory he did—or travel the roads that made his observations possible.

CHAPTER 42 (II.XV)

Of how the buildings for the Lord-Incas were constructed, and the highways to travel through the kingdom [of Peru].

One of the things that most took my attention when I was observing and setting down the things of this kingdom was how and in what way the great, splendid highways we see throughout it could be built, and the number of men that must have been required, and what tools and instruments they used to level the mountains and cut through the rock to make them as broad and good as they are. For it seems to me that if the Emperor were to desire another highway built like the one from Quito to Cuzco, or that which goes from Cuzco to Chile, truly I do not believe he could do it, with all his power and the men at his disposal, unless he followed the method the Incas employed. For if it were a question of a road fifty leagues long, or a hundred, or two hundred, we can assume that, however rough the land, it would not be too difficult, working hard, to do it. But there were so long, one of them more than 1100 leagues, over mountains so rough and dismaying that in certain places one could not see bottom, and some of the sierras so sheer and barren that the road had to be cut through the living

Source: Pedro Cieza de León, *The Incas*, trans. Harriet de Onis, ed. Victor Wolfgang von Hagen (Norman: University of Oklahoma Press, 1959), 135–137.

rock to keep it level and the right width. All this they did with fire and picks.

. . .

When a Lord-Inca had decided on the building of one of these famous highways, no great provisioning or levies or anything else was needed except for the Lord-Inca to say, let this be done. The inspectors then went through the provinces, laying out the route and assigning Indians from one end to the other to the building of the road. In this way, from one boundary of the province to the other, at its expense and with its Indians, it was built as laid out, in a short time; and the others did the same, and, if necessary, a great stretch of the road was built at the same time, or all of it. When they came to the barren places, the Indians of the lands nearest by came with victuals and tools to do the work, and all was done with little effort and joyfully, because they were not oppressed in any way, nor did the Incas put overseers to watch them.

Aside from these, great fine highways were built, like that which runs through the valley of Xaquixahuana, and comes out of the city of Cuzco and goes by the town of Muhina. There were many of these highways all over the kingdom, both in the highlands and the plains. Of all, four are considered the main highways, and they are those which start from the city of Cuzco, at the square, like a crossroads, and go to the different provinces of the kingdom. As these monarchs held such a high opinion of themselves, when they set out on one of these roads, the royal person with the necessary guard took one [road], and the rest of the people another. So great was their pride that when one of them died, his heir, if he had to travel to a distant place, built his road larger and broader than that of his predecessor, but this was only if this Lord-Inca set out on some conquest, or [performed] some act so noteworthy that it could be said the road built for him was longer.

WORKING WITH SOURCES

1. How were the Incas' roads a manifestation of royal power, at least in Cieza de León's estimation?
2. What technical challenges faced the Incan road builders, and how did they overcome them?

15.5 Garcilaso de la Vega, "The Walls and Gates of Cuzco," 1609–1616

The Incan city of Cuzco was an elongated triangle formed by the confluence of two rivers. At one end, enormous, zigzagging walls followed the contours of a steep hill. The walls were built with stone blocks weighing up to 100 tons and cut so precisely that no mortar was needed. The ruins of the walls were still visible after the Spanish siege of 1536 (as they are today), and they were a marvel to Garcilaso de la Vega, when he viewed them in the mid-sixteenth century. Garcilaso was born in 1539, the decade of the conquest of Peru, to a Spanish conqueror and a Native American princess, a second cousin of the last two Inca rulers. As a young man, Garcilaso left his native Peru never to return. Toward the end of his life he retired to a secluded Spanish village, where he wrote his general history of the Incas. He was particularly proud of the monumental achievements of his Incan relatives, and of the power that their construction projects represented.

Source: Garcilaso de la Vega, *Royal Commentaries of the Incas and General History of Peru,* trans. Harold V. Livermore (Austin: University of Texas Press, 1966), vol. 1, 463–468.

CHAPTER XXVII

The fortress of Cuzco; the size of its stones.

The Inca kings of Peru made marvelous buildings, fortresses, temples, royal palaces, gardens, storehouses, roads, and other constructions of great excellence, as can be seen even today from their remaining ruins, though the whole building can scarcely be judged from the mere foundations.

The greatest and most splendid building erected to show the power and majesty of the Incas was the fortress of Cuzco, the grandeur of which would be incredible to anyone who had not seen it, and even those who have seen it and considered it with attention imagine, and even believe, that it was made by enchantment, the handiwork of demons, rather than of men. Indeed the multiplicity of stones, large and small, of which the three **circumvallations** are composed (and they are more like rocks than stones) makes one wonder how they could have been quarried, for the Indians had neither iron nor steel to work them with. And the question of how they were conveyed to the site is no less difficult a problem, since they had no oxen and could not make wagons: nor would oxen and wagons have sufficed to carry them. They were in fact heaved by main force with the aid of thick cables. The roads by which they were brought were not flat, but rough mountainsides with steep slopes, up and down which the rocks were dragged by human effort alone.

. . .

CHAPTER XXVIII

The three circumvallations, the most remarkable part of the work.

Circumvallations: Walls built around the city.

On the other side, opposite this wall, there is a large level space. From this direction the ascent to the top of the hill is a gradual one up which an enemy could advance in order of battle. The Incas therefore made three concentric walls on the slopes, each of which would be more than two hundred fathoms long. They are in the shape of a half moon, for they close together at the ends to meet the other wall of smooth masonry on the side facing the city. The first of these three walls best exhibits the might of the Incas, for although all three are of the same workmanship, it is the most impressive and has the largest stones, making the whole construction seem incredible to anyone who has not seen it, and giving an impression of awe to the careful observer who ponders on the size and number of the stones and the limited resources of the natives for cutting and working them and setting them in their places.

. . .

Almost in the middle of each wall there was a gate, and these gates were each shut with a stone as high and as thick as the wall itself which could be raised and lowered. The first of these was called Tiupuncu, "gate of sand," since the plain is rather sandy or gravelly at this point: *tiu* is "sand," or "a sandy place," and *puncu*, "gate, door." The second is called Acahuana Puncu, after the master mason, whose name was Acahuana, the syllable *ca* being pronounced deep down in the throat. The third is Viracocha Puncu, dedicated to the god Viracocha, the phantom we have referred to at length, who appeared to Prince Viracocha Inca and forewarned him of the rising of the Chancas, as a result of which he was regarded at the defender and second founder of Cuzco, and therefore given this gate with the request that he should guard it and defend the fortress as he had guarded the city and the whole empire in the past.

WORKING WITH SOURCES

1. Why did the Incas feel the need to fortify Cuzco so heavily, and would these preparations have been successful in typical battle situations?
2. What aspect of the city's walls most arouses Garcilaso's admiration and wonder, and why?

16. THE WESTERN EUROPEAN OVERSEAS EXPANSION AND OTTOMAN-HABSBURG STRUGGLE, 1450–1650

16.1 Christopher Columbus, *The Book of Prophecies*, 1501–1502

Although he is more famous for his voyages—and for the richly detailed accounts he made of them—Columbus (1451–1506) also composed a book of prophetic revelations toward the end of his life, entitled *El Libro de las Profecias*. Written after his third voyage to the Americas, the book traced the development of God's plans for the end of the world, which could be hastened along, particularly by a swift and decisive move to reclaim Jerusalem from Muslim control. When Jerusalem was once more restored to Christian sovereignty, Columbus predicted, Jesus could return to earth, and all of the events foreseen in the Book of Revelation (and in various medieval revelations, as well) could unfold. It is helpful to place the plans for Columbus's original voyage in 1492 against the backdrop of his religious beliefs, as he encourages Ferdinand and Isabella to take their rightful place in God's mystical plan—as well as in Columbus's own cartographic charts.

Letter from the Admiral to the King and Queen [Ferdinand and Isabella]

. . .

Most exalted rulers: At a very early age I began sailing the sea and have continued until now. This profession creates a curiosity about the secrets of the world. I have been a sailor for forty years, and I have personally sailed to all the known regions. I have had commerce and conversation with knowledgeable people of the clergy and the laity. Latins and Greeks, Jews and Moors, and with many others of different religions. Our Lord has favored my occupation and has given me an intelligent mind. He has endowed me with a great talent for seamanship; sufficient ability in astrology, geometry, and arithmetic; and the mental and physical dexterity required to draw spherical maps of cities, rivers and mountains, islands and ports, with everything in its proper place.

During this time I have studied all kinds of texts: cosmography, histories, chronicles, philosophy, and other disciplines. Through these writings, the hand of Our Lord opened my mind to the possibility of sailing to the Indies and gave me the will to attempt the voyage. With this burning ambition I came to your Highnesses. Everyone who heard about my enterprise rejected it with laughter and ridicule. Neither all the sciences that I mentioned previously nor citations drawn from them were of any help to me. Only Your Highnesses had faith and perseverance. Who could doubt that this flash of understanding was the work of the Holy Spirit, as well as my own? The Holy Spirit illuminated his holy and sacred Scripture, encouraging me in a very strong and clear voice from the forty-four books of the Old Testament, the four evangelists, and twenty-three epistles from the blessed apostles, urging me to proceed. Continually, without

Source: Christopher Columbus, *The Book of Prophecies*, ed. Roberto Rusconi, trans. Blair Sullivan (Berkeley: University of California Press, 1997), vol. 3, 67–69, 75–77.

ceasing a moment, they insisted that I go on. Our Lord wished to make something clearly miraculous of this voyage to the Indies in order to encourage me and others about the holy temple.

. . .

Most of the prophecies of holy Scripture have already been fulfilled. The Scriptures say this and the Holy Church loudly and unceasingly is saying it, and no other witness is necessary. I will, however, speak of one prophecy in particular because it bears on my argument and gives me support and happiness whenever I think about it.

I have greatly sinned. Yet, every time that I have asked, I have been covered by the mercy and compassion of Our Lord. I have found the sweetest consolation in throwing off all my cares in order to contemplate his marvelous presence.

I have already said that for the voyage to the Indies neither intelligence nor mathematics nor world maps were of any use to me; it was the fulfillment of Isaiah's prophecy. This is what I want to record here in order to remind Your Highnesses and so that you can take pleasure from the things I am going to tell you about Jerusalem on the basis of the same authority. If you have faith in this enterprise, you will certainly have the victory.

. . .

I said above that much that has been prophesied remains to be fulfilled, and I say that these are the world's great events, and I say that a sign of this is the acceleration of Our Lord's activities in this world. I know this from the recent preaching of the gospel in so many lands.

The Calabrian abbot Joachim said that whoever was to rebuild the temple on Mount Zion would come from Spain.

The cardinal Pierre d'Ailly wrote at length about the end of the religion of Mohammed and the coming of the Antichrist in his treatise *De concordia astronomicae veritatis et narrationis historicae* [*On the agreement between astronomical truth and historical narrative*]; he discusses, particularly in the last nine chapters, what many astronomers have said about the ten revolutions of Saturn.

WORKING WITH SOURCES

1. How does Columbus appeal to the "crusading" goals of Ferdinand and Isabella, and why?
2. Would this appeal have found favor with the monarchs, given their other actions in Spain in 1492?

16.2 Thomas the Eparch and Joshua Diplovatatzes, "The Fall of Constantinople," 1453

The siege and conquest of Constantinople by the Ottoman Turks under Mehmet II (r. 1451–1481) was one of the turning points of world history. Unfolding over two months between April 5 and May 29, 1453, the siege exposed the inability of the Byzantine emperor Constantine XI to withstand a sustained and massive attack. Outnumbering the defenders 11 to 1, the Ottomans battered Constantinople's walls with heavy cannons and took advantage of the natural weaknesses of the

Source: William L. North from the Italian version in A. Pertusi, ed., *La Caduta di Constantinopoli: Le testimonianze dei contemporanei* (Milan: Mondadori, 1976), 234–239, available online at https://apps.carleton.edu/curricular/mars/assets/Thomas_the_Eparch_and_Joshua_Diplovatatzes_for_MARS_website.pdf.

city's geography. This account, told by two survivors and (self-proclaimed) eyewitnesses to the siege and its aftermath, details some of the specific stages of the defeat—and the suffering for Christians that came as a result.

When the Turk then drew near to Pera in the fortified zone, he seized all the boats he could find and bound them to each other so as to form a bridge which permitted the combatants to fight on the water just as they did on land. The Turks had with them thousands of ladders which they placed against the walls, right at the place which they had fired [their cannon] and breached the wall, just as they did at the cemetery of St. Sebold. The Genoese handled this breach; they wanted to protect it with their ships because they had so many. In the army of the Turk the order had been given fifteen days before the attack that each soldier would carry a ladder, whether he was fighting on land or sea. There also arrived galleys full of armed men: it seemed that they were Genoese and that they had come to aid the besieged, but in fact they were Turks and they were slipping into the gates. Just as this was becoming less worrisome and the city seemed secure, there arrived under the flag of the Genoese several ships which repelled the Turks with great losses.

At dawn on Monday, 29 May, they began an attack that lasted all night until Tuesday evening and they conquered the city. The commander of the Genoese, who was leading the defense of the breach, pretended to be wounded and abandoned his battle station, taking with him all his people. When the Turks realized this, they slipped in through the breach. When the emperor of the Greeks saw this, he exclaimed in a loud voice: "My God, I have been betrayed!" and he suddenly appeared with his people, exhorting the others to stand firm and defend themselves. But then the gate was opened and the crush of people became such that the emperor himself and his [men] were killed by the Turks and the traitors.

Then the Turks ran to the Hagia Sophia, and all those whom they had imprisoned there, they killed in the first heat of rage. Those whom they found later, they bound with a cord around their neck and their

hands tied behind their backs and led them out of the city. When the Turk learned that the emperor had been killed in Constantinople, he captured the Grand Duke who was governing in the emperor's stead and had the Grand Duke's son beheaded and then the Grand Duke himself. Then he seized one of the Grand Duke's daughters who was quite beautiful and made her lie on the great altar of Hagia Sophia with a crucifix under her head and then raped her. Then the most brutish of the Turks seized the finest noble women, virgins, and nuns of the city and violated them in the presence of the Greeks and in sacrilege of Christianity. Then they destroyed all the sacred objects and the bodies of the saints and burned everything they found, save for the cross, the nail, and the clothing of Christ: no one knows where these relics ended up, no one has found them. They also wanted to desecrate the image of the Virgin of St. Luke by stabbing six hundred people in front of it, one after another, like madmen. Then they took prisoner those who fell into their hands, tied them with a rope around the neck and calculated the value of each one. Women had to redeem themselves with their own bodies, men by fornicating with their hands or some other means. Whoever was able to pay the assessed amount could remain in his faith and whoever refused had to die. The Turk who had become governor of Constantinople, named Suleiman in German, occupied the temple of Hagia Sophia to practice his faith there. For three days the Turks sacked and pillaged the city, and each kept whatever he found—people and goods—and did with them whatever he wished.

. . .

All this was made known by Thomas the Eparch, a count of Constantinople, and Joshua Diplovatatzes. Thutros of Constantinople translated their Greek into "welisch" and Dumita Exswinnilwacz and Matheus Hack of Utrecht translated their welisch into German.

WORKING WITH SOURCES

1. What does this account suggest about the preparedness of the Turks for the sack of Constantinople—and the lack of preparation on the part of the Byzantine defenders?
2. What details indicate that the taking of Constantinople was seen as a "religious" war on the Ottoman side?

16.3 Evliya Çelebi, "A Procession of Artisans at Istanbul," ca. 1638

Born on the Golden Horn and raised in the Sultan's palace in Istanbul, Çelebi traveled throughout Ottoman domains between 1640 and 1680. He published an account of his travels and experiences as the *Seyahatname*, or *Book of Travels*. In the first of his ten books in the document, Çelebi provides a lengthy description of Istanbul around the year 1638, including a panoramic view of 1,100 artisan and craft guilds. The numbers and diversity of trades represented underscore the extent of Ottoman commerce—as well as the pride of place each of the city's working people claimed as their due.

The numbers in brackets refer to the order of listing in this chapter.

I: *Ship-captains [7] vs. Saddlers [30]*
Following the bakers [6], the saddlers wished to pass, but the ship-captains and sea-merchants raised a great fuss. When Sultan Murad got wind of the matter, he consulted with the ulema and the guild shaikhs. They all agreed that it made sense for the ship-captains to proceed after the bakers, because it was they who transported the wheat, and the bakers were dependent on them, and also because Noah was their patron saint.

Comment: the saddlers do not reappear until much later, between the tanners [29] and the shoemakers [31].

. . .

III: *Egyptian Merchants [9] vs. Butchers [10]*
Following the procession of these Mediterranean Sea captains, the butchers were supposed to pass, according to imperial decree. But all the great Egyptian merchants, including the dealers in rice, hemp, Egyptian reed mats, coffee and sugar gathered together and began quarreling with the butchers. Finally they went before the sultan and said: "My padishah, our galleons are charged with transporting rice, lentils, coffee and hemp. They cannot do without us, nor we without them. Why should these bloody and tricky butchers come between us? Plagues have arisen from cities where they shed their blood, and for fear of this their stalls and shambles in other countries are outside of the city walls. They are a bloody and filthy band of ill-omen. We, on the other hand, always make Istanbul plentiful and cheap with grains of all sorts."

Now the butchers' eyes went bloodshot. "My padishah," they said, "Our patron saint is Butcher Cömerd and our occupation is with sheep, an animal which the Creator has made the object of mercy, and whose flesh He has made lawful food for the strengthening of His servants' bodies. Bread and meat are mentioned as the foremost of God's gifts to mankind: with a small portion of meat, a poor man can subsist for five or six days. We make our living with such a lawful trade, and are known for our generosity (*cömerdlik*). It is we who make Istanbul plentiful and

Source: Robert Dankoff, *An Ottoman Mentality: The World of Evliya Çelebi*, 2nd ed. (Leiden, the Netherlands: Brill, 2006), 86–89.

cheap. As for these merchants and dealers and profiteers: concerning them the Koran says (2:275), 'God has made selling lawful and profiteering unlawful'. They are such a despised group that after bringing their goods from Egypt they store it in magazines in order to create a shortage, thus causing public harm through their hoarding.

. . .

"Egyptian sugar? But in the Koran the rivers of paradise are praised as being made 'of pure honey' (47:15). Now we have honey from Turkey, Athens, Wallachia, Moldavia, each with seventy distinct qualities. Furthermore, if my padishah wished, thousands of quintals of sugar could be produced in Alanya, Antalya, Silifke, Tarsus, Adana, Payas, Antakya, Aleppo, Damascus, Sidon, Beyrut, Tripoli and other such provinces—enough to make it plentiful and cheap throughout the world—so why do we need your sugar?

"As for coffee: it is an innovation; it prevents sleep; it dulls the generative powers; and coffee houses are dens of sedition. When roasted it is burnt; and in the legal compilations known as *Bezzaziye* and *Tatarhaniye* we have the dictum that 'Whatever is carbonized is absolutely forbidden'—this holds even for burnt bread. Spiced sherbet, pure milk, tea, fennel, salep, and almond-cream—all these are more wholesome than coffee."

. . .

To these objections of the butchers, the Egyptian merchants replied:

. . . "It is true that Turkey has no need of sugar and hemp, and that European sugar is also very fine. But tell us this, O band of butchers: what benefit and return do you offer to the public treasury?"

The butchers had nothing to say to this, and the Egyptian merchants continued: "My padishah, the goods arriving in our galleons provide the public treasury an annual revenue of 11,000 purses from customs dues. As a matter of justice (*'adalet ederseñiz*) we ought to have precedence in the Muhammadan procession, and the butchers ought to come after us." The *şeyhülislam* Yahya Efendi and Mu'id Ahmed Efendi cited the hadith, "The best of men is he who is useful to mankind," and the sultan gave the Egyptian merchants a noble rescript authorizing them to go first, and the butchers to go second.

WORKING WITH SOURCES

1. Why did the order in which they appeared in the procession matter so much to these particular groups?
2. How did appeals to the Quran accentuate or diminish their case to be placed ahead in the procession?

16.4   Ogier Ghiselin de Busbecq, "The Court of Suleiman the Magnificent," 1581

Ghiselin (1522–1592) was a Flemish ambassador who represented the Austrian Habsburgs at the court of Suleiman the Magnificent (1520–1566) in Istanbul. In 1581, he published an account of his time among the Ottomans as *Itinera Constantinopolitanum et Amasianum* (*Travels in Constantinople and Asia Minor*). In this segment of his travel narrative, he draws attention to the personal habits

Source: Wayne S. Vucinich, *The Ottoman Empire: Its Record and Legacy* (Princeton, NJ: Van Nostrand, 1965), 127–129.

and behaviors of a contemporary emperor—one who saw himself as the heir to the Romans as well as to the other monarchs who had held Constantinople/Istanbul.

The Sultan was seated on a very low ottoman, not more than a foot from the ground, which was covered with a quantity of costly rugs and cushions of exquisite workmanship; near him lay his bow and arrows. His air, as I said, was by no means gracious, and his face wore a stern, though dignified, expression. On entering we were separately conducted into the royal presence by the chamberlains, who grasped our arms. . . . After having gone through a pretense of kissing his hand, we were conducted backwards to the wall opposite his seat, care being taken that we should never turn our backs on him. The Sultan then listened to what I had to say; but the language I held was not at all to his taste, for the demands of his Majesty breathed a spirit of independence and dignity . . . and so he made no answer beyond saying in a tetchy way, "Giusel, giusel," i.e. well, well . . .

. . .

I was greatly struck with the silence and order that prevailed in this great crowd. There were no cries, no hum of voices, the usual accompaniments of a motley gathering, neither was there any jostling; without the slightest disturbance each man took his proper place according to his rank. The Agas, as they call their chiefs, were seated, to wit, generals, colonels (*bimbashi*), and captains (*soubashi*). Men of a lower position stood. The most interesting sight in this assembly was a body of several thousand Janissaries, who were drawn up in a long line apart from the rest; their array was so steady and motionless that, being at a little distance, it was some time before I could make up my mind as to whether they were human beings or statues; at last I received a hint to salute them, and saw all their heads bending at the same moment to return my bow.

. . .

When the cavalry had ridden past, they were followed by a long procession of Janissaries, but few of whom carried any arms except their regular weapon, the musket. They were dressed in uniforms of almost the same shape and colour, so that you might recognize them to be the slaves. . . . There is only one thing in which they are extravagant, viz., plumes, head-dresses, etc., and veterans who formed the rear guard were specially distinguished by ornaments of this kind. The plumes which they insert in their frontlets might well be mistaken for a walking forest.

WORKING WITH SOURCES

1. Why were order and discipline apparently so important at Suleiman's court?
2. Why might Ghiselin have found the Janissaries so particularly impressive?

16.5   Janissary Musket, ca. 1750–1800

The Janissaries constitute the most famous and centralized of the Ottomans' military institutions. A feared and respected military fource, the Janissaries were Christian-born males who had been seized from their homes as boys, converted to Islam, and then trained as future soldiers and administrators for the Turks. Under the direct orders of the sultan and his viziers, the Janissaries were equipped with the latest military innovations. In the early fifteenth century, these units received cannons and matchlock muskets. The muskets continued their evolution in the Janissaries' hands, becoming the standard equipment for Ottoman and other armies.

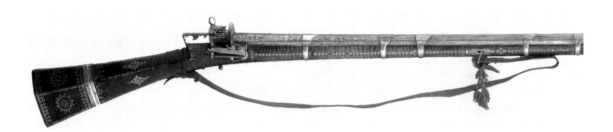

WORKING WITH SOURCES

1. What does the elaborate decoration of the musket suggest about its psychological, as well as its practical, effects?
2. Was this firearm likely to have been produced by indigenous, rather than European, gunsmiths? Why or why not?

© INTERFOTO / Alamy

17. THE RENAISSANCE, NEW SCIENCES, AND RELIGIOUS WARS IN EUROPE, 1450–1750

17.1 Examination of Lady Jane Grey, London, 1554

Jane Grey, the granddaughter of Henry VIII's sister Mary, was born in 1537, the same year as Edward VI, the only surviving son of the king who had sought a male heir so desperately. Jane, who like Edward was raised in the Protestant religion Henry had introduced to England, proved a diligent and intellectually gifted teenager. In spite of her youth and gender, Jane corresponded with Protestant authorities on the Continent, but fast-moving events in England precluded further study. When Edward died without an heir in 1553, the throne passed, by prearranged agreement, to his fiercely Catholic half-sister Mary.

However, in order to forestall a Catholic successor—and the dramatic rollback of the Protestant reforms instituted by Henry's and Edward's Church of England—Jane's relatives proclaimed her queen. Her rule lasted a mere nine days. She was imprisoned in the Tower of London by Mary, who was then forced to consider whether Jane's execution was warranted. Shortly before Jane's death, at age 16, Queen Mary sent her own chaplain, Master Feckenham (sometimes rendered as "Fecknam") to try to reconcile Jane to the Catholic faith. The results of this attempt were triumphantly recorded in John Foxe's *Acts and Monuments*, published after the Protestant Queen Elizabeth had triumphed over Mary and the Catholics. Although the conversation recorded here is not a trial transcript—and is a highly partisan account—it does distill some of the central issues that divided Catholics and Protestants in an extremely chaotic and violent period.

FECKNAM: "I am here come to you at this present, sent from the queen [Mary] and her council, to instruct you in the true doctrine of the right faith: although I have so great confidence in you, that I shall have, I trust, little need to travail with you much therein."

JANE: "Forsooth, I heartily thank the queen's highness, which is not unmindful of her humble subject: and I hope, likewise, that you no less will do your duty therein both truly and faithfully, according to that you were sent for."

. . .

FECKNAM: "How many sacraments are there?"

JANE: "Two: the one the sacrament of baptism, and the other the sacrament of the Lord's Supper."

FECKNAM: "No, there are seven."

JANE: "By what Scripture find you that?"

FECKNAM: "Well, we will talk of that hereafter. But what is signified by your two sacraments?"

JANE: "By the sacrament of baptism I am washed with water and regenerated by the Spirit, and that washing is a token to me that I am the child of God. The sacrament of the Lord's

Source: "The Examination of Lady Jane Grey (1554)," from Denis R. Janz, ed., *A Reformation Reader: Primary Texts with Introductions*, 2nd ed. (Minneapolis, MN: Fortress, 2008), 360–362, taken from *The Acts and Monuments of John Foxe* (London: Seeleys, 1859), 415–417.

Supper, offered unto me, is a sure seal and testimony that I am, by the blood of Christ, which he shed for me on the cross, made partaker of the everlasting kingdom."

FECKNAM: "Why? What do you receive in that sacrament? Do you not receive the very body and blood of Christ?"

JANE: "No, surely, I do not so believe. I think that at the supper I neither receive flesh nor blood, but bread and wine: which bread when it is broken, and the wine when it is drunken, put me in remembrance how that for my sins the body of Christ was broken, and his blood shed on the cross; and with that bread and wine I receive the benefits that come by the breaking of his body, and shedding of his blood, for our sins on the cross."

FECKNAM: "Why, doth not Christ speak these words, 'Take, eat, this is my body?' Require you any plainer words? Doth he not say, it is his body?"

JANE: "I grant, he saith so; and so he saith, 'I am the vine, I am the door'; but he is never the more for that, the door or the vine. Doth not St. Paul say, 'He calleth things that are not, as though they were?' God forbid that I should say, that I eat the very natural body and blood of Christ: for then either I should pluck away my redemption, or else there were two bodies, or two Christs. One body was tormented on the cross, and if they did eat another body, then had he two bodies: or if his body were eaten, then was it not broken upon the cross; or if it were broken upon the cross, it was not eaten of his disciples."

. . .

With these and like such persuasions he would have had her lean to the [Catholic] church, but it would not be. There were many more things whereof they reasoned, but these were the chiefest.

After this, Fecknam took his leave, saying, that he was sorry for her: "For I am sure," quoth he, "that we two shall never meet."

JANE: "True it is," said she, "that we shall never meet, except God turn your heart; for I am assured, unless you repent and turn to God, you are in an evil case. And I pray God, in the bowels of his mercy, to send you his Holy Spirit; for he hath given you his great gift of utterance, if it please him also to open the eyes of your heart."

WORKING WITH SOURCES

1. What does this source reveal about the religious education of young people in the extended royal household during the final years of Henry VIII and the reign of Edward VI?
2. How does the literal interpretation of the Bible enter into this discussion, and why?

17.2   Sebastian Castellio, *Concerning Whether Heretics Should Be Persecuted*, 1554

In October 1553, the extraordinarily gifted Spanish scientist Michael Servetus was executed with the approval and the strong support of John Calvin and his followers in Geneva. The charge was heresy, specifically for denying the existence of the Trinity and the divinity of Christ, and the method of execution—burning at the stake—elicited commentary and protest from across

Source: Sebastian Castellio, *Concerning Heretics, Whether They Are to Be Persecuted and How They Are to Be Treated, A Collection of the Opinions of Learned Men Both Ancient and Modern,* trans. Roland H. Bainton (New York: Octagon, 1965), 132–134.

Europe. One of the fullest and most sophisticated protests against this execution was issued by Sebastian Castellio, a professor of Greek language and New Testament theology in the Swiss city of Basel. His book *De Haereticis* is a collection of opinions, drawn from Christian writers, from both before and after the Protestant Reformation and across 15 centuries. It is more than an academic exercise, however, as this dedication of the Latin work to a German noble demonstrates.

From the Dedication of the book to Duke Christoph of Württemberg:

. . . And just as the **Turks** disagree with the Christians as to the person of Christ, and the Jews with both the Turks and the Christians, and the one condemns the other and holds him for a heretic, so Christians disagree with Christians on many points with regard to the teaching of Christ, and condemn one another and hold each other for heretics. Great controversies and debates occur as to baptism, the Lord's Supper, the invocation of the saints, justification, free will, and other obscure questions, so that Catholics, Lutherans, Zwinglians, Anabaptists, monks, and others condemn and persecute one another more cruelly than the Turks do the Christians. These dissensions arise solely from ignorance of the truth, for if these matters were so obvious and evident as that there is but one God, all Christians would agree among themselves on these points as readily as all nations confess that God is one.

What, then is to be done in such great contentions? We should follow the counsel of Paul, "Let not him that eateth despise him that eateth not. . . . To his own master he standeth or falleth." [Romans 14:3–4] Let not the Jews or Turks condemn the Christians, nor let the Christians condemn the Jews or Turks, but rather teach and win them by true religion and justice, and let us, who are Christians, not condemn one another, but, if we are wiser than they, let us also be better and more merciful. This is certain that the better a man knows the truth, the less is he inclined to condemn, as appears in the case of Christ and the apostles. But he who lightly condemns others shows thereby that he knows nothing precisely, because he cannot bear others, for to know is to know

how to put into practice. He who does not know how to act mercifully and kindly does not know the nature of mercy and kindness, just as he who cannot blush does not know the nature of shame.

If we were to conduct ourselves in this fashion we should be able to dwell together in concord. Even though in some matters we disagreed, yet should we consent together and forbear one another in love, which is the bond of peace, until we arrive at the unity of the faith [Ephesians 4:2–3]. But now, when we strive with hate and persecutions we go from bad to worse. Nor are we mindful of our office, since we are wholly taken up with condemnation, and the Gospel because of us is made a reproach unto the heathen [Ezekiel 22:4], for when they see us attacking one another with the fury of beasts, and the weak oppressed by the strong, these heathen feel horror and detestation for the Gospel, as if it made men such, and they abominate even Christ himself, as if he commanded men to do such things. We rather degenerate into Turks and Jews than convert them into Christians. Who would wish to be a Christian, when he saw that those who confessed the name of Christ were destroyed by Christians themselves with fire, water, and the sword without mercy and more cruelly treated than brigands and murderers? Who would not think Christ a **Moloch**, or some such god, if he wished that men should be immolated to him and burned alive? Who would wish to serve Christ on condition that a difference of opinion on a controversial point with those in authority would be punished by burning alive at the command of Christ himself more cruelly than in the bull of **Phalaris**, even

---

Turks: Muslims.

Moloch: A Phoenician deity who, according to the Bible, demanded the sacrifice of human children.

Phalaris: Tyrant in pre-Christian Sicily who burned victims alive in a giant bronze bull.

though from the midst of the flames he should call with a loud voice upon Christ, and should cry out that he believed in Him? Imagine Christ, the judge of all, present. Imagine Him pronouncing the sentence and applying the torch. Who would not hold Christ for a Satan? What more could Satan do than burn those who call upon the name of Christ?

WORKING WITH SOURCES

1. Was Castellio minimizing the significant theological disputes that had arisen as a result of the Reformation? Were his objections directly applicable to the Servetus case?
2. What did Castellio see as the practical, as well as the theological, consequences of burning those perceived to be "heretics"? Is he convincing on this point?

17.3   Duc de Saint-Simon, "The Daily Habits of Louis XIV at Versailles," ca. 1715

A minor noble at Louis XIV's court at Versailles, Louis de Rouvroy, the duc de Saint-Simon (1675–1755), would achieve lasting fame after his death with the publication of his copious, frank, and witty observations of the court. While resident at Versailles for brief periods after 1702 until the king's death in 1715, Saint-Simon paid particular attention to the maneuverings of his fellow aristocrats. He managed to garner the resentment of many of them, especially the king's illegitimate children, "the Bastards," who held a prominent place at court. His accounts of the daily routine of life at Versailles, and the central position of the king who had famously declared, "L'état, c'est moi!," are often applied today to spectacles that can also be described as at once grand and a little absurd.

At eight o'clock the chief valet de chambre on duty, who alone had slept in the royal chamber, and who had dressed himself, awoke the King. The chief physician, the chief surgeon, and the nurse (as long as she lived), entered at the same time. The latter kissed the King; the others rubbed and often changed his shirt, because he was in the habit of sweating a great deal. At the quarter [hour], the grand chamberlain was called (or, in his absence, the first gentleman of the chamber), and those who had, what was called the *grandes entrées*. The chamberlain (or chief gentleman) drew back the curtains which had been closed again, and presented the holy water from the vase, at the head of the bed. These gentlemen stayed but a moment, and that was the time to speak to the King, if any one had anything to ask of him; in which case the rest stood aside. When, contrary to custom, nobody had aught to say, they were there but for a few moments. He who had opened the curtains and presented the holy water, presented also a prayer-book. Then all passed into the cabinet of the council. A very short religious service being over, the King called, they re-entered. The same officer gave him his dressing-gown; immediately after, other privileged courtiers entered, and then everybody, in time to find the King putting on his shoes and stockings, for he did almost everything

Source: Memoirs of the Duc de Saint-Simon, trans. Bayle St. John, ed. W. H. Lewis (New York: Macmillan, 1964), 140–141, 144–145.

himself and with address and grace. Every other day we saw him shave himself; and he had a little short wig in which he always appeared, even in bed, and on medicine days. He often spoke of the chase, and sometimes said a word to somebody. No toilette table was near him; he had simply a mirror held before him.

As soon as he was dressed, he prayed to God, at the side of his bed, where all the clergy present knelt, the cardinals without cushions, all the laity remaining standing; and the captain of the guards came to the balustrade during the prayer, after which the King passed into his cabinet.

He found there, or was followed by all who had the entrée, a very numerous company, for it included everybody in any office. He gave orders to each for the day; thus within half a quarter of an hour it was known what he meant to do; and then all this crowd left directly. The bastards, a few favourites, and the valets alone were left. It was then a good opportunity for talking with the King; for example, about plans of gardens and buildings; and conversation lasted more or less according to the person engaged in it.

. . .

At ten o'clock his supper was served. The captain of the guard announced this to him. A quarter of an hour after the King came to supper, and from the antechamber of Madame de Maintenon [his principal mistress] to the table again, any one spoke to him who wished. This supper was always on a grand scale, the royal household (that is, the sons and daughters of France), at table, and a large number of courtiers and ladies present, sitting or standing, and on the evening before the journey to Marly all those ladies who wished to take part in it. That was called presenting yourself for Marly. Men asked in the morning, simply saying to the King, "Sire, Marly." In later years, the King grew tired of this, and a valet wrote up in the gallery the names of those who asked. The ladies continued to present themselves.

. . .

The King, wishing to retire, went and fed his dogs; then said good night, passed into his chamber to the *ruelle* of his bed, where he said his prayers, as in the morning, then undressed. He said good night with an inclination of the head, and whilst everybody was leaving the room stood at the corner of the mantelpiece, where he gave the order to the colonel of the guards alone. Then commenced what was called the *petit coucher*, at which only the specially privileged remained. That was short. They did not leave until he got into bed. It was a moment to speak to him.

Ruelle: The "little path" between a bed and the wall.

WORKING WITH SOURCES

1. Why does Saint-Simon pay particular attention to moments of the day during which a courtier could speak directly with the king?
2. What does the combination of religious and secular pursuits in the king's daily habits suggest about life at his court?

17.4 Giorgio Vasari, *The Life of Michelangelo Buonarroti*, 1550

Trained as a painter, architect, and goldsmith, Giorgio Vasari (1511–1574) practiced various artistic trades, but is most renowned today as the first art historian. His *Lives of the Most Eminent Painters, Sculptors, and Architects*, first published in 1550, is the principal source of information about the most prominent artists of the European Renaissance. Having studied under the great artist

Michelangelo Buonarroti (1475–1564), Vasari was particularly keen to tell this story. In these scenes from his biography of Michelangelo, Vasari draws attention to his master's early training, as well as the prominent roles Lorenzo il Magnifico de' Medici and ancient sculpture played in his artistic development.

In those days Lorenzo de' Medici the Magnificent kept Bertoldo the sculptor in his garden near Piazza San Marco, not so much as the custodian or guardian of the many beautiful antiquities he had collected and assembled there at great expense, but rather because he wished above all else to create a school for excellent painters and sculptors. . . . Thus, Domenico [Ghirlandaio] gave him some of his best young men, including among others Michelangelo and Francesco Granacci; and when they went to the garden, they found that Torrigiani, a young man of the Torrigiani family, was there working on some clay figures in the round that Bertoldo had given him to do.

After Michelangelo saw these figures, he made some himself to rival those of Torrigiani, so that Lorenzo, seeing his high spirit, always had great expectations for him, and, encouraged after only a few days, Michelangelo began copying with a piece of marble the antique head of an old and wrinkled faun with a damaged nose and a laughing mouth, which he found there. Although Michelangelo had never before touched marble or chisels, the imitation turned out so well that Lorenzo was astonished, and when Lorenzo saw that Michelangelo, following his own fantasy rather than the antique head, had carved its mouth open to give it a tongue and to make all its teeth visible, this lord, laughing with pleasure as was his custom, said to him: "But you should have known that old men never have all their teeth and that some of them are always missing." In that simplicity of his, it seemed to Michelangelo, who loved and feared this lord, that Lorenzo was correct; and as soon as Lorenzo left, he immediately broke a tooth on the head and dug out the gum in such a way that it seemed the tooth had fallen out, and anxiously awaited Lorenzo's return, who, after coming back and seeing Michelangelo's simplicity and excellence, laughed about it on more than one occasion, recounting it to his friends as if it were miraculous. . . .

. . .

Around this time it happened that Piero Soderini saw the statue [the *David*, finished in 1504], and it pleased him greatly, but while Michelangelo was giving it the finishing touches, he told Michelangelo that he thought the nose of the figure was too large. Michelangelo, realizing that the Gonfaloniere [a civic official in Florence] was standing under the giant and that his viewpoint did not allow him to see it properly, climbed up the scaffolding to satisfy Soderini (who was behind him nearby), and having quickly grabbed the chisel in his left hand along with a little marble dust that he found on the planks in the scaffolding, Michelangelo began to tap lightly with the chisel, allowing the dust to fall little by little without retouching the nose from the way it was. Then, looking down at the Gonfaloniere who stood there watching, he ordered:

"Look at it now."

"I like it better," replied the Gonfaloniere: "you've made it come alive."

Thus Michelangelo climbed down, and, having contented this lord, he laughed to himself, feeling compassion for those who, in order to make it appear that they understand, do not realize what they are saying; and when the statue was finished and set in its foundation, he uncovered it, and to tell the truth, this work eclipsed all other statues, both modern and ancient, whether Greek or Roman; and it can be said that neither the Marforio in Rome, nor the Tiber and the Nile of the Belvedere, nor the colossal statues of Monte Cavallo can be compared to this David, which Michelangelo completed with so much measure and beauty, and so much skill.

Source: Giorgio Vasari, *The Lives of the Artists* (New York: Oxford University Press, 1998), 418–420; 427–428.

WORKING WITH SOURCES

1. How do these anecdotes illustrate the relationship between artists and their patrons (and funders) during the Renaissance?
2. How did Michelangelo deal with the legacy of artists from Greco-Roman antiquity?

17.5 Galileo Galilei, Letter to the Grand Duchess Christina de' Medici, 1615

This famous letter is often cited as an early sign of Galileo's inevitable conflict with church authorities over the Copernican system of planetary motion—and the theory's theological, as well as its scientific, ramifications. Galileo (1564–1642) would be condemned to house arrest in 1632 and forced to make a public repudiation of the heliocentric theory first advanced by Copernicus in the sixteenth century. However, Galileo's connection to the renowned Medici family of Florence was also cause for comment—and caution—from 1610, when he received an appointment and their implicit endorsement.

Constructing a telescope in 1609 (which he proudly claimed could "magnify objects more than 60 times"), Galileo trained it on the moons of Jupiter, which he tracked over several days in 1610. Having named these objects for the Medici family, he rushed these and many other astronomical observations into print in the *Sidereus Nuncius* (*The Starry Messenger*). Inviting other scientists to "apply themselves to examine and determine" these planetary motions, Galileo demonstrated a preference for the Copernican theory and elicited sharp responses, particularly from church officials. In 1615, the dowager Grand Duchess Christina, mother of his patron, Cosimo II, expressed her own reservations about the implications of the Copernican theory for a passage in the Old Testament. Galileo's response attempts, or seems to attempt, to reconcile experimental science and received religion.

Thus let these people apply themselves to refuting the arguments of Copernicus and of the others, and let them leave its condemnation as erroneous and heretical to the proper authorities; but let them not hope that the very cautious and very wise Fathers and the Infallible One with his absolute wisdom are about to make rash decisions like those into which they would be rushed by their special interests and feelings. For in regard to these and other similar propositions which do not directly involve the faith, no one can doubt that the Supreme Pontiff always [*Pope*] has the absolute power of permitting or condemning them; however, no creature has the power of making them be true or false, contrary to what they happen to be by nature and de facto. So it seems more advisable to first become sure about the necessary and immutable truth of the matter, over which no one has control, than to condemn one side when such certainty is lacking; this would imply a loss of freedom of decision and of choice insofar as it would give necessity to things which are presently indifferent, free, and dependent on the will of the supreme authority.

Source: Galileo Galilei, *The Essential Galileo*, ed. and trans. Maurice A. Finocchiaro (Indianapolis: Hackett, 2008), §4.2.5—4.2.6, 140–144.

Pope—pushing his decisions

Context: Counter information
Galileo Recantation

In short, if it is inconceivable that a proposition should be declared heretical when one thinks that it may be true, it should be futile for someone to try to bring about the condemnation of the earth's motion and sun's rest unless he first shows it to be impossible and false.

There remains one last thing for us to examine: to what extent it is true that the Joshua passage [Joshua 10:12–13] can be taken without altering the literal meaning of the words, and how it can be that, when the sun obeyed Joshua's order to stop, from this it followed that the day was prolonged by a large amount.

. . .

I think therefore, if I am not mistaken, that one can clearly see that, given the Ptolemaic system, it is necessary to interpret the words in a way different from their literal meaning. Guided by St. Augustine's very useful prescriptions, I should say that the best nonliteral interpretation is not necessarily this, if anyone can find another which is perhaps better and more suitable. So now I want to examine whether the same miracle could be understood in a way more in accordance with what we read in Joshua, if to the Copernican system we add another discovery which I recently made about the solar body. However, I continue to speak with the same reservations—to the effect that I am not so enamored with my own opinions as to want to place them ahead of those of others; nor do I believe it is impossible to put forth interpretations which are better and more in accordance with the Holy Writ.

Let us first assume in accordance with the opinion of the above-mentioned authors, that in the Joshua miracle the whole system of heavenly motions was stopped, so that the stopping of only one would not introduce unnecessarily universal confusion and great turmoil in the whole order of nature.

. . .

Furthermore, what deserves special appreciation, if I am not mistaken, is that with the Copernican system one can very clearly and very easily give a literal meaning to another detail which one reads about the same miracle; that is, that the sun stopped in the middle of heaven. Serious theologians have raised a difficulty about this passage: it seems very probable that, when Joshua asked for the prolongation of the day, the sun was close to setting and not at the meridian; for it was then about the time of the summer solstice, and consequently the days were very long, so that if the sun had been at the meridian then it does not seem likely that it would have been necessary to pray for a lengthening of the day in order to win a battle, since the still remaining time of seven hours or more could very well have been sufficient.

. . .

We can remove this and every other implausibility, if I am not mistaken, by placing the sun, as the Copernican system does and as it is most necessary to do, in the middle, namely, at the center of the heavenly orbs and of the planetary revolutions; for at any hour of the day, whether at noon or in the afternoon, the day would have been lengthened and all heavenly turnings stopped by the sun stopping in the middle of the heavens, namely, at the center of the heavens, where it is located. Furthermore, this interpretation agrees all the more with the literal meaning inasmuch as, if one wanted to claim that the sun's stopping occurred at the noon hour, then the proper expression to use would have been to say that it "stood still at the meridian point," or "at the meridian circle," and not "in the middle of the heaven"; in fact, for a spherical body such as heaven, the middle is really and only the center.

WORKING WITH SOURCES

1. How does Galileo deal with the apparently irreconcilable conclusions of science and the Bible?
2. How would you characterize Galileo's tone in his analysis of the verses from the Book of Joshua?

18. NEW PATTERNS IN NEW WORLDS: COLONIALISM AND INDIGENOUS RESPONSES IN THE AMERICAS, 1500–1800

18.1   Hernán Cortés, *Second Letter from Mexico to Emperor Charles V*, 1522

With a handful of untrained and poorly equipped soldiers, Hernán Cortés overthrew the powerful Aztec civilization between 1519 and 1520. Born in Spain around 1485, Cortés decided to inform the king of Spain (and Holy Roman emperor) Charles V of his achievements, in a series of written updates. Despite their ostensible purpose, these "letters" were designed for more than the edification and delight of the emperor. Like Julius Caesar's dispatches from the Gallic Wars of the 50s BCE—in which at least one million Gauls were killed and another million enslaved—these accounts were designed for broad public consumption. Each letter was sent to Spain as soon as it was ready, and it seems likely that Cortés's father, Martín, arranged for their immediate publication. Over the course of these five published letters, although Cortés developed a persona for himself as a conquering hero and agent of imperial power, he also exposed the ruthlessness and brutality of his "conquest" of Mexico.

From henceforth they offered themselves as vassals of Your Sacred Majesty and swore to remain so always and to serve and assist in all things that Your Highness commanded them. A notary set all this down through the interpreters which I had. Still I determined to go with them; on the one hand, so as not to show weakness and, on the other, because I hoped to conduct my business with Mutezuma from that city because it bordered on his territory, as I have said, and on the road between the two there is free travel and no frontier restrictions.

When the people of Tascalteca saw my determination it distressed them considerably, and they told me many times that I was mistaken, but since they were vassals of Your Sacred Majesty and my friends they would go with me to assist me in whatever might happen. Although I opposed this and asked them not to come, as it was unnecessary, they followed me with some 100,000 men, all well armed for war, and came within two leagues of the city. After much persuasion on my part they returned, though there remained in my company some five or six thousand of them. That night I slept in a ditch, hoping to divest myself of these people in case they caused trouble in the city, and because it was already late enough and I did not want to enter too late. The following morning, they came out of the city to greet me with many trumpets and drums, including many persons whom they regard as priests in their temples, dressed in traditional vestments and singing after their fashion, as they do in the temples. With such ceremony they led us into the city and gave us very good quarters, where all those in my company were most comfortable. There they brought us food, though not sufficient.

. . .

Source: Hernán Cortés: Letters from Mexico, edited and translated by Anthony Pagden (Yale University Press, 1986), 72–74.

During the three days I remained in that city they fed us worse each day, and the lords and principal persons of the city came only rarely to see and speak with me. And being somewhat disturbed by this, my interpreter, who is an Indian woman from Putunchan, which is the great river of which I spoke to Your Majesty in the first letter, was told by another Indian woman and a native of this city that very close by many of Mutezuma's men were gathered, and that the people of the city had sent away their women and children and all their belongings, and were about to fall on us and kill us all; and that if she wished to escape she should go with her and she would shelter her. All this she told to Gerónimo de Aguilar, an interpreter whom I acquired in Yucatán, of whom I have also written to Your Highness; and he informed me. I then seized one of the natives of this city who was passing by and took him aside secretly and questioned him; and he confirmed what the woman and the natives of Tascalteca had told me. Because of this and because of the signs I had observed, I decided to forestall an attack, and I sent for some of the chiefs of the city, saying that I wished to speak with them. I put them in a room and meanwhile warned our men to be prepared, when a harquebus was fired, to fall on the many Indians who were outside our quarters and on those who were inside. And so it was done, that after I had put the chiefs in the room, I left them bound up and rode away and had the harquebus fired, and we fought so hard that in two hours more than three thousand men were killed.

. . .

After fifteen or twenty days which I remained there the city and the land were so pacified and full of people that it seemed as if no one were missing from it, and their markets and trade were carried on as before. I then restored the friendly relations between this city of Curultecal and Tascalteca, which had existed in the recent past, before Mutezuma had attracted them to his friendship with gifts and made them enemies of the others.

WORKING WITH SOURCES

1. Does Cortés offer a justification for his treatment of the people of Tascalteca? Why or why not?
2. What were the risks associated with Cortés's reliance on translators as he conquered the natives of Mexico?

18.2 Marina de San Miguel's Confessions before the Inquisition, Mexico City, 1598–1599

The Inquisition was well established in Spain at the time of Cortés's conquest in the 1520s. A tribunal of the Holy Office of the Inquisition came in the conquistadors' wake, ultimately established at Mexico City in 1571 with authority to regulate Catholic morality throughout "New Spain." Most of the Inquisition trials concerned petty breaches of religious conduct, but others dealt with the much more serious crime of heresy. In November 1598, the Inquisition became alarmed about the rise of a group who believed that the Day of Judgment was at hand. Among the group denounced to the Holy Office was Marina de San Miguel, a Spanish-born woman who held

Source: Jacqueline Holler, "The Spiritual and Physical Ecstasies of a Sixteenth-Century Beata: Marina de San Miguel Confesses Before the Mexican Inquisition," in Richard Boyer and Geoffrey Spurling, eds., *Colonial Lives: Documents on Latin American History, 1550–1850* (New York: Oxford University Press, 2000), 79–98.

a high status due to her mystical visions. Her confessions, offered between November 1598 and January 1599, reveal the degree to which confessions of "deviance" could be extorted from a victim. In March 1601, Marina was stripped naked to the waist and paraded upon a mule. Forced to confess her errors, she was sentenced to 100 lashes with a whip.

First Confession

In the city of Mexico, Friday, November 20, 1598. The Lord Inquisitor *licenciado* don Alonso de Peralta in his morning audience ordered that a woman be brought before him from one of the secret prisons of this Holy Office. Being present, she swore an oath *en forma devida de derecho** under which she promised to tell the truth here in this audience and in all the others that might be held until the determination of her case, and to keep secret everything that she might see or believe or that might be talked about with her or that might happen concerning this her case.

. . .

She was asked if she knows, presumes, or suspects the cause for her arrest and imprisonment in the prisons of the Holy Office. . . . The inquisitor said that with her illness she must have imagined it. And she says that she wants to go over her memory so that she can tell the truth about everything that she might remember.

With this the audience ceased, because it was past eleven. The above was read and she approved it and signed it. And she was ordered to return to her cell, very admonished to examine her memory as she was offered to do.

. . .

Third Confession

In the city of Mexico, Tuesday, November 24, 1598. . . .

She said that what she has remembered is that in the course of her life some spiritual things have happened to her, which she has talked about to some people. And she believes that they have been the cause of her imprisonment, because they were scandalized by what she told them.

. . .

And then she opened her eyes and began to shake and get up from the bench on which she was seated, saying, "My love, help me God, how strongly you have given me this." And among these words she said to the Lord Inquisitor that when she is given these trances, she should be shaken vigorously to awaken her from her deep dream. Then she returned to being as though sleeping. The inquisitor called her by her name and she did not respond, nor the second time. And the third time she opened her eyes and made faces, and made signs with her hands to her mouth.

. . .

Sixth Confession

In the city of Mexico, Monday, January 25, 1599. . . .

She said that it's like this. . . . She has been condemned to hell, because for fifteen years she has had a sensual temptation of the flesh, which makes her perform dishonest acts with her own hands on her shameful parts. She came to pollution [orgasm] saying dishonest words that provoke lust, calling by their dishonest names many dirty and lascivious things. She was tempted to this by the devil, who appeared to her internally in the form of an Angel of Light, who told her that she should do these things, because they were no sin. This was to make her abandon her scruples. And the devil appeared to her in the form of Christ our Redeemer, in such a way that she might uncover her breasts and have carnal union with him. And thus, for fifteen years, she has had carnal union occasionally from month to month, or every two months. And if it had been more she would accuse herself of that too, because she is only trying to save her soul, with no regard to honor or the world. And the carnal act that the devil as Angel of Light and in the form of Christ had with her was the same as if she had had it with a man. And he kissed her, and she enjoyed it, and she felt a great ardor in her whole body, with particular delight and pleasure.

. . .

Eighth Confession

In the city of Mexico, Wednesday, January 27, 1599. . . .

But all the times she had the copulation with the devil in the form of Christ she doubted whether it was the devil or not, from which doubts one can infer that she did not believe as firmly as she ought to have that such things could not possibly be from Christ. In this she should urgently discharge her conscience. . . .

. . .

After the *Ninth Confession*:
In the city of Mexico, Tuesday, Day of the Purification of our Lady, February 2, 1599, the Lord Inquisitor in his afternoon audience ordered Marina de San Miguel brought before him. And once present she was told that if she has remembered anything in her case she should say it, and the truth, under the oath that she has made.

She said no. . . .

WORKING WITH SOURCES

1. What does this document indicate about the working methods of the Inquisition (and their "successes") in Mexico in the 1590s?
2. Does the Inquisition seem to have been more concerned about Marina's sexuality than her mystical "experiences?"

18.3   Nahuatl Land Sale Documents, Mexico, ca. 1610s

After the conquest of the Aztec imperial capital of Tenochtitlan, Spaniards turned their attention to the productive farmland in the surrounding countryside, which was inhabited by Nahuatl-speaking native people. By the late sixteenth century, Spaniards began to expand rapidly into this territory. They acquired estates in a variety of ways, from royal grants to open seizure of property. Nevertheless, the purchase of plots of land from individual Nahuas was also common—although sometimes the sellers came to regret the transaction and petitioned higher authorities for redress of their grievances.

Here in the *altepetl* Santo Domingo Mixcoac, Marquesado del Valle, on the first day of July of the year 1612, I, Joaquín de San Francisco, and my wife, Juana Feliciana, citizens here in the *altepetl* of Santa María Purificación Tlilhuacan, sell to Dr. Diego de León Plaza, *teopixqui*, one field and house that we have in the *tlaxilacalli* Tlilhuacan next to the house of Juan Bautista, Spaniard. Where we are is right in the middle of [in between] their houses. And now we receive [the money] in person. The reason we sell it is that we have no children to whom it might belong. For there is another land and house, but [the land] here we can no longer [work] because it is really in the middle of [land belonging to] Spaniards. [The land] is not *tributario*, for my father, named Juan Altamirano, and my mother, María Catalina, really left it to me. And now I give it to [the doctor] very voluntarily. And now he is personally giving me 130 pesos. Both my wife and I receive it in person before the witnesses. And the tribute will be remedied with [the price]; it will pay it. The land [upon which tribute is owed] is at Colonanco. It is adjacent to the land of

Altepetl: City-state.
Teopixqui: Priest, in Nahuatl.
Tlaxilacalli: Subunit of an *altepetl*.

Source: Rebecca Horn, "Spaniards in the Nahua Countryside: Dr. Diego de León Plaza and Nahuatl Land Sale Documents" (Mexico, Early Seventeenth Century), in Richard Boyer and Geoffrey Spurling, eds., *Colonial Lives: Documents on Latin American History, 1550–1850* (New York: Oxford University Press, 2000), 102–103, 108–109.

Miguel de Santiago and Lucas Pérez. And the witnesses [are] Antonio de Fuentes and señora Inés de Vera and Juana de Vera, Spanish women (and the Nahuas) Juan Josef, Gabriel Francisco, María, Mariana, and Sebastián Juan. And because we do not know how to write, I, Joaquín [de San] Francisco, and my wife asked a witness to set down [a signature] on our behalf [along with the notary?] Juan Vázquez, Spaniard. Witnesses, Antonio de Fuentes, [etc.] Before me, Matías Valeriano, notary. And both of them, he and his wife [Joaquín de San Francisco and Juana Feliciana], received the 140 pesos each three months, [presumably paid in installments?] before the witnesses who were mentioned. Before me, Matías Valeriano, notary.

. . .

[Letter of complaint to the authorities of Santo Domino Mixcoac, on the behalf of a group of Nahuas, undated:]

We are citizens here in Santo Domingo Mixcoac. We state that we found out that Paula and Juana and María and Catalina and Inés and Anastacia complain about the *teniente* before you [the *corregidor*, *gobernador*, *regidores*, etc.]. It is Antonio de Fuentes whom they

_____

Teniente: Lieutenant.

are accusing because they say he mistreats them. [They say] he robs [people's land].

. . .

And now [the] Spaniard Napolles disputes with the *teniente*. And Napolles goes around to each house exerting pressure on, forcing many people [to say "get rid of the *teniente*"]. [He says:] "Let there be no officer of the justice. I will help you expel the *teniente* because we will be happy if there is no officer of the law on your land." Napolles, Spaniard, keeps a woman at his house and he is forcing her. For this reason [the authorities] arrested him for concubinage. They gave him a fine about which he became very angry and they arrested him. He stole four pigs, the property of a person named Francisco Hernández, Spaniard, and because of that they arrested him. He was scorched [burned] for their relatives accuse them.

. . .

And so now with great concern and with bowing down we implore you [the *corregidor*, *gobernador*, and *regidores*, etc.] and we ask for justice. Everyone knows how [the blacks and *mestizos*] mistreat us. They don't go to confession. They are already a little afraid and are already living a little better. And we ask for justice. Let them be punished. We who ask it are Juan Joseph, Francisco de San Juan, and Francisco Juan.

WORKING WITH SOURCES

1. Why do the documents incorporate Nahuatl terms at some times but not at others?
2. How do the documents illustrate the various levels of justice available to native people and to "Spaniards"?

18.4 *The Jesuit Relations*, French North America, 1649

_____

The Jesuit Relations are the most important documents attesting to the encounter between Europeans and native North Americans in the seventeenth century. These annual reports of French missionaries from the Society of Jesus document the conversions—or attempted conversions—of the various indigenous peoples in what is today the St. Lawrence River basin and the Great Lakes region.

_____

Source: Paul Ragueneau, "Relation of 1648–49," in Allan Greer, ed., *The Jesuit Relations: Natives and Missionaries in Seventeenth-Century North America* (Boston: Bedford/St. Martin's, 2000), 112–115.

When they arrived on the banks of the St. Lawrence in 1625, French Jesuits were entering a continent still very much under control of First Nations peoples, who were divided by their own ethnic and linguistic differences. Even the catch-all terms "Huron" and "Iroquois" masked their nature as confederacies, composed of several distinct nations, who had joined together prior to the arrival of Europeans.

When the Jesuits made headway with one group, they usually lost initiative with the group's rivals—and sometimes found themselves in the midst of a conflict that they could barely understand or appreciate. This section of the *Relations* concerns the torture and murder of Jean Brébeuf, who had lived among the Hurons at various points from the 1620s through the 1640s, observing their culture and systematically attempting to convert them to Catholicism. However, when an Iroquois raiding party invaded his settlement, the depth of the Hurons' Christian commitment—and his own—would be tested.

The sixteenth day of March in the present year, 1649, marked the beginning of our misfortunes—if an event, which no doubt has been the salvation of many of God's elect, can be called a misfortune.

The Iroquois, enemies of the Hurons, arrived by night at the frontier of this country. They numbered about a thousand men, well furnished with weapons, most of them carrying firearms obtained from their allies, the Dutch. We had no knowledge of their approach, although they had started from their country in the autumn, hunting in the forests throughout the winter, and had made a difficult journey of nearly two hundred leagues over the snow in order to take us by surprise. By night, they reconnoitered the condition of the first place upon which they had designs. It was surrounded by a pine stockade fifteen or sixteen feet in height, and a deep ditch with which nature had strongly fortified this place on three sides. There remained only a small space that was weaker than the others.

It was at this weak point that the enemy made a breach at daybreak, but so secretly and promptly that he was master of the place before anyone could mount a defense. All were then sleeping deeply, and they had no time to recognize the danger. Thus this village was taken, almost without striking a blow and with only ten Iroquois killed. Part of the Hurons—men, women, and children—were massacred then and there, while the others were made captives and were reserved for cruelties more terrible than death.

. . .

The enemy did not stop there, but followed up his victory, and before sunrise he appeared in arms to attack the town of St. Louis, which was fortified with a fairly good stockade. Most of the women and the children had just gone from it upon hearing the news which had arrived regarding the approach of the Iroquois. The people of greatest courage, about eighty persons, being resolved to defend themselves well, courageously repulsed the first and the second assaults, killing about thirty of the enemy's boldest men, in addition to many wounded. But finally, the larger number prevailed, as the Iroquois used their hatchets to undermine the palisade of stakes and opened a passage for themselves through some considerable breaches.

About nine o'clock in the morning, we perceived from our house at St. Marie the fire which was consuming the cabins of that town, where the enemy, after entering victoriously, had reduced everything to desolation. They cast into the flames the old, the sick, the children who had not been able to escape, and all those who, being too severely wounded, could not have followed them into captivity. At the sight of those flames, and by the color of the smoke which issued from them, we understood sufficiently what was happening, for this town of St. Louis was no more than a league distant from us. Two Christians who escaped the fire arrived about this time and confirmed this.

In this town of St. Louis were at that time two of our fathers, Father Jean de Brébeuf and Father Gabriel

Lalemant, who had charge of a cluster of five towns. These formed but one of the eleven missions of which we have spoken above, and we call it the mission of St. Ignace.

Some Christians had begged the fathers to preserve their lives for the glory of God, which would have been as easy for them as for the more than five hundred persons who went away at the first alarm, for there was more than enough time to reach a place of safety. But their zeal could not permit such a thing, and the salvation of their flock was dearer to them than the love of their own lives. They employed the moments left to them as the most precious which they had ever had in the world, and through the heat of the battle their hearts were on fire for the salvation of souls. One was at the breach, baptizing the **catechumens**, and the other was giving absolution to the **neophytes**. Both of them urged the Christians to die in the sentiments of

___

Catechumens: Native converts who had not yet been baptized.
Neophytes: Recently baptized Christians.

piety with which they consoled them in their miseries. Never was their faith more alive, nor their love for their good fathers and pastors more keenly felt.

An infidel, seeing the desperate situation, spoke of taking flight, but a Christian named Etienne Annaotaha, the most esteemed in the country for his courage and his exploits against the enemy, would never allow it. "What!" he said. "Could we ever abandon these two good fathers, who have exposed their lives for us? Their love for our salvation will be the cause of their death, for there is no longer time for them to flee across the snows. Let us then die with them, and we shall go together to heaven." This man had made a general confession a few days previously, having had a presentiment of the danger awaiting him and saying that he wished that death should find him disposed for Heaven. And indeed he, as well as many other Christians, had abandoned themselves to fervor in a manner so extraordinary that we shall never be sufficiently able to bless the guidance of God over so many predestined souls. His divine providence continues lovingly to guide them in death as in life.

WORKING WITH SOURCES

1. How well do the Jesuits seem to have understood the conflicts among native peoples in this region?
2. How was Ragueneau's reporting of the battle designed to highlight the "success" of the mission, despite an apparent setback?

18.5 The Salem Witch Trials, British North America, 1692

The witch hunt that took place in Salem, Massachusetts, in 1692 has been frequently (if sensationally) depicted in modern films and plays. But a reading of the extant documents used in the trial of the supposed witches provides a more nuanced insight into the process of denunciation, conviction, and execution that unfolded in this persecution, which was among the last in the Western world. Although the Salem witch hunt resulted in the conviction of 30 and the execution of 19, the total number of persons who had been formally accused reached 164. Doubts about the guilt of those executed eventually led to a reconsideration of the procedures used in the trial, and the governor of the colony abruptly suspended the trials in the autumn of 1692. In spite of the admission by some of the Salem jurors that they had been mistaken, the judgments passed on seven of the convicted were not reversed until 2001.

Source: Brian P. Levack, ed., *The Witchcraft Sourcebook* (New York: Routledge, 2004), 225–226, 228–229.

Samuel Gray of Salem, aged about 42 years, testifieth and saith that about fourteen years ago, he going to bed well one [a.m.] one Lord's Day at night, and after he had been asleep some time, he awakened and looking up, saw the house light as if a candle or candles were lighted in it and the door locked, and that little fire there was raked up. He did then see a woman standing between the cradle in the room and the bedside and seemed to look upon him. So he did rise up in his bed and it vanished or disappeared. Then he went to the door and found it locked, and unlocking and opening the door, he went to the entry door and looked out and then again did see the same woman he had a little before seen in the room and in the same garb she was in before. Then he said to her, "What in the name of God do you come for?" Then she vanished away, so he locked the door again and went to bed, and between sleeping and waking he felt something come to his mouth or lips cold, and thereupon started and looked up again and did see the same woman with some thing between both her hands holding before his mouth upon which she moved. And the child in the cradle gave a great screech out as if it was greatly hurt and she disappeared, and taking the child up could not quiet it in some hours from which time the child that was before a very lively, thriving child did pine away and was never well, although it lived some months after, yet in a sad condition and so died. Some time after within a week or less he did see the same woman in the same garb and clothes that appeared to him as aforesaid, and although he knew not her nor her name before, yet both by the countenance and garb doth testify that it was the same woman that they now call Bridget Bishop, alias Oliver, of Salem. Sworn Salem, May 30th 1692.

. . .

The deposition of Joseph Ring at Salisbury, aged 27 years, being sworn, saith that about the latter end of September last, being in the wood with his brother Jarvis Ring hewing of timber, his brother went home with his team and left this deponent alone to finish the hewing of the piece for him for his brother to carry when he came again. But as soon as his brother was gone there came to this deponent the appearance of Thomas Hardy of the great island of Puscataway, and by some impulse he was forced to follow him to the house of Benovy Tucker, which was deserted and about a half a mile from the place he was at work in, and in that house did appear Susannah Martin of Amesbury and the aforesaid Hardy and another female person which the deponent did not know. There they had a good fire and drink—it seemed to be cider. There continued most part of the night, [the] said Martin being then in her natural shape and talking as if she used to. But towards the morning the said Martin went from the fire, made a noise, and turned into the shape of a black hog and went away, and so did the other. Two persons go away, and this deponent was strangely carried away also, and the first place he knew was by Samuel Woods' house in Amesbury.

. . .

The deposition of Thomas Putnam, aged 40 years and [Edward Putnam] aged 38 years, who testify and say that we have been conversant with the afflicted persons or the most of them, as namely Mary Walcott, Mercy Lewes, Elizabeth Hubbard, Abigail Williams, Sarah Bibber and Ann Putnam junior and have often heard the aforementioned persons complain of Susannah Martin of Amesbery [sic] torturing them, and we have seen the marks of several bites and pinches which they say Susannah Martin did hurt them with, and also on the second day of May 1692, being the day of the examination of Susannah Martin, the aforenamed persons were most grievously tortured during the time of her examination, for upon a glance of her eyes they were struck down or almost choked and upon the motion of her finger we took notes they were afflicted, and if she did but clench her hands or hold her head aside the afflicted persons aforementioned were most grievously tortured, complaining of Susannah Martin for hurting them.

WORKING WITH SOURCES

1. What do these documents suggest about the (supposed) powers of witches, especially in terms of acting at a distance upon their victims?
2. Although all of the witnesses in this set of documents were men, do they reveal something about the connection between witchcraft accusations and gender?

19. AFRICAN KINGDOMS, THE ATLANTIC SLAVE TRADE, AND THE ORIGINS OF BLACK AMERICA, 1450–1800

19.1 Abd al-Rahman al-Saadi on the Scholars of Timbuktu, ca. 1655

Born in Timbuktu in 1596, Abd al-Rahman al-Saadi wrote, in Arabic, a chronicle entitled *Tarikh al-Sudan* (*History of the Sudan*). The document addresses the political, cultural, and religious history of the Songhay state in the fifteenth and sixteenth centuries, and it also offers detailed accounts of various states in the Niger River valley into al-Saadi's own day. Al-Saadi was particularly interested in the impact of Islamic thought and culture on the African kingdoms, as the following excerpt demonstrates. The document was discovered by a German explorer in the 1850s during his visit to Timbuktu.

This is an account of some of the scholars and holymen who dwelt in Timbuktu generation after generation—may God Most High have mercy on them, and be pleased with them, and bring us the benefit of their *baraka* in both abodes —and of some of their virtues and noteworthy accomplishments. In this regard, it is sufficient to repeat what the trustworthy shaykhs have said, on the authority of the righteous and virtuous Friend of God, locus of manifestations of divine grace and wondrous acts, the jurist *Qāḍī* Muhammad al-Kābarī—may God Most High have mercy on him. He said: "I was the contemporary of righteous folk of Sankore, who were equaled in their righteousness only by the Companions of the Messenger of God—may God bless him and grant him peace and be pleased with all of them."

Among them were (1) the jurist al-Hājj, grand father of *Qāḍī* 'Abd al-Rahmān b. Abī Bakr b. al-Hājj. He held the post of *qāḍī* during the last days of Malian rule, and was the first person to institute recitation of half a *hizb* of the Qur'ān for teaching purposes in the Sankore mosque after both the mid-afternoon and the evening worship. He and his brother Sayyid Ibrā hīm the jurist left Bīru to settle in Bangu. His tomb there is a well-known shrine, and it is said he is a *badal*. The following account is related on the authority of our virtuous and ascetic shaykh, the jurist al-Amīn b. Ahmad, who said, "In his day the Sultan of Mossi came campaigning as far as Bangu, and people went out to fight him. It so happened that a group of people were sitting with al-Hājj at that moment, and he uttered something over [a dish of] millet and told them to eat it. They all did so except for one man, who was his son-in-law, and he declined to do so because of their relationship by marriage. Then the holyman said to them, "Go off and fight. Their arrows will do

---

Hizb: Segment.
Badal: Fifth rank in the Sufi hierarchy.

Source: Abd al-Rahman al-Saadi, *Timbuktu and the Songhay Empire*, trans. John Hunwick (Leiden, the Netherlands: Brill, 2003), 38–40.

you no harm." All of them escaped harm except for the man who did not eat, and he was killed in that battle. The Sultan of Mossi and his army were defeated and driven off, having gained nothing from the people of Bangu, thanks to the *baraka* of that sayyid.

From him is descended the Friend of God Most High the jurist Ibrāhīm, son of the Friend of God Most High, the jurist *Qāḍī* 'Umar who lived in Yindubu'u, both of whom were righteous servants of God. It was Askiya *al-ḥājj* Muhammad who appointed 'Umar *qāḍī* of that place. From time to time one of his sister's sons used to visit Timbuktu, and the jurist *Qāḍī* Mahmūd complained to Askiya *al-ḥājj* Muhammad that this man was slandering them to the people of Yindubu'u. When the Askiya visited Tila the jurist *Qāḍī* 'Umar came with a group of men from Yindubu'u to pay him a courtesy call. The Askiya inquired after his sister's son, so 'Umar presented him to him. The Askiya said, "You are the one who was been sowing discord between the jurist Mahmūd and your maternal uncle." The *qāḍī* was annoyed, and retorted, "You, who appointed one *qāḍī* in Timbuktu and another in Yindubu'u, are the one sowing discord." Then he got up angrily and went off to the waterfront, saying to his companions, "Let us go off and cross the river and be on our way." When they got there, he wanted to cross it, but they said, "It is not yet time for the ferry. Be patient until it comes." He replied, "What if it does not come?" They realised that he was prepared to cross the river without a boat. So they restrained him and sat him down until the ferry came, and they all crossed over together—may God have mercy on them and bring us benefit through them. Amen!

WORKING WITH SOURCES

1. Why did the scholars and holy men of Timbuktu draw a visitor's attention?
2. Are there indications in this document of a culture that was still fusing Islamic and non-Islamic traditions together?

19.2   Letter of Nzinga Mbemba (Afonso I) of Kongo to the King of Portugal, 1526

A Portuguese sailor came into contact with the Kingdom of Kongo, which occupied a vast territory along the Congo River in central Africa, in 1483. When he returned in 1491, he was accompanied by Portuguese priests and Portuguese products, and in the same year the Kongolese king and his son were baptized as Catholics. When the son succeeded his father in 1506, he took the Christian name Afonso and promoted the introduction of European culture and religion within his kingdom. His son Henrique was educated in Portugal and became a Catholic bishop. However, Afonso's kingdom began to deteriorate in subsequent decades, as the Portuguese made further inroads into his territory, pursuing ruthless commercial practices and trading in slaves captured in his dominions. In 1526, the king sent desperate letters to King João III of Portugal, urging him to control his own subjects and to respect the alliance—and the common Catholic faith—that bound the Europeans and the Africans.

Sir, Your Highness should know how our Kingdom is being lost in so many ways that it is convenient to provide for the necessary remedy, since this is caused by the excessive freedom given by your agents and officials to the men and merchants who are allowed to come to this Kingdom to set up shops with

Source: https://www2.stetson.edu/secure/history/hy10430/afonso.html

goods and many things which have been prohibited by us, and which they spread throughout our Kingdoms and Domains in such an abundance that many of our vassals, whom we had in obedience, do not comply because they have the things in greater abundance than we ourselves; and it was with these things that we had them content and subjected under our vassalage and jurisdiction, so it is doing a great harm not only to the service of God, but the security and peace of our Kingdoms and State as well.

And we cannot reckon how great the damage is, since the mentioned merchants are taking every day our natives, sons of the land and the sons of our noblemen and vassals and our relatives, because the thieves and men of bad conscience grab them wishing to have the things and wares of this Kingdom which they are ambitious of; they grab them and get them to be sold; and so great, Sir, is the corruption and licentiousness that our country is being completely depopulated, and Your Highness should not agree with this nor accept it as in your service. And to avoid it we need from those (your) Kingdoms no more than some priests and a few people to teach in schools, and no other goods except wine and flour for the holy sacrament. That is why we beg of Your Highness to help and assist us in this matter, commanding your factors that they should not send here either merchants or wares, because it is our will that in these Kingdoms there should not be any trade of slaves nor outlet for them. Concerning what is referred [to] above, again we beg of Your Highness to agree with it, since otherwise we cannot remedy such an obvious damage. Pray Our Lord in His mercy to have Your Highness under His guard and let you do forever the things of His service. I kiss your hands many times. . . .

(At our town of Kongo, written on the sixth day of July in 1526.)

Moreover, Sir, in our Kingdoms there is another great inconvenience which is of little service to God, and this is that many of our people, keenly desirous as they are of the wares and things of your Kingdoms, which are brought here by your people, and in order to satisfy their voracious appetite, seize many of our people, freed and exempt men, and very often it happens that they kidnap even noblemen and the sons of noblemen, and our relatives, and take them to be sold to the white men who are in our Kingdoms; and for this purpose they have concealed them; and others are brought during the night so that they might not be recognized.

And as soon as they are taken by the white men they are immediately ironed and branded with fire, and when they are carried to be embarked, if they are caught by our guards' men the whites allege that they have bought them but they cannot say from whom, so that it is our duty to do justice and to restore to the freemen their freedom, but it cannot be done if your subjects feel offended, as they claim to be.

And to avoid such a great evil we passed a law so that any white man living in our Kingdoms and wanting to purchase goods in any way should first inform three of our noblemen and officials of our court whom we rely upon in this matter, and these are Dom Pedro Manipanza and Dom Manuel Manissaba, our chief usher, and Goncalo Pires our chief freighter, who should investigate if the mentioned goods are captives or free men, and if cleared by them there will be no further doubt nor embargo for them to be taken and embarked. But if the white men do not comply with it they will lose the aforementioned goods. And if we do them this favor and concession it is for the part Your Highness has in it, since we know that it is in your service too that these goods are taken from our Kingdom, otherwise we should not consent to this. . . . (date of letter, October 18, 1526.)

WORKING WITH SOURCES

1. What do these documents indicate about the intersections of international commerce and the slave trade?
2. In what terms does King Afonso issue his protest to the Portuguese king, and why?

19.3   Documents Concerning the Slave Ship *Sally*, Rhode Island, 1765

Rhode Islanders were the principal American slave traders during the eighteenth century, during which a total of approximately 1,000 slave-trading voyages set out from the colony to Africa. The "triangular trade" between the Atlantic seaboard, the Caribbean, and West Africa was the main source of great wealth for many families in this small British settlement. Among these families was that of John Brown, whose donation to a struggling college in Providence would lead to the renaming of the institution in his honor. Aware of their university's explicit connection to the profitable and lethal slave trade, archivists at Brown University have attempted to tell the full story of voyages like that of the *Sally*. In the excerpts that follow, lines from the ship's log are annotated with details of the events they describe.

December 11, 1764: At James Fort, on the River Gambia

By early December, the Sally had arrived at James Fort, the primary British slave "factory" on Africa's Windward Coast. Located fifteen miles from the mouth of the Gambia River, James Fort was the collection point for slaves coming down from the interior, and British and North American ships routinely stopped there to acquire provisions and slaves. On December 11, Hopkins purchased thirteen Africans from Governor Debatt, the British official who ran the fort, in exchange for 1,200 gallons of rum and sundry stores.

June 8, 1765: "Woman Slave hanged her Self between Decks"

While most slave ships worked their way along the coast, the Sally appears to have remained largely in one place, apparently at a small British slave "factory" near the mouth of the River Grande, in what is today Guinea-Bissau. Hopkins traded rum with passing slave ships, acquiring manufactured goods like cloth, iron bars, and guns, which he then used to acquire slaves. On June 8, 1765, he purchased his 108th captive. That same day, an enslaved woman committed suicide. She was the second captive to die on the ship.

Newport July 17, 1765
Sir

Having heard by Capt Morris that you had Lost all your Hands in the River Basa I came down here, last Evening on purpose to Take Some method to suply the misfortune as much as Possable, by the Two Vessels Just about sailing from this place Capt Briggs & Capt Moor but Receiving your Letter of ye 15th May this morning which giving us Such favourable accounts of your Circumstance from what we had heard Quite aleviates our Misfortune and prevents dewing any thing further than Writing you by these opertunitys principaly to Inform you that (Notwithstanding our first orders to you & our Letter to Barbadoes of ye 4th Ultimo advising you to go to South Carolina,) that the market there is Surpriseingly Glutted with Slaves So that it will not by any means do to go there Therefore Recomend if you Can get £20 Sterling for your Well Slaves Land at Barbadoes to sell there . . . and Lay out ye Neet proceed in 30 hogshead Rum 8 or 10 hogshead Sugar & 3 or 4 Baggs of Cotton the remainder in full Weight money or Good Bills but money full Weight is 5percent better for us than bills and proceed home, without giving yourself any further trouble about Loading with Salt But if your Slaves Should be in good order and you Cannot get that proceed to Jamaica and there Dispose of them for ye same of pay & proceed home, but Notwithstanding what we here advise if you

Source: From John Carter Brown Library http://cds.library.brown.edu/projects/sally/documents.html

think any other port in the Westindes will Do better Considering all ye Risque, you are At full Liberty to go and Inshort do by Vessel & Cargo in that Respect as if She wass your own all friends and particularly your family is Well

M

2

Burroughs is this morning gone to Providence in order to Carry your Letter to Mrs Hopkins. you may depend. . . . Friends nor money shall not be Wanting to make the Insurance you Wish for to your Wife whose Letter Mr Burrows opend in order to Relieve the aprehentions of his father & family from ye Maloncholy Tale Brought by Capt Morris

I am for Self & Co. your Assured Frend
MB

Copy Letter
to Capt Esek

Hopkins July
1765

July 17, 1765: The Browns receive word from Hopkins

In June, 1765, after months with no news from the Sally, the Browns received reports that the ship and crew had been lost. Those rumors were contradicted on July 17, when a letter belatedly arrived from Hopkins, safe on the River Grande. Though Hopkins reported the loss of one crewman and substantial loss of his cargo through leakage, the Browns were elated. Your letter "Quite Aleviates our Misfortune," they wrote.

Original in the John Carter Brown Library at Brown University

Log Book From the Slave Ship *Sally*

August 20, 1765: The Sally embarks for the Americas
On August 20, 1765, more than nine months after his arrival on the African coast, Hopkins acquired his 196th and final captive. Nineteen Africans had already died on the ship. A twentieth captive, a "woman all Most dead," was left behind as a present for Anthony, the ship's "Linguister," or translator. At least twenty-one Africans had been sold to other slave traders on the coast, bringing the Sally's "cargo" to about 155 people.

August 28, 1765: "Slaves Rose on us was obliged fire on them and Destroyed 8"
Four more Africans died in the first week of the Sally's return voyage. On August 28, desperate captives staged an insurrection, which Hopkins and the crew violently suppressed. Eight Africans died immediately, and two others later succumbed to their wounds. According to Hopkins, the captives were "so Desperited" after the failed insurrection that "Some Drowned them Selves Some Starved and Others Sickened & Dyed."

October, 1765: The Sally arrives in the West Indies
The Sally reached the West Indies in early October, 1765, after a transatlantic passage of about seven weeks. After a brief layover in Barbados, the ship proceeded to Antigua, where Hopkins wrote to the Browns, alerting them to the scope of the disaster. Sixty-eight Africans had perished during the passage, and twenty more died in the days immediately following the ship's arrival, bringing the death toll to 108. A 109th captive would later die en route to Providence.

November 16, 1765: "Sales of Negroes at Public Vendue"
When they dispatched the Sally, the Brown brothers instructed Hopkins to return to Providence with four or five "likely lads" for the family's use. The rest of the Sally survivors were auctioned in Antigua. Sickly and emaciated, they commanded extremely low prices at auction. The last two dozen survivors were auctioned in Antigua on November 16, selling, in one case, for less than £5, scarcely a tenth of the value of a "prime slave."

"Brig Sally's Account Book".

WORKING WITH SOURCES

1. How do these documents illuminate the economic and market forces that were bound up in the transatlantic slave trade?
2. What were the practical consequences of viewing human slaves as a commercial product?

19.4   *The Interesting Narrative of the Life of Olaudah Equiano, 1789*

This autobiography of a slave who would emerge as a leading voice in the abolitionist cause has been enormously significant for understanding Atlantic slavery. Equiano claimed to have been born a prince among the Igbo people of modern Nigeria around 1745, kidnapped as a child, and

Source: Henry Louis Gates, Jr., ed., *The Classic Slave Narratives* (New York: Mentor, 1987), 99–100, 102–103.

transported across the ocean to the West Indies and Virginia. Named by his first (of several) masters after the sixteenth-century king Gustav I of Sweden, "Gustavus Vas[s]a" would travel throughout the southern American colonies and the Caribbean, always longing to achieve his freedom. Shaming his Quaker master into honoring a promise, Equiano was freed in 1765, but he continued to suffer the indignities and risks attending a free black man living in a slave society. His published memoir was designed to galvanize antislavery forces, and his work elicited sufficient sympathy and respect to contribute to the abolition of the British slave trade (though not slavery itself) in 1807.

We set sail once more for Montserrat, and arrived there safe; but much out of humour with our friend, the silversmith. When we had unladen the vessel, and I had sold my venture, finding myself master of about forty-seven pounds, I consulted my true friend, the Captain, how I should proceed in offering my master the money for my freedom. He told me to come on a certain morning, when he and my master would be at breakfast together. Accordingly, on that morning I went, and met the Captain there, as he had appointed. When I went in I made my obeisance to my master, and with my money in my hand, and many fears in my heart, I prayed him to be as good as his offer to me, when he was pleased to promise me my freedom as soon as I could purchase it. This speech seemed to confound him; he began to recoil; and my heart that instant sunk within me. "What," said he, "give you your freedom? Why, where did you get the money? Have you got forty pounds sterling?" "Yes, sir," I answered. "How did you get it?" replied he. I told him, "very honestly." The Captain then said he knew I got the money very honestly and with much industry, and that I was particularly careful. On which my master replied, I got money much faster than he did; and said he would not have made me the promise which he did, had he thought I should have got the money so soon. "Come, come," said my worthy Captain, clapping my master on the back. "Come, Robert, (which was his name) I think you must let him have his freedom. You have laid your money out very well; you have received good interest for it all this time, and here is now the principal at last. I know Gustavus has earned you more than a hundred a year, and he will still save you money, as he will not leave you. Come, Robert, take the money." My master then said, he would not be worse than his promise; and, taking the money, told me to go to the Secretary at the Register Office, and get my manumission drawn up.

These words of my master were like a voice from heaven to me: in an instant all my trepidation was turned into unutterable bliss, and I most reverently bowed myself with gratitude, unable to express my feelings, but by the overflowing of my eyes, and a heart replete with thanks to God; while my true and worthy friend, the Captain, congratulated us both with a peculiar degree of heartfelt pleasure.

. . .

During our stay at this place [Savannah, Georgia], one evening a slave belonging to Mr. Read, a merchant of Savannah, came near our vessel, and began to use me very ill. I entreated him, with all the patience of which I was master, to desist, as I knew there was little or no law for a free negro here. But the fellow, instead of taking my advice, persevered in his insults, and even struck me. At this I lost all temper, and fell on him, and beat him soundly. The next morning his master came to our vessel, as we lay alongside the wharf, and desired me to come ashore that he might have me flogged all round the town, for beating his negro slave! I told him he had insulted me, and had given the provocation by first striking me. I had also told my Captain the whole affair that morning, and desired him to go along with me to Mr. Read, to prevent bad consequences; but he said that it did not signify, and if Mr. Read said any thing he would make matters up, and desired me to go to work, which I accordingly did.

The Captain being on board when Mr. Read came and applied to him to deliver me up, he said he knew nothing of the matter, I was a free man. I was astonished and frightened at this, and thought I had better keep where I was, than go ashore and be flogged round the town, without judge or jury. I therefore refused to stir; and Mr. Read went away, swearing he would bring all the constables in the town, for he would have me out of the vessel. When he was gone, I thought his threat might prove too true to my sorrow; and I was confirmed in this belief, as well by the many instances I had seen of the treatment of free negroes, as from a fact that had happened within my own knowledge here a short time before.

There was a free black man, a carpenter, that I knew, who for asking a gentleman that he had worked for, for the money he had earned, was put into gaol; and afterwards this oppressed man was sent from Georgia, with false accusations, of an intention to set the gentleman's house on fire, and run away with his slaves. I was therefore much embarrassed, and very apprehensive of a flogging at least. I dreaded, of all things, the thoughts of being stripped, as I never in my life had the marks of any violence of that kind. At that instant a rage seized my soul, and for a little I determined to resist the first man that should attempt to lay violent hands on me, or basely use me without a trial; for I would sooner die like a free man, than suffer myself to be scourged, by the hands of ruffians, and my blood drawn like a slave.

WORKING WITH SOURCES

1. What did being free mean to Equiano? Was he disappointed in his change of status?
2. What role does the captain play in the narrative at this point?

19.5 Casta Paintings, Mexico, Eighteenth Century

Some of the most remarkable visual records of colonial Mexico are the series of paintings called "caste" paintings, illustrating every racial combination of Spanish, *mestizo*, black, Native American, and other types thought possible in the New Spain of the eighteenth and early nineteenth centuries. Casta paintings were always created in a series, and each picture usually contains a male-female couple and at least one child. Occasionally more than one child and even other animal or human figures are depicted. At the top or bottom of the painting is an inscription that explains the racial mix shown in the image. At least 50 groups of these paintings have been identified, although very few survive today in complete series.

Source: De Espanol y Negra, Mulato (From Spaniard and Black, Mulatto), attributed to Jose de Alcibar, c. 1760 Denver Art Museum: Collection of Frederick and Jan Mayer Photo © James O. Milmoe.

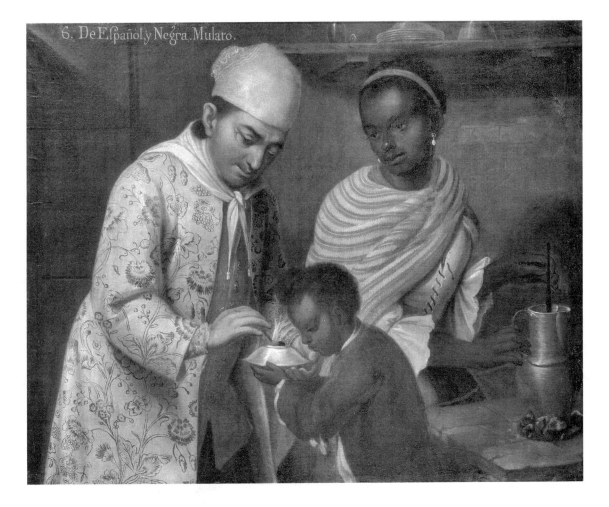

6. De Español, y Negra. Mulato.

WORKING WITH SOURCES

1. How do the inscription and the image work together, and what was the entire painting meant to convey?
2. Analyze the clothing styles depicted in the painting; do these clothes provide any indication of a "reality" that may appear in the work?

20. THE MUGHAL EMPIRE: MUSLIM RULERS AND HINDU SUBJECTS, 1400–1750

20.1   Babur, *The Baburnama*, ca. 1528

Zahiruddin Muhammad Babur (1483–1530) was born a prince of Fergana in Transoxiana (modern Uzbekistan and Tajikistan), a region that had been conquered (briefly) by the army of Alexander the Great in the 320s BCE and more recently by Babur's ancestor Timur-i Lang, or Tamerlane (r. 1370–1405). Driven from his homeland, Babur conquered neighboring kingdoms and moved south into Afghanistan, capturing Kabul in 1504. By 1519, he stepped up his raids into northern India, and his highly mobile, if vastly outnumbered, army defeated Sultan Ibrahim Lodi at Panipat in 1526. Victory at Panipat was followed by the conquest of the Lodi capital of Agra and further defeats of Hindu leaders in northern India. Babur's dynasty would become known as the Mughals (from "Mongols"), but his legacy can also be gauged from the success of his memoirs, the *Baburnama*. Composed and reworked throughout his life, the *Baburnama* is the first true autobiography in Islamic literature, and it can be read for insights into his own character as well as the military tactics he employed on the battlefield.

On Wednesday afternoon the twenty-eighth of Rajab [May 10], I entered Agra and camped in Sultan Ibrahim's quarters.

From the year 910 [1504–05], when Kabul was conquered, until this date I had craved Hindustan. Sometimes because my **begs** had poor opinions, and sometimes because my brothers lacked cooperation, the Hindustan campaign had not been possible and the realm had not been conquered. Finally all such impediments had been removed. None of my little begs and officers were able any longer to speak out in opposition to my purpose. In 925 [1519] we led the army and took Bajaur by force in two or three **gharis**, massacred the people, and came to Bhera. The people of Bhera paid ransom to keep their property from being plundered and pillaged, and we took four

hundred thousand shahrukhis worth of cash and goods, distributed it to the army according to the number of liege men, and returned to Kabul.

From that date until 932 [1525–26], we led the army to Hindustan five times within seven or eight years. The fifth time, God through his great grace vanquished and reduced a foe like Sultan Ibrahim and made possible for us a realm like Hindustan. From the time of the Apostle until this date only three padishahs gained dominion over and ruled the realm of Hindustan. The first was Sultan Mahmud Ghazi, who, with his sons, occupied the throne of Hindustan for a long time. The second was Sultan Shihabuddin Ghuri and his slaves and followers, who ruled this kingdom for many years. I am the third. My accomplishment, however, is beyond comparison with theirs, for when Sultan Mahmud subdued Hindustan, the throne of Khurasan was under his control, the rulers of Khwarazm and the marches were obedient to him, and

---

Begs: Subordinates.
Ghari: Measure of time, about 24 minutes.

Source: The Baburnama: Memoirs of Babur, Prince and Emperor, trans. and ed. Wheeler M. Thackston (New York: Oxford University Press, 1996), 328–329, 330, 331.

the padishah of Samarkand was his underling. If his army was not two hundred thousand strong, it must have been at least one hundred thousand. Moreover, his opponents were rajahs. There was not a single padishah in all of Hindustan. Every rajah ruled independently in a different region.

. . .

Hindustan is a vast and populous kingdom and a productive realm. To the east and south, in fact to the west too, it ends at the ocean. To the north is a mountain range that connects the mountains of the Hindu Kush, Kafiristan, and Kashmir. To the northwest are Kabul, Ghazni, and Kandahar. The capital of all Hindustan is Delhi. After Sultan Shihabuddin Ghuri's reign until the end of Sultan Firozshah's, most of Hindustan was under the control of the Delhi sultans. Up to the time that I conquered Hindustan, five Muslim padishahs and two infidels had ruled there. Although the mountains and jungles are held by many petty rays and rajahs, the important and independent rulers were the following five.

. . .

Of the infidels, the greater in domain and army is the rajah of Vijayanagar. The other is Rana Sanga, who had recently grown so great by his audacity and sword. His original province was Chitor. When the sultans of Mandu grew weak, he seized many provinces belonging to Mandu, such as Ranthambhor, Sarangpur, Bhilsan, and Chanderi. Chanderi had been in the *daru'l-harb* for some years and held by Sanga's highest-ranking officer, Medini Rao, with four or five thousand infidels, but in 934 [1528], through the grace of God, I took it by force within a ghari or two, massacred the infidels, and brought it into the bosom of Islam, as will be mentioned.

All around Hindustan are many rays and rajahs. Some are obedient to Islam, while others, because they are so far away and their places impregnable, do not render obedience to Muslim rulers.

Daru'l-harb: "Abode of war," Islamic term for non-Islamicized countries.

WORKING WITH SOURCES

1. Why was it important for Babur to display his knowledge of the history and geography of Hindustan?
2. Was he driven by a "crusading" goal to liberate Hindustan from control by the "infidels" and convert its inhabitants to Islam?

20.2 Muhammad Dara Shikuh, *The Mingling of Two Oceans*, ca. 1650s

The eldest son of Shah Jahan, the fifth Mughal emperor, Dara Shikuh was defeated by his younger brother in a struggle for power in 1658. The victorious brother, Muhiuddin, ruled as the Emperor Aurangzeb, and he had Dara declared, by a court of nobles and clergy, an apostate from Islam and assassinated in 1659. Dara left behind a remarkable series of writings, advocating an enlightened program of harmonizing the various, bitterly opposed religions of the subcontinent. He had developed friendships with Sikhs, followed a Persian mystic, and completed a translation of

Source: Muhammad Dara Shikuh, *The Mingling of Two Oceans*, trans. and ed. M. Mafuz ul-Haq (Calcutta: Asiatic Society of Bengal, 1929), 50–53.

50 Upanishads from their original Sanskrit into Persian in 1657. His most famous work, the *Majma-ul-Bahrain* (*The Mingling of Two Oceans*), addressed the overlapping ideas of Hindu and Muslim mysticism. His attempt to combine the traditions into a coherent whole may have been rejected by his fervently Muslim brother, but he also represents a strain of ecumenical thought within the Mughal Empire.

X. Discourse on the Vision of God (*Rūyat*).

The Indian monotheists call the Vision of God, *Sāchātkār*, that is, to see God with the (ordinary) eyes of the forehead. Know that the Vision of God, either by the Prophets, may peace be on them, or by the perfect divines, may their souls be sanctified, whether in this or the next world and whether with the outer or the inner eyes, cannot be doubted or disputed; and the "men of the Book" (*ahl-i-kitāb*), the perfect divines and the seers of all religions—whether they are believers in the Kur'ān, the Vedas, the Book of David or the Old and the New Testaments—have a (common) faith in this respect. Now, one who disbelieves the beholding of God is a thoughtless and sightless member of his community, the reason being: if the Holy Self is Omnipotent, how can He not have the potency to manifest Himself? This matter has been explained very clearly by the 'Ulamā of the Sunnī Sect. But, if it is said, that (even) the Pure Self (*dhāt-i-baht*) can be beheld, it is an impossibility; for the Pure Self is elegant and undetermined, and, as He cannot be determined, He is manifest in the veil of elegance only, and as such cannot be beheld, and such beholding is an impossibility. And the suggestion that He can be beheld in the next and not in this world, is groundless, for if He is Omnipotent, He is potent to manifest Himself in any manner, anywhere and at any time He likes. (I hold) that one who cannot behold Him here (i.e., in this world) will hardly behold Him there (i.e. in the next world); as He has said in the Holy verse: "And whoever is blind in this, he shall (also) be blind in the hereafter." [*Qur'an* 17:72]

The *Mu'tazila* and the *Shī'a* doctors, who are opposed to *rūyat* (Beholding), have committed a great blunder in this matter, for had they only denied the capability of beholding the Pure Self, there would have been some justification, but their denial of all forms of *rūyat* is a great mistake; the reason being that most of the Prophets and perfect divines have beheld God with their ordinary eyes and have heard His Holy words without any intermediary and, now, when they are, by all means, capable of hearing the words of God, why should they not be capable of beholding Him? Verily, they must be so; and, just as it is obligatory to have faith in God, the Angels, the (revealed) Books, the Prophets, the Destiny, the Good and the Evil, and the Holy Places, etc., so it is obligatory and incumbent to have faith in *rūyat*.

. . .

Now, the beholding of God is of five kinds: first, in dream with the eyes of heart; secondly, beholding Him with the ordinary eyes; thirdly, beholding Him in an intermediate state of sleep and wakefulness, which is a special kind of Selflessness; fourthly, (beholding Him) in (a stage of) special determination; fifthly, beholding the One Self in the multitudinous determinations of the internal and external worlds. In such a way beheld our Prophet, may peace be on him, whose "self" had disappeared from the midst and the beholder and the beheld had merged in one and his sleep, wakefulness and selflessness looked as one and his internal and the external eyes had become one unified whole—such is the state of perfect *rūyat*, which is not confined either to this or the next world and is possible everywhere and at every period.

XI. Discourse on the Names of God, the Most High (*Asmāi Allāh Ta'ālā*).

Know that the names of God, the Most High, are numberless and beyond comprehension. In the language of the Indian divines, the Absolute, the Pure, the Hidden of the hidden and the Necessary Self is known as *asan*, *tirgun*, *nirankār*, *niranjan*, *sat* and *chit*. If knowledge is attributed to Him, the Indian divines designate Him as *chitan*, while the Muslims call Him *'Alīm* (Knowing).

WORKING WITH SOURCES

1. To what extent, and in what specific ways, did Dara Shikuh represent an ecumenical spirit with respect to Islam and other religions?
2. How does Dara Shikuh anticipate and address the objections of others within the Muslim community?

20.3 Edicts of Aurangzeb, 1666–1679

When he became emperor in 1658, Aurangzeb attempted a radical "Islamification" of Mughal India, imposing a strict interpretation of Sharia law and implementing reforms that he thought would benefit Muslims more than adherents of other religions. Repudiating his great-grandfather Akbar's vision of religious transcendence and harmony but stopping short of forcible conversion, Aurangzeb offered incentives to non-Muslims to convert, destroyed many of their temples, and reimposed the hated *jizya* tax. This tax on Hindus had been abolished by Akbar in 1564, and its reinstatement by Aurangzeb in 1679 triggered mass protests and violent reactions from authorities in many cities. Revolts among Sikhs and among Hindus left the Mughal Empire weakened and in decline by the time of Aurangzeb's death in 1707. An excerpt from his proscriptions is offered below.

Exhibit No. 6: Keshava Rai Temple. "Even to look at a temple is a sin for a Musalman," Aurangzeb. Umurat-i-Hazur Kishwar-Kashai Julus (R.Yr.) 9, Rabi II 24 / 13 October 1666.
'It was reported to the Emperor (Aurangzeb) that in the temple of Keshava Rai at Mathura, there is a stone railing presented by Bishukoh (one without dignity i.e. Prince Dara, Aurangzeb's elder brother). On hearing of it, the Emperor observed, "In the religion of the Musalmans it is improper even to look at a temple and this Bishukoh has installed this kathra (barrier railing). Such an act is totally unbecoming of a Musalman. This railing should be removed (forthwith)." His Majesty ordered Abdun Nabi Khan to go and remove the kathra, which is in the middle of the temple. The Khan went and removed it. After doing it he had audience. He informed that the idol of Keshava Rai is in the inner chamber. The railing presented by Dara was in front of the chamber and, formerly, it was of wood. Inside the kathra used to stand the sevakas of the shrine (pujaris etc.) and outside it stood the people (khalq)'.

Exhibit No. 7: Demolition of Kalka's Temple - I. Siyah Waqa'i- Darbar Regnal Year 10, Rabi I, 23 / 3 September 1667.
'The asylum of Shariat (Shariat Panah) Qazi Abdul Muqaram has sent this arzi to the sublime Court: a man known to him told him that the Hindus gather in large numbers at Kalka's temple near Barahapule (near Delhi); a large crowd of the Hindus is seen here. Likewise, large crowds are seen at (the mazars) of Khwaja Muinuddin, Shah Madar and Salar Masud Ghazi. This amounts to bid'at (heresy) and deserves consideration. Whatever orders are required should be issued.

Source: http://www.aurangzeb.info/2008/06/exhibit-no_7171.html.

Saiyid Faulad Khan was thereupon ordered (by the Emperor) to send one hundred beldars to demolish the Kalka temple and other temples in its neighbourhood which were in the Faujdari of the Khan himself; these men were to reach there post haste, and finish the work without a halt'.

Exhibit No. 8: Demolition of Kalka Temple II. Siyah Akhbarat-i-Darbar-i-Mu'alla Julus 10, Rabi II 3/12 September 1667.

'Saiyad Faulad Khan reported that in compliance with the orders, beldars were sent to demolish the Kalka temple which task they have done. During the course of the demolition, a Brahmin drew out a sword, killed a bystander and then turned back and attacked the Saiyad also. The Brahmin was arrested'.

Exhibit No. 16: Reimposition of Jizyah by Aurangzeb. (2nd April 1679)

'As all the aims of the religious Emperor were directed to the spreading of the law of Islam and the overthrow of the practices of the infidels, he issued orders to the high diwani officers that from Wednesday, the 2nd April 1679/1st Rabi I, in obedience to the Quranic injunction, "till they pay commutation money (Jizyah) with the hand in humility," and in agreement with the canonical tradition, Jizyah should be collected from the infidels (zimmis) of the capital and the provinces. Many of the honest scholars of the time were appointed to discharge the work (of collecting Jizyah). May God actuate him (Emperor Aurangzeb) to do that which He loves and is pleased with, and make his future life better than the present'.

WORKING WITH SOURCES

1. How did the legacy of Akbar's and Dara's ecumenism influence Aurangzeb's policies?
2. What was the stated purpose of the reimposition of financial penalties on non-Muslims? Was this policy likely to have the effect he intended?

20.4   Muhammad Ghawth Gwaliori, *The Five Jewels,* ca. 1526

muslim area of India

In sixteenth-century Hindustan, the Sufi mystic Muhammad Ghawth Gwaliori claimed to have experienced an astounding ascension through multiple heavenly spheres up to the throne of God. This intensely personal experience, which he underwent in his 20s, occurred within a volatile political and social context. Born around 1501, Ghawth left home at age 12 to further his religious education and to undertake a series of mystic initiations that prepared him for his ascension in 1526. Ghawth lived during the rule of Humayun, when Mughal control was still tentative, and Akbar was still a young man. After his mystical experiences made him famous, Ghawth was seen as a spiritual support for the Mughal regime. When Humayun fell from power in 1540, Ghawth was persecuted by a group of Afghan warlords who followed a more orthodox form of Islam and attacked the reality—as well as the political implications—of his mystical experiences.

Source: Excerpts from Scott A. Kugle, "Heaven's Witness: The Uses and Abuses of Muhammad Ghawth's Mystical Ascension," *Journal of Islamic Studies* 14 (2003): 17–20.

multiple heavenly spirits

We reached the limit of the fourth heavenly sphere; the sphere split open; the stars waned like glowing crescents. I passed up into the heaven. The spirits of all the prophets came forward to greet me. They all shook my hand joyfully, along with the angels of that sphere. They praised me and their faces lit up, saying, "We have been waiting for so long, asking the Lord when you would be passing by this way. On the day that the Prophet ascended along this route, there were with him some saints, and you were one of them. However, at that time, you were in the form of pure spirit. In contrast, this time you are fully attached to your body! This is a completely new and different spectacle." They stood around amazed at my appearance. I ascended with 'Alī and Abū Bakr, until we neared the limit of the fifth heavenly sphere.

1st prophet
4th

The fourth heaven split open; the stars flared up, blazing brightly. I ascended into the fifth heavenly sphere. Such wondrous and strange things came into sight while all the angels of that sphere came forward into my presence. They carried in their hands pages, like those of a book. I asked, "What are these pages?" They answered, "These are the registers of Might which will consume the people consigned to the flames. They haven't been displayed yet or made public, but they record all the people's deeds." I asked, "Where are the people of the flames?" They invited me to come this way in order to see. When I came forward, I saw a chamber formed from the purest substance of Divine wrath. In it, there were many beings sitting, all in the shape of women. One woman among them was explaining clearly the meaning of Divine unity [*tawhīd*]. I asked, "Who is that woman who is teaching so eloquently?" They answered, "That is the mother of all humankind, Eve!"

I rushed forward to greet her and pay my respects, and asked her, "Why have you, a true Muslim, appeared in the midst of all the people who are overcome by Divine wrath?" Eve replied, "We are the most comprehensive, most perfect and most beautiful of all the manifestations of the Divine. We are called 'the People of Divine Might' who are the manifestation of Allah's attribute of utter singularity." I requested Eve to explain this to me further; she said, "The authority of Allah's beauty is delegated to the prophets, and that authority has already come to its full completion long ago and its delegation is now over. Then the saints were raised up and were given authority. To the saints was delegated the authority of Allah's beauty mixed with Allah's might. Now listen, these women whom you see here are the messengers who will be sent to the people punished in hell fire. They are called 'the People of Divine Might.' They each wish to raise people up from the fires of hell into the realm of pure Divine might. The Prophet himself revealed this from the inner world when he said, 'Women are the emissaries of Satan.'"

. . .

The heaven split open and we ascended into it. The essences both lofty and lowly appeared before me. I hesitated there, thinking that, if I don't understand the appearance of these essences, I will have no way to advance religious knowledge and intuitive knowledge [*'ilm-i dīnī o 'ilm-i ladūnī*]. My thoughts inclined to find out what religious knowledge really looked like. At that moment, Jesus spoke to me, saying, "Have you ever seen the four Imams [who fashioned the structure of Islamic law]?" I answered, "No." Jesus directed me to look at a certain place in the vastness; there I saw the four Imams standing together, each disputing with the others, saying, "No, no, the certain truth is this, not that." I thought to myself, if this is the outer knowledge of religion, then what is the inner knowledge of intuition? The thought simply flashed in my mind, but I didn't say anything to that effect. Just then, all the Divine names of Allah emerged, each in the particular dimension of its knowability, from the realm of the primal archetypes. Each took a distinct shape, giving rise to the whole multitude of perceptible and existent forms. I could see the continuity between the Divine names and all the created forms that arose from their various natures. I could see the universe contained within the relation between the Divine names that prepared the universe for its worldly existence.

WORKING WITH SOURCES

1. What do the inclusion of Ali, Eve, and Jesus in Ghawth's mystical vision suggest about religious culture in sixteenth-century Hindustan?
2. What might one learn from Ghawth's vision about the Sufi view of gender and the roles of women?

20.5 Calico Textile, ca. 1806

Calico was a fine printed cotton cloth first imported to England from Calicut, on the western shore of the subcontinent, by the British East India Company. A domestic manufacture of calico-inspired textiles followed, as English artisans attempted to mimic the bright colors, careful weaving, and intricate designs of Indian cloth. This example commemorates Vice Admiral Lord Nelson, a British naval hero of the Napoleonic Wars and the American War of Independence. Nelson, who died in the Battle of Trafalgar in 1806, was buried in St. Paul's Cathedral after an elaborate funeral service.

WORKING WITH SOURCES

1. What specific elements are incorporated into this commemorative calico, and how are they symbolic of Nelson's military career?
2. How were the interests of the British East Indies Company furthered by internal conflict on the subcontinent in the seventeenth and eighteenth centuries?

Source: National Maritime Museum, London.

21. REGULATING THE "INNER" AND "OUTER" DOMAINS: CHINA AND JAPAN, 1500–1800

21.1 Treaty between Koxinga and the Dutch Government, Formosa, 1662

In the seventeenth century, the Manchus crossed the Great Wall, captured Beijing, and founded a new regime, the Qing, or "pure," dynasty. Some Ming loyalists fled to the island of Formosa (Taiwan), off the Chinese coast, where they expelled the Dutch. The Europeans had established a trading base on the island, and the document below demonstrates the negotiated surrender of this fort to Koxinga.

Treaty made and agreed upon; from the one side, by His Highness the LORD TEIBINGH TSIANTE TEYSIANCON KOXIN, who has besieged Castle Zeelandia on Formosa since 1st May 1661 up till this 1st day of February 1662; and from the other side, as representing the Dutch Government, by the Governor of the said Castle, FREDERIK COYETT, and his Council, consisting of the undernoted eighteen Articles:

Article 1
All hostilities committed on either side to be forgotten.

Article 2
Castle Zeelandia, with its outworks, artillery, remaining war materiel, merchandise, money, and other properties belonging to the Honourable Company, to be surrendered to LORD KOXINGA.

Article 3
Rice, bread, wine, arack, meat, pork, oil, vinegar, ropes, canvas, pitch, tar, anchors, gunpowder, bullets, and linen, with such other articles as may be required by the besieged during their voyage to Batavia, to be taken aboard the Company's ships in keeping with instructions from the before-mentioned Governor and Council.

Article 4
All private movable property inside the Castle or elsewhere belonging to officers of the Dutch Government, shall first be inspected by LORD KOXINGA's delegates, and then placed on board the said ships.

. . .

Article 9
Every servant of the Company, now imprisoned by the Chinese in Formosa, shall be liberated within eight or ten days, and those who are in China, as soon as possible. Servants of the Company who are not imprisoned in Formosa shall be granted a free pass to reach the Company's ships in safety.

Article 10
The said LORD KOXINGA shall now return to the Company the four captured boats, with all their accessories.

Article 11
He shall also provide a sufficient number of vessels to take the Honourable Company's people and goods to their ships.

Source: William Campbell, *Formosa under the Dutch* (London: Kegan Paul, Trench, Trubner, 1903), 455–456.

Article 12
Vegetables, flesh-meat, and whatever else may be necessary to sustain the Company's people during their stay, shall daily be provided by His Highness's subjects at a reasonable price.

Article 13
So long as the Honourable Company's people remain on land before embarkation, no soldier or other subject of LORD KOXINGA shall be permitted to enter the Castle (unless on service for the Company), to approach the outworks nearer than the **gabions**, or to proceed further than the palisades erected by order of His Highness.

Article 14
No other than a white flag shall float from the Castle until the Honourable Company's people have marched out.

. . .

Article 18
All misunderstandings, and every important matter overlooked in this Agreement, shall immediately be dealt with to the satisfaction of both parties, upon notice having been given on either side.

LORD CHEN CH'ENG-KUNG, [L. S.]
FREDERIK COYETT, [L. S.]

Gabion: A cage or box filled with rocks or sand; used in military fortifications.

WORKING WITH SOURCES

1. How and why did the forces of Lord Koxinga attempt to negotiate a less humiliating surrender for the Dutch? What were the long-term goals of both sides to the treaty?
2. Is Koxinga negotiating with the Dutch government, or more with a private corporation in the area?

21.2 Matteo Ricci, *China in the Sixteenth Century,* ca. 1600

When European Christian missionaries first came to Ming China, they made very little progress in converting the Chinese, in large part due to their limited training in Chinese language and culture. When he arrived in China in 1583, the Jesuit Matteo Ricci (1552–1610) encouraged his followers to immerse themselves in the language and to become conversant with the rich traditions of Chinese literature. He also came to be respected by, and especially helpful to, the emperor, as he offered his expertise in the sciences and mathematics to the imperial court. With a European Jesuit (Adam Schall von Bell) as the official court astronomer to Kangxi, there were reports that the Emperor himself considered converting to Catholicism. Nevertheless, not every encounter between Chinese and Europeans went so smoothly, as the following anecdote from Ricci's diary reveals.

Of late they [the Chinese] had become quite disturbed by the coming of the Portuguese, and particularly so because they can do nothing about it, due to the great profit reaped from Portuguese traders by the public treasury and by certain influential merchants. Without referring to the public treasury or to the merchants who come from every other province, they complain that the foreign commerce raises the

---

price of all commodities and that outsiders are the only ones to profit from it. As an expression of their contempt for Europeans, when the Portuguese first arrived they were called foreign devils, and this name is still in common use among the Cantonese.

The citizens of Sciauquin have their own particular reasons for hating the strangers. They are afraid that the Portuguese merchants will get into the interior of the realm with the missionaries, and their fears are not without some foundation. The frequent visits of the Fathers to the town of Macao and their growing intimacy with the Governor have already aroused their antipathy. There is nothing that stirs them up like a wide-spreading slander, and they had a good one in the story that the tower which had been built at such great expense, and with so much labor, was erected at the request of the foreign priests. This probably had its origin in the fact that the tower was completed while the Fathers were building their mission houses. This false rumor had such an effect that the people called it the Tower of the Foreigners instead of The Flowery Tower, as it was named. As a result of the animosity which grew out of this incident, when they realized that they could not drive out the Mission, as they wanted to, they took to insulting the missionaries whenever an occasion occurred or they could trump up a reason for doing so. It was quite annoying and dangerous to be made a continual target for stones hurled from the tower, when people came there every day to play games, the purpose for which these towers are built. Not a stone was thrown at the Mission House from the high tower nearby that missed its roof as a target. These showers of stones were heaviest when they knew that there were only one or two of the servants at home. Another silly reason for their taking offense was that the doors of our house, which were kept open for inspection while it was being built, were now kept closed according to the rule of our Society. What they wanted to do was to use the house as they did their temples of idols, which are always left wide open and are often the scenes of uncouth frivolity.

It happened one day, when their insolence became really unbearable, that one of our servants ran out and seized a boy, who had been throwing stones at the house, and dragging him inside threatened to bring him to court. Attracted by the shrieking of the boy, several men, who were known in the neighborhood, ran into the house to intercede for the culprit, and Father Ricci ordered that he be allowed to depart without further ado. Here was a good pretext for a major calumny, and two of the neighbors who disliked the Fathers went into conference with a bogus relative of the boy, who knew something about court procedure. Then they trumped up a story that the boy had been seized by the Fathers and hidden in their house for three days, that he had been given a certain drug, well known to the Chinese, which prevented him from crying out, and that the purpose of it all was to smuggle him back to Macao, where they could sell him into slavery. The two men were to be called in as witnesses.

. . .

[A trial takes place before the Governor, and he hears the "witnesses" to the crime.]

. . .

Finally, in order to save the Father present from any embarrassment, he [the Governor] declared him [Ricci] wholly innocent and . . . his next move was to summon the three members of the building commission, who were at the tower on the day the incident occurred. The plaintiff requested that he call in the neighbors also, the real authors of the charge, who had a full knowledge of all its details. The Governor dismissed the multitude and, as he was leaving, he forbade the Father to leave the court. In the meantime, and in deep humiliation, the Father betook himself to prayer, commending his cause and its solution to God, to the Blessed Mother and to the Saints.

. . .

Then he [the Governor] told the missionary and his interpreter and the three Commissioners that he had heard enough of this affair, and that they might return to their homes and their business.

. . .

On the following day the Governor sent a solemn document to be posted at the main entrance of the Mission House. This notice, after explaining that the foreigners were living here with permission of the Viceroy, stated that certain unprincipled persons, contrary to right and reason, were known to have molested the strangers living herein, wherefore: he, the Governor, strictly forbade under severest penalty that anyone from now on should dare to cause them further molestation.

WORKING WITH SOURCES

1. What seems to have been Ricci's attitude toward Chinese customs and religious practices?
2. To what extent did trade rights and religious goals intersect in this setting? What was in the immediate and long-term interests of the Chinese "hosts" of the mission?

21.3 Emperor Qianlong's Imperial Edict to King George III, 1793

The reign of Qianlong (r. 1736–1795) marked both the high point and the beginning of the decline of the Qing dynasty. Several European nations, driven by their desire to corner the market on the lucrative Chinese trade, sent representatives to Qianlong's court. In 1793, Great Britain dispatched Lord Macartney, its first envoy to China, to obtain safe and favorable trade relations for his country. In response, Qianlong composed a letter to King George III (r. 1760–1820) detailing his objections and conditions, which Macartney conveyed back to Britain. The terms of this letter underscore Qianlong's subtle understanding of global economic conditions and the maintenance of a balance between the interests of various nations.

You, O King, live beyond the confines of many seas, nevertheless, impelled by your humble desire to partake of the benefits of our civilisation, you have dispatched a mission respectfully bearing your memorial. Your Envoy has crossed the seas and paid his respects at my Court on the anniversary of my birthday. To show your devotion, you have also sent offerings of your country's produce.

I have perused your memorial: the earnest terms in which it is couched reveal a respectful humility on your part, which is highly praiseworthy. In consideration of the fact that your Ambassador and his deputy have come a long way with your memorial and tribute, I have shown them high favour and have allowed them to be introduced into my presence. To manifest my indulgence, I have entertained them at a banquet and made them numerous gifts. I have also caused presents to be forwarded to the Naval Commander and six hundred of his officers and men, although they did not come to Peking, so that they too may share in my all-embracing kindness.

As to your entreaty to send one of your nationals to be accredited to my Celestial Court and to be in control of your country's trade with China, this request is contrary to all usage of my dynasty and cannot possibly be entertained. It is true that Europeans, in the service of the dynasty, have been permitted to live at Peking, but they are compelled to adopt Chinese dress, they are strictly confined to their own precincts and are never permitted to return home. You are presumably familiar with our dynastic regulations. Your proposed Envoy to my Court could not be placed in a position similar to that of European officials in Peking who are forbidden to leave China, nor could he, on the other hand, be allowed liberty of movement and the privilege of corresponding with his own country; so that you would gain nothing by his residence in our midst.

Source: E. Backhouse and J. O. Bland, *Annals and Memoirs of the Court of Peking* (Boston: Houghton Mifflin, 1914), 322–331.

Moreover, our Celestial dynasty possesses vast territories, and tribute missions from the dependencies are provided for by the Department for Tributary States, which ministers to their wants and exercises strict control over their movements. It would be quite impossible to leave them to their own devices. Supposing that your Envoy should come to our Court, his language and national dress differ from that of our people, and there would be no place in which to bestow him. It may be suggested that he might imitate the Europeans permanently resident in Peking and adopt the dress and customs of China, but, it has never been our dynasty's wish to force people to do things unseemly and inconvenient. Besides, supposing I sent an Ambassador to reside in your country, how could you possibly make for him the requisite arrangements? Europe consists of many other nations besides your own: if each and all demanded to be represented at our Court, how could we possibly consent? The thing is utterly impracticable. How can our dynasty alter its whole procedure and system of etiquette, established for more than a century, in order to meet your individual views? If it be said that your object is to exercise control over your country's trade, your nationals have had full liberty to trade at Canton for many a year, and have received the greatest consideration at our hands. Missions have been sent by Portugal and Italy, preferring similar requests. The Throne appreciated their sincerity and loaded them with favours, besides authorising measures to facilitate their trade with China. You are no doubt aware that, when my Canton merchant, Wu Chao-ping, who was in debt to foreign ships, I made the Viceroy advance the monies due, out of the provincial treasury, and ordered him to punish the culprit severely. Why then should foreign nations advance this utterly unreasonable request to be represented at my Court? Peking is nearly two thousand miles from Canton, and at such a distance what possible control could any British representative exercise?

. . .

Yesterday your Ambassador petitioned my Ministers to memorialise me regarding your trade with China, but his proposal is not consistent with our dynastic usage and cannot be entertained. Hitherto, all European nations, including your own country's

barbarian merchants, have carried on their trade with our Celestial Empire at Canton. Such has been the procedure for many years, although our Celestial Empire possesses all things in prolific abundance and lacks no product within its own borders. There was therefore no need to import the manufactures of outside barbarians in exchange for our own produce. But as the tea, silk and porcelain which the Celestial Empire produces, are absolute necessities to European nations and to yourselves, we have permitted, as a signal mark of favour, that foreign *hongs* [merchant firms] should be established at Canton, so that your wants might be supplied and your country thus participate in our beneficence. But your Ambassador has now put forward new requests which completely fail to recognise the Throne's principle to "treat strangers from afar with indulgence," and to exercise a pacifying control over barbarian tribes, the world over. Moreover, our dynasty, swaying the myriad races of the globe, extends the same benevolence towards all. Your England is not the only nation trading at Canton. If other nations, following your bad example, wrongfully importune my ear with further impossible requests, how will it be possible for me to treat them with easy indulgence? Nevertheless, I do not forget the lonely remoteness of your island, cut off from the world by intervening wastes of sea, nor do I overlook your excusable ignorance of the usages of our Celestial Empire. I have consequently commanded my Ministers to enlighten your Ambassador on the subject, and have ordered the departure of the mission. But I have doubts that, after your Envoy's return he may fail to acquaint you with my view in detail or that he may be lacking in lucidity, so that I shall now proceed . . . to issue my mandate on each question separately. In this way you will, I trust, comprehend my meaning. . . .

. . .

(7) Regarding your nation's worship of the Lord of Heaven, it is the same religion as that of other European nations. Ever since the beginning of history, sage Emperors and wise rulers have bestowed on China a moral system and inculcated a code, which from time immemorial has been religiously observed by the myriads of my subjects. There has been no hankering after heterodox doctrines. Even

the European (missionary) officials in my capital are forbidden to hold intercourse with Chinese subjects; they are restricted within the limits of their appointed residences, and may not go about propagating their religion. The distinction between Chinese and barbarian is most strict, and your Ambassador's request that barbarians shall be given full liberty to disseminate their religion is utterly unreasonable.

It may be, O King, that the above proposals have been wantonly made by your Ambassador on his own responsibility, or peradventure you yourself are ignorant of our dynastic regulations and had no intention of transgressing them when you expressed these wild ideas and hopes. . . . If, after the receipt of this explicit decree, you lightly give ear to the representations of your subordinates and allow your barbarian merchants to proceed to Chêkiang and Tientsin, with the object of landing and trading there, the ordinances of my Celestial Empire are strict in the extreme, and the local officials, both civil and military, are bound reverently to obey the law of the land. Should your vessels touch the shore, your merchants will assuredly never be permitted to land or to reside there, but will be subject to instant expulsion. In that event your barbarian merchants will have had a long journey for nothing.

WORKING WITH SOURCES

1. How did Qianlong attempt to keep China and Great Britain on an equal footing, and in what specific regards?
2. How effectively does the emperor balance courtesy and warning in his letter?

21.4 Chikamatsu Monzaemon, *Goban Taiheiki*, 1710

This one-act puppet play is one of the first fictionalized (though only thinly disguised) treatments of a famous event that occurred in Tokugawa Japan in 1701–1703. The historical incident began with a knife attack by the daimyo (feudal lord) Asano Naganori on an imperial official named Kira Yoshinaka. Whatever the justice of the provocation, Asano had committed a serious breach in conduct and was forced to pay the most severe penalty. Even though Kira had suffered only a minor wound to his face, Asano was commanded to commit *seppuku*, ritual suicide. When he did so, his 47 samurai vassals were left leaderless (*rōnin*), but they swore to avenge Asano's memory by killing Kira.

In January 1703, the 47 rōnin entered Kira's home, chasing him and killing several of his retainers and wounding others, including Kira's grandson. When they finally trapped and overcame Kira, the rōnin cut off his head and brought it to their master's grave. However, they then decided to turn themselves in to the authorities and commit seppuku themselves, true to their code until the bitter end. In order to elude the censors, Chikamatsu altered the names, condensed some of the main details, and offered a judge that was more sympathetic to the rōnin cause. The essential story would reemerge repeatedly in popular culture (both Japanese and non-Japanese) down to the present day.

Source: Jacqueline Miller, "A Chronicle of Great Peace Played Out on a Chessboard: Chikamatsu Monzaemon's Goban Taiheiki," *Harvard Journal of Asiatic Studies* 46 (1986): 221–267, 263–267.

NARRATOR: Just then someone announces that the messenger from the shogun, Hatakeyama Sakyō no Dayū, has come. The puffed-up samurai are cowed and prostrate themselves to the left and right of the gate. The doors are opened from inside and Hatakeyama meets face to face with the old priest.

HATAKEYAMA: "Last night the retainers of En'ya Hangan forced their way into the mansion of Kō no Moronao in order to take revenge on the enemy of their lord, and killed him. As samurai, this has earned them both merit and praise. But they showed no respect for the fact that the shogun's palace was in the vicinity and disturbed the peace of Kamakura. It is the shogun's decision that these men be placed in the charge of Niki and Ishidō, and he orders that today they all cut open their bellies in front of the grave of En'ya. He also grants the head of Moronao to his only son, Moroyasu, and orders you to deliver it to him."

NARRATOR: The head priest accepts the written decree. He prepares a container for the head and sees to it that the arrangements are properly carried out.

HATAKEYAMA: "Let a member of Lord Moroyasu's household who has some semblance of respectability receive the head."

NARRATOR: At this, a chief retainer, Misumi no Gunji, announces his name in an imposing fashion, but there seems to be little honor for him when he returns with heavy heart, bearing the head of his useless master. Told that they ought to begin their preparations right away, the priests place En'ya's shrine in the center. They then place tatami mats to the right and left and spread white sand in front to soak up the blood that will be spilled. Behind they draw a white curtain and set out cushions covered in white silk. And on footed trays they place the knives for the suicides of the more than forty men.

Samurai throughout Kamakura pay solemn visits to the shrines, praying to the tutelary gods of warriors that they themselves, as military men, will be favored with the same good fortune. Poets write sheaves of verse about grief, and litterateurs search for rhymes to express their sorrow. Everyone, regardless of rank, age or sex, regrets this parting and they jostle each other in their haste to gather at the Kōmyōji. There, the scene in front of the gates resembles a fair.

Now the time has come—it is noon. As the moment of death approaches, the official observer, the Lord of Nagoya in Bizen, arrives at the Kōmyōji. Then, beginning with those who will act as seconds, all the officials, including the recording clerks and supervisors, accept their respective commissions and take their places on this formal occasion.

. . .

LORD OF NAGOYA: "The shogun declares that the forty and more retainers of En'ya Hangan, in avenging their late lord by killing Kō no Moronao, committed an act of unprecedented loyalty, with each man worth a thousand. He is deeply impressed and would like to save their lives, but they erred in taking up arms in this age of great peace and by troubling the shogun's direct vassal. The government has no choice but to order them to commit seppuku. Under strong officers there are no weak soldiers. Your loyalty has reminded him of the benevolence of En'ya Hangan while he was alive. There is no doubt about the claim to succession of En'ya's only son, Takeōmaro, and the shogun decrees that he shall govern the two provinces of Izumo and Hōki. Go to the underworld and report this to your lord with gratitude. Now quickly cut your bellies!"

NARRATOR: He announces this in a loud voice, and the men lower their heads, weeping or laughing in their joy. One by one they remove their sleeveless over-robes. Yuranosuke takes the knife and stabs himself in the left side. As he does so, Rikiya, too, stabs himself. One by one they all stab themselves and, having done so, pull the blade across. At the same time and in the same place, sitting to the right and left of their master's grave, they have all cut their bellies, for the bond over three lives is strong. Finally all have been beheaded by their seconds, and the temple quickly becomes a graveyard. The *rōnin* leave their names on stones that will stand for ages to come. The foundation of the success of their lord's descendants and house, their prosperity and unbounded good fortune, lies in those

honest hearts filled with loyalty and filial spirit. They conformed to the laws of both heaven and earth, and the gods and buddhas graciously watched over them.

WORKING WITH SOURCES

1. Why does the court official express sympathy for the rōnin and still persist in enforcing the sentence against them?
2. Is Chikamatsu's admiration for the actions of the rōnin justified by the historical reality of the period and original circumstances?

21.5   Honda Toshiaki, "Secret Plan for Managing the Country," 1798

Drawing on the conclusions of his "Western" education, Japanese economist Honda Toshiaki (1749–1821) advocated a three-pronged plan of action to level the playing field between the Tokugawa Shogunate and European powers. Having studied mathematics as a young man, Honda learned the Dutch language and studied Dutch medicine, astronomy, and military science. The choice of Dutch was fortuitous, since these were the only Europeans permitted to remain in Japan after 1639. Nevertheless, it was the prowess of these particular Europeans in shipping and trade, dependent on a scientific and mathematical knowledge of navigation, that most interested Honda. This section of his "Secret Plan" addresses the need for the emperor to control ships and shipping in order to ensure Japanese prosperity.

As long as there are no government-owned ships and the merchants have complete control over transport and trade, the economic conditions of the samurai and farmers grow steadily worse. In years when the harvest is bad and people die of starvation, the farmers perish in greater numbers than any other class. Fields are abandoned and food production is still further reduced. There is then insufficient food for the nation and much suffering. Then the people will grow restive and numerous criminals will have to be punished. In this way citizens will be lost to the state. Since its citizens are a country's most important

possession, it cannot afford to lose even one, and it is therefore most unfortunate that any should be sentenced to death. It is entirely the fault of the ruler if the life of even a single subject is thereby lost.

. . .

Some daimyo have now ceased to pay their retainers their basic stipends. These men have had half their property confiscated by the daimyo as well, and hate them so much that they find it impossible to contain their ever accumulating resentment. They finally leave their clan and become bandits. They wander lawlessly over the entire country, plotting

Source: From Sources of Japanese Tradition Volume 2, edited by Ryusaku Tsunoda, William Theodore de Bary, and Donald Keene. Copyright © 1964 Columbia University Press, pg. 51–53. Reprinted with permission of the publisher.

with the natives who live on the shore, and thus entering a career of piracy. As they become ever more entrenched in their banditry one sees growing a tendency to revert to olden times.

It is because of the danger of such occurrences that in Europe a king governs his subjects with solicitude. It is considered to be the appointed duty of a king to save his people from hunger and cold by shipping and trading. This is the reason why there are no bandits in Europe. Such measures are especially applicable to Japan, which is a maritime nation, and it is obvious that transport and trade are essential functions of the government.

Ships which are at present engaged in transport do not leave coastal waters and put out to sea. They always have to skirt along the shore, and can navigate only by using as landmarks mountains or islands within visible range. Sometimes, as it inevitably happens, they are blown out to sea by a storm and lose their way. Then, when they are so far away from their familiar landmarks that they can no longer discern them, they drift about with no knowledge of their location. This is because they are ignorant of astronomy and mathematics, and because they do not possess the rules of navigation. Countless ships are thereby lost every year. Not only does this represent an enormous annual waste of produce, but valuable subjects also perish. If the methods of navigation were developed, the loss at sea of rice and other food products would be reduced, thus effecting a great saving. This would not only increase the wealth of the nation, but would help stabilize the prices of rice and other produce throughout Japan. The people, finding that they are treated equally irrespective of occupation and that the methods of government are fair, would no longer harbor any resentment, but would raise their voices in unison to pray for the prosperity of the rulers. By saving the lives of those subjects who would otherwise be lost at sea every year, we shall also be able to make up for our past shame, and will keep foreign nations from learning about weak spots in the institutions of Japan from Japanese sailors shipwrecked on their shores. Because of these and numerous other benefits to be derived from shipping, I have termed it the third imperative need.

WORKING WITH SOURCES

1. How does Toshiaki use comparisons to European practices to solidify his case regarding imperial control of shipping?
2. How does he envision the ideal relationship between the emperor and his people? What should be the emperor's central principle in ruling?

22. PATTERNS OF NATION-STATE FORMATION IN THE ATLANTIC WORLD, 1750–1871

22.1 *Declaration of the Rights of Man and of the Citizen, August 26, 1789*

When the Third Estate reconstituted itself as the National Assembly in June 1789, among the first measures it considered was a universal declaration of the rights and duties of individual French citizens. A proposal was made by the Marquis de Lafayette to this effect in July, but swift-moving events in Paris, such as the fall of the Bastille on July 14, moved the Revolution in new directions. Undaunted, a subcommittee continued to debate the document, editing a draft proposal of 24 articles down to 17. Like the Declaration of Independence in the American colonies (1776), this document was a compromise statement, drawn up and edited by committee; and yet, like the American Declaration, it is a stirring statement of Enlightenment principles concerning both the individual's role in the state and the ultimate source of all government.

The representatives of the French people, constituted as a National Assembly, and considering that ignorance, neglect, or contempt of the rights of man are the sole causes of public misfortunes and governmental corruption, have resolved to set forth in a solemn declaration the natural, inalienable, and sacred rights of man: so that by being constantly present to all the members of the social body this declaration may always remind them of their rights and duties; so that by being liable at every moment to comparison with the aim of any and all political institutions the acts of the legislative and executive powers may be the more fully respected; and so that by being founded henceforward on simple and incontestable principles the demands of the citizens may always tend toward maintaining the constitution and the general welfare.

In consequence, the National Assembly recognizes and declares, in the presence and under the auspices of the Supreme Being, the following rights of man and the citizen:

1. Men are born and remain free and equal in rights. Social distinctions may be based only on common utility.

2. The purpose of all political association is the preservation of the natural and imprescriptible rights of man. These rights are liberty, property, security, and resistance to oppression.

3. The principle of all sovereignty rests essentially in the nation. No body and no individual may exercise authority which does not emanate expressly from the nation.

4. Liberty consists in the ability to do whatever does not harm another; hence the exercise of the natural rights of each man has no other limits than those which assure to other members of society the enjoyment of the same rights. These limits can only be determined by the law.

Source: Lynn Hunt, ed. and trans., *The French Revolution and Human Rights: A Brief Documentary History* (Boston: Bedford St. Martin's, 1996), 77–79.

5. The law only has the right to prohibit those actions which are injurious to society. No hindrance should be put in the way of anything not prohibited by the law, nor may any one be forced to do what the law does not require.

6. The law is the expression of the general will. All citizens have the right to take part, in person or by their representatives, in its formation. It must be the same for everyone whether it protects or penalizes. All citizens being equal in its eyes are equally admissible to all public dignities, offices, and employments, according to their ability, and with no other distinction than that of their virtues and talents.

. . .

11. The free communication of thoughts and opinions is one of the most precious of the rights of man. Every citizen may therefore speak, write, and print freely, if he accepts his own responsibility for any abuse of this liberty in the cases set by the law.

12. The safeguard of the rights of man and the citizen requires public powers. These powers are therefore instituted for the advantage of all, and not for the private benefit of those to whom they are entrusted.

13. For maintenance of public authority and for expenses of administration, common taxation is indispensable. It should be apportioned equally among all the citizens according to their capacity to pay.

14. All citizens have the right, by themselves or through their representatives, to have demonstrated to them the necessity of public taxes, to consent to them freely, to follow the use made of the proceeds, and to determine the means of apportionment, assessment, and collection, and the duration of them.

. . .

17. Property being an inviolable and sacred right, no one may be deprived of it except when public necessity, certified by law, obviously requires it, and on the condition of a just compensation in advance.

WORKING WITH SOURCES

1. To what extent does the declaration mix specific provisions and general principles of human rights?

2. How does the document aim to uphold the "common utility"? How is the "public necessity" to be determined?

22.2 Olympe de Gouges, *The Declaration of the Rights of Woman*, September 1791

Women were not included among the new officeholders of Revolutionary France, nor were they members of the National Assembly, which supposedly represented all members of the country's Third Estate. An immediate question arose concerning the extent to which the benefits of the Revolution should be extended to females (as well as to slaves throughout France's global empire). Some men did advocate the extension of these rights and privileges, but women also took action

Source: Lynn Hunt, ed. and trans., *The French Revolution and Human Rights: A Brief Documentary History* (Boston: Bedford St. Martin's, 1996), 124–126.

in their own cause. Among these was the "Cercle Social" (Social Circle), a group of female activists who coordinated their publishing activities on behalf of women and their own goals in the developing Revolution.

One of the leaders of this group was Marie Gouze (1748–1793), who, under her pen name "Olympe de Gouges," attacked both the institution of slavery and the oppression of women in 1791. A playwright, pamphleteer, and political activist, de Gouges published this thoughtful meditation on what the National Assembly should declare concerning "the rights of woman" (as opposed merely to "the rights of man"). Other members of the Social Circle were arrested as the Revolution entered its radical phase, but Olympe de Gouges was executed by guillotine in November 1793.

To be decreed by the National Assembly in its last sessions or by the next legislature.

Preamble

Mothers, daughters, sisters, female representatives of the nation ask to be constituted as a national assembly. Considering that ignorance, neglect, or contempt for the rights of woman are the sole causes of public misfortunes and governmental corruption, they have resolved to set forth in a solemn declaration the natural, inalienable, and sacred rights of woman: so that by being constantly present to all the members of the social body this declaration may always remind them of their rights and duties; so that by being liable at every moment to comparison with the aim of any and all political institutions the acts of women's and men's powers may be the more fully respected; and so that by being founded henceforward on simple and incontestable principles the demands of the citizenesses may always tend toward maintaining the constitution, good morals, and the general welfare.

In consequence, the sex that is superior in beauty as in courage, needed in maternal sufferings, recognizes and declares, in the presence and under the auspices of the Supreme Being, the following rights of woman and the citizeness.

1 Woman is born free and remains equal to man in rights. Social distinctions may be based only on common utility.

2 The purpose of all political association is the preservation of the natural and imprescriptible rights of woman and man. These rights are liberty, property, security, and especially resistance to oppression.

3 The principle of all sovereignty rests essentially in the nation, which is but the reuniting of woman and man. No body and no individual may exercise authority which does not emanate expressly from the nation.

4 Liberty and justice consist in restoring all that belongs to another; hence the exercise of the natural rights of woman has no other limits than those that the perpetual tyranny of man opposes to them; these limits must be reformed according to the laws of nature and reason.

5 The laws of nature and reason prohibit all actions which are injurious to society. No hindrance should be put in the way of anything not prohibited by these wise and divine laws, nor may anyone be forced to do what they do not require.

6 The law should be the expression of the general will. All citizenesses and citizens should take part, in person or by their representatives, in its formation. It must be the same for everyone. All citizenesses and citizens, being equal in its eyes, should be equally admissible to all public dignities, offices, and employments, according to their ability, and with no other distinction than that of their virtues and talents.

. . .

11 The free communication of thoughts and opinions is one of the most precious of the rights of woman, since this liberty assures the recognition of children by their fathers. Every citizeness may therefore say freely, I am the mother of your child; a barbarous prejudice [against unmarried women having children] should not force her to hide the truth, so long as responsibility is accepted for any abuse of this liberty in cases determined by the law [women are not allowed to lie about the paternity of their children].

12 The safeguard of the rights of woman and citizeness requires public powers. These powers are instituted for the advantage of all and not for the private benefit of those to whom they are entrusted.

13 For maintenance of public authority and for expenses of administration, taxation of women and men is equal; she takes part in all forced labor service, in all painful tasks; she must therefore have the same proportion in the distribution of places, employments, offices, dignities, and in industry.

14 The citizenesses and citizens have the right, by themselves or through their representatives, to have demonstrated to them the necessity of public taxes.

The citizenesses can only agree to them upon admission of an equal division, not only in wealth, but also in the public administration, and to determine the means of apportionment, assessment, and collection, and the duration of the taxes.

. . .

17 Property belongs to both sexes whether united or separated; it is for each of them an inviolable and sacred right, and no one may be deprived of it as a true patrimony of nature, except when public necessity, certified by law, obviously requires it, and then on condition of a just compensation in advance.

WORKING WITH SOURCES

1. What does de Gouges consider woman's "natural and reasonable" share in the "common" life of a society?
2. To what extent does biology determine the particular roles and sufferings of women? Are women (in de Gouges's context) to be considered the superior element of human society as a result?

22.3 Voltaire, "Torture," from the *Philosophical Dictionary*, 1769

Voltaire (the pen name of François-Marie Arouet) epitomized the Enlightenment. His *Dictionnaire philosophique* (*Philosophical Dictionary*), the first edition of which appeared in 1764, distilled his thought on philosophical matters in what he self-deprecatingly called an "alphabetical abomination." Voltaire invariably found ways to deploy humor in the pursuit of serious moral, religious, and ethical truths, as the continued popularity of his "contes philosophiques" (philosophical tales), including *Candide, Zadig,* and *Micromégas*, attests.

In this "dictionary," arranged alphabetically according to the entry's title (in French), Voltaire tackled matters like atheism, fanaticism, the soul, superstition, and tolerance. His tone is always light and witty, despite the weightiness of (and the violence associated with) the subject matter. Inspired by ongoing court cases and interrogation methods, Voltaire added the following miraculous little essay on the use (and, in some countries, disuse) of torture as a legal instrument to the 1769 version of the *Dictionary*. His satirical approach resonates today, as issues of what constitutes torture and how it ought to be applied continue to dominate our political discourse.

Source: Voltaire, *Philosophical Dictionary*, ed. and trans. Theodore Besterman (Harmondsworth, UK: Penguin, 1972), 394–396.

Although there are few articles on jurisprudence in these respectable alphabetical reflections, a word must nevertheless be said about torture, otherwise named the question. It is a strange way to question one. Yet it was not invented by the merely curious. It would appear that this part of our legislation owes its first origin to a highwayman. Most of these gentlemen are still in the habit of squeezing thumbs, burning the feet of those who refuse to tell them where they have put their money, and questioning them by means of other torments.

The conquerors, having succeeded these thieves, found this invention of the greatest utility. They put it into practice when they suspected that some vile plot was being hatched against them, as, for instance, that of being free, a crime of divine and human lèse-majesté. The accomplices had to be known; and to arrive at this knowledge those who were suspected were made to suffer a thousand deaths, because according to the jurisprudence of these first heroes anyone suspected of having had so much as a disrespectful thought about them was worthy of death. And once a man has thus deserved death it matters little whether appalling torments are added for a few days or even several weeks. All this even had something of the divine about it. Providence sometimes tortures us by means of the stone, gravel, gout, scurvy, leprosy, pox great and small, griping of the bowels, nervous convulsions, and other executants of the vengeance of providence.

Now since the first despots were images of divinity, as all their courtiers freely admitted, they imitated it so far as they could.

. . .

The grave magistrate who has bought for a little money the right to conduct these experiments on his fellow creatures tells his wife at dinner what happened during the morning. The first time her ladyship is revolted, the second time she acquires a taste for it, for after all women are curious, and then the first thing she says to him when he comes home in his robes is: "My angel, did you give anyone the question today?"

The French, who are considered to be a very humane people, I do not know why, are astonished that the English, who have had the inhumanity to take the whole of Canada from us [in 1760 and ratified in 1763, as a result of the Seven Years' War], have renounced the pleasure of applying the question.

. . .

In 1700 the Russians were regarded as barbarians. We are now only in 1769, and an **empress** has just given this vast state laws that would have done honour to Minor, to Numa, and to Solon if they had had enough intelligence to compose them. The most remarkable of them is universal toleration, the second is the abolition of torture. Justice and humanity guided her pen, she has reformed everything. Woe to a nation which, long civilized, is still led by atrocious ancient practices! "Why should we change our jurisprudence?" it asks. "Europe uses our cooks, our tailors, our wig-makers; therefore our laws are good."

Empress: Catherine the Great.

WORKING WITH SOURCES

1. Does Voltaire make a convincing case that the use of torture results from excessive curiosity and a warped desire to inflict suffering?
2. How does he ridicule the continuation of "ancient" practices into modern times, and how does this essay reflect the values of the philosophical Enlightenment?

22.4   Edmund Burke, *Reflections on the Revolution in France*, 1790

Born in Dublin to a Protestant father and a Catholic mother, Edmund Burke (1729–1797) struggled to build a political career in Georgian England. Having established a reputation for brilliant thinking and speaking, he entered Parliament in 1766. One of his principal causes in the 1760s and 1770s was the defense of the American colonists in their conflict with the mother country. Burke opposed the English government's position that England was sovereign over the colonies and could tax the colonists as she saw fit. By contrast, Burke insisted that a "right" was not an abstract principle and that policy should be guided by actual circumstances. When the French Revolution began in 1789, Burke surprised some of his political allies by speaking against it, mainly because he believed that "reason" and "rights" were not absolute principles that justified violent change. His statement against the extremes of revolution, published in November 1790, became the basis for a form of political ideology known as conservatism.

It is no wonder, therefore, that with these ideas of everything in their constitution and government at home, either in church or state, as illegitimate and usurped, or at best as a vain mockery, they look abroad with an eager and passionate enthusiasm. Whilst they are possessed by these notions, it is vain to talk to them of the practice of their ancestors, the fundamental laws of their country, the fixed form of a constitution whose merits are confirmed by the solid test of long experience and an increasing public strength and national prosperity. They despise experience as the wisdom of unlettered men; and as for the rest, they have wrought underground a mine that will blow up, at one grand explosion, all examples of antiquity, all precedents, charters, and acts of parliament. They have "the rights of men." Against these there can be no prescription, against these no agreement is binding; these admit no temperament and no compromise; anything withheld from their full demand is so much of fraud and injustice. Against these their rights of men let no government look for security in the length of its continuance, or in the justice and lenity of its administration.

. . .

Government is not made in virtue of natural rights, which may and do exist in total independence of it, and exist in much greater clearness and in a much greater degree of abstract perfection; but their abstract perfection is their practical defect. By having a right to everything they want everything. Government is a contrivance of human wisdom to provide for human *wants*. Men have a right that these wants should be provided for by this wisdom. Among these wants is to be reckoned the want, out of civil society, of a sufficient restraint upon their passions. Society requires not only that the passions of individuals should be subjected, but that even in the mass and body, as well as in the individuals, the inclinations of men should frequently be thwarted, their will controlled, and their passions brought into subjection. This can only be done *by a power out of themselves*, and not, in the exercise of its function, subject to that will and to those passions which it is its office to bridle and subdue. In this sense the restraints on men, as well as their liberties, are to be reckoned among their rights. But as the liberties and the restrictions vary with times and circumstances and admit to infinite modifications, they cannot be settled upon

Source: Edmund Burke, *Reflections on the Revolution in France*, ed. Thomas H. D. Mahoney (Indianapolis: Liberal Arts, 1955), 66, 68–69, 70–71, 73–74.

any abstract rule; and nothing is so foolish as to discuss them upon that principle.

. . .

The pretended rights of these theorists are all extremes; and in proportion as they are metaphysically true, they are morally and politically false. The rights of men are in a sort of *middle*, incapable of definition, but not impossible to be discerned. The rights of men in governments are their advantages; and these are often in balances between differences of good, in compromises sometimes between good and evil, and sometimes between evil and evil. Political reason is a computing principle: adding, subtracting, multiplying, and dividing, morally and not metaphysically, or mathematically, true moral denominations.

. . .

In France, you are now in the crisis of a revolution and in the transit from one form of government to another—you cannot see that character of men exactly in the same situation in which we see it in this country. With us it is militant; with you it is triumphant; and you know how it can act when its power is commensurate to its will. I would not be supposed to confine these observations to any description of men or to comprehend all men of any description within them—No! far from it. I am as incapable of that injustice as I am of keeping terms with those who profess principles of extremities and who, under the name of religion, teach little else than wild and dangerous politics. The worst of these politics of revolution is this: they temper and harden the breast in order to prepare it for the desperate strokes which are sometimes used in extreme occasions. But as these occasions may never arrive, the mind receives a gratuitous taint; and the moral sentiments suffer not a little when no political purpose is served by the depravation. This sort of people are so taken up with their theories about the rights of man that they have totally forgotten his nature. Without opening one new avenue to the understanding, they have succeeded in stopping up those that lead to the heart. They have perverted in themselves, and in those that attend to them, all the well-placed sympathies of the human breast.

WORKING WITH SOURCES

1. Is Burke's protest against the Revolution merely the result of his estimation of its "extremist" nature?
2. Is Burke justified in drawing a connection between metaphysical theorizing and physical violence? Did he provide an accurate prediction of "the Terror," still to come?

22.5   Thomas Paine, *Rights of Man*, 1791

As a young man in England, Thomas Paine worked a series of low-paying, menial jobs, most of which he was quickly fired from, being perceived as an uncooperative "troublemaker." In 1774, at the age of 37, seeming to be a total failure in every profession he had attempted, he hired passage on a ship to the American colonies. Fortunately, Paine possessed a letter of recommendation from Benjamin Franklin, whom he had met after a scientific lecture in London. On the strength of this letter, Paine found employment as a printer and writer in Philadelphia, and soon became the editor of a journal called the *Pennsylvania Magazine*. Incensed by the abuses to which the colonists

Source: The Life and Major Writings of Thomas Paine, ed. Philip S. Foner (New York: Citadel, 1945), 316–317, 340–341.

were subject, he encouraged his fellow Americans to make a formal break with Britain. He also wrote and published a series of editorials protesting the American institution of slavery, castigating those who were agitating for their own "liberty" while denying it so cruelly to others.

Paine published his thoughts on independence in pamphlet form in January 1776 under the title *Common Sense*. So popular was the document that General Washington ordered that it be read aloud to his troops as they froze along the Delaware River on Christmas Eve 1776. Declaring, "These are the times that try men's souls," Paine continued to offer encouragement to the soldiers in pamphlets later published as *The American Crisis*, and his efforts on behalf of the American cause were recognized by many of the founding fathers of the country during the Revolution.

When he heard about the storming of the Bastille in Paris in July 1789, Paine rushed to France to be a part of this new revolution. Soon afterward, he had the honor of delivering the key to the Bastille from the Marquis de Lafayette to Washington, at which time, he declared, his heart "leaped with joy." When Burke's *Reflections* on the Revolution were published in 1790, Paine felt he had been betrayed by his former friend, with whom he had had many conversations and a meeting of minds in the American cause. As a result, he published *The Rights of Man*, a strong rebuke of Burke's philosophy and commentary, in February 1791. The work was dedicated to the first president of the United States, George Washington.

The three first articles [of the Declaration of the Rights of Man and of the Citizen] are the basis of liberty, as well individual as national; nor can any country be called free, whose government does not take its beginning from the principles they contain, and continue to preserve them pure; and the whole of the Declaration of Rights is of more value to the world, and will do more good, than all the laws and statutes that have yet been promulgated.

In the declaratory exordium which prefaces the Declaration of Rights, we see the solemn and majestic spectacle of a nation opening its commission, under the auspices of its Creator, to establish a Government; a scene so new, and so transcendently unequalled by any thing in the European world, that the name of a revolution is diminutive of its character, and it rises into a regeneration of man.

What are the present governments of Europe, but a scene of iniquity and oppression? What is that of England? Do not its own inhabitants say, It is a market where every man has his price, and where corruption is common traffic, at the expense of a deluded people? No wonder, then, that the French Revolution is traduced.

Had it confined itself merely to the destruction of flagrant despotism, perhaps Mr. Burke and some others had been silent. Their cry now is, "It is gone too far": that is, it has gone too far for them. It stares corruption in the face, and the venal tribe are all alarmed. Their fear discovers itself in their outrage, and they are but publishing the groans of a wounded vice.

But from such opposition, the French Revolution, instead of suffering, receives an homage. The more it is struck, the more sparks it will emit; and the fear is, it will not be struck enough. It has nothing to dread from attacks: Truth has given it an establishment; and Time will record it with a name as lasting as his own.

Having now traced the progress of the French Revolution through most of its principal stages, from its commencement, to the taking of the Bastille, and its establishment by the Declaration of Rights, I will close the subject with the energetic apostrophe of M. de Lafayette—*May this great monument, raised to Liberty, serve as a lesson to the oppressor, and an example to the oppressed!*

. . .

From the Revolutions of America and France, and the symptoms that have appeared in other countries, it is evident that the opinion of the world is changed with respect to systems of government, and that revolutions are not within the compass of political calculations. The progress of time and circumstances, which men assign to the accomplishment of great changes, is too mechanical to measure the force of the mind, and the rapidity of reflection, by which revolutions are generated. All the old governments have received a shock from those that already appear, and which were once more improbable, and are a greater subject of wonder, than a general revolution in Europe would be now.

When we survey the wretched condition of man under the monarchical and hereditary systems of government, dragged from his home by one power, or driven by another, and impoverished by taxes more than by enemies, it becomes evident that those systems are bad, and that a general revolution in the principle and construction of governments is necessary.

What is government more than the management of the affairs of a nation? It is not, and from its nature cannot be, the property of any particular man or family, but of the whole community, at whose expense it is supported; and though by force or contrivance it has been usurped into an inheritance, the usurpation cannot alter the right of things. Sovereignty, as a matter of right, appertains to the nation only, and not to any individual; and a nation has at all times an inherent indefeasible right to abolish any form of government it finds inconvenient, and establish such as accords with its interest, disposition, and happiness. The romantic and barbarous distinction of [making] men into kings and subjects, though it may suit the condition of courtiers, cannot that of citizens; and is exploded by the principle upon which governments are now founded. Every citizen is a member of the sovereignty, and, as such, can acknowledge no personal subjection; and his obedience can be only to the laws.

WORKING WITH SOURCES

1. How does Paine defend the Revolution against the charge of "extremism," as levied by Burke and others?
2. Why does Paine think it dangerous to romanticize kings and queens?

23. CREOLES AND CAUDILLOS: LATIN AMERICA IN THE NINETEENTH CENTURY, 1790–1917

23.1 Memoirs of General Antonio López de Santa Anna, 1872

Santa Anna (1794–1876) is recognized today by Americans, and especially by Texans, primarily for his successful siege of the Alamo in March 1836. However, he also epitomized the caudillo type in nineteenth-century Mexico, dominating his country's political life and weathering a series of highs and lows throughout his long career. Although he served as president for 11 nonconsecutive terms (some of only a few months) over a period of 22 years, Santa Anna is more famous for his military achievements and losses—including some extraordinary adventures. For example, in an 1838 battle against the French at Veracruz, Santa Anna's leg was shattered during a cannon volley. The leg was amputated and buried with full military honors. Exiled multiple times, to Cuba, Jamaica, Colombia, and even the United States, Santa Anna devoted his final years to compiling his memoirs, an excerpt of which is translated below. This passage details his turbulent political career—at least from his perspective—in the early 1840s.

Sixty-two days after my foot had been amputated, Gen. Guadalupe Victoria called on me at the instigation of the government. He informed me that a revolution was threatening, and that the government desired me to take [Anastasio] Bustamante's place as temporary president in this time of trial. How well the people knew me! They knew I would never desert my principles and would always be on hand when my country needed me!

I was carried to the capital on a litter. Although my trip was made with extreme care, the hardships of the journey and the change of climate weakened me. However, despite my poor health, I assumed the office of president immediately. The tasks involved completely overwhelmed me, but I pulled through. The government forces triumphed throughout the country.

Gen. Gabriel Valencia captured and executed the hope of the revolution, José A. Mejia, in the vicinity of the town of Acajeta. The dreaded threat of revolution died, and peace was restored.

Bustamante once again took up the reins of government, and I retired to [my estate] to complete my recovery. However, Bustamante's loss of prestige with the people caused his government to fail. In the town of Guadalajara, in the early months of 1841, arrangements were made for Bustamante to abdicate and for the reform of the Constitution of 1824. In Tacubaya, a council of generals agreed upon basic ground rules to help bring about these reforms, and once again I assumed the office of provisional president. . . .

Source: Antonio López de Santa Anna, *The Eagle: The Autobiography of Santa Anna*, ed. and trans. Ann Fears Crawford (Austin, TX: Pemberton, 1967), 65–69, as excerpted in James A. Wood and John Charles Chasteen, *Problems in Modern Latin American History: Sources and Interpretations*, 3rd ed. (Lanham, MD: Rowman & Littlefield, 2009), 79–81.

In order to conform to public opinion, I called together a group of prominent citizens from all states in the nation to instigate needed reforms. This group drew up *The Principles of Political Organization* on June 12, 1844. This constitution was circulated by the government, and each of the states accepted and ratified it without dissension.

In September 1844, my beloved wife died. Greater sorrow I had never known! General of Division Valentín Canalizo substituted for me while I devoted myself to family matters.

During the first session under our new Constitution, I was duly elected president and called to the capital to administer the customary oath. The election saddened me even more. My deep melancholy drove me to abhor the glamorous life of the capital and to prefer a life of solitude. I resigned the noble office to which I had been called, but the public intruded upon my privacy, pleading that I return. My friends, with the greatest of good faith, also begged me to resume my office. Their pleas led me to sacrifice myself to the public good. I withdrew my resignation.

Near the end of October, General [Mariano] Paredes rebelled against the government in Guadalajara. When the news was communicated to me by the government, they ordered me to take the troops quartered in Jalapa and march to the capital. I instantly obeyed the orders. Paredes had been relieved of his command of the Capital District due to excesses of intoxication while he was commanding his troops. He bore a grudge and was determined to take revenge. In our country one spark was sufficient to set aflame a revolution.

I was marching toward Guadalajara under orders, when I received the news of an upheaval in the capital. The situation seemed serious, and I halted my advance. Details of the revolt in the capital arrived soon after my halt. The messenger read me the following infamous words:

> The majority of Congress openly favor the Paredes revolution. The government, in self-defense or wishing to avoid revolution, has issued a decree by which the sessions of Congress have been suspended. This decree has served as a pretext for General José J. Herrera to join the revolt. Rioters have torn down the bronze bust of President Santa Anna that stood in the Plaza del Mercado. They have also taken his amputated foot from the cemetery of Santa Paula and proceeded to drag it through the streets to the sounds of savage laughter.

I interrupted the narrator, exclaiming "Stop! I don't wish to hear any more! Almighty God! A member of my body, lost in the service of my country, dragged from the funeral urn, broken into bits to be made sport of in such a barbaric manner!" In that moment of grief and frenzy, I decided to leave my native country, object of my dreams and of my illusions, for all time.

WORKING WITH SOURCES

1. How were Santa Anna's personal setbacks interwoven with his political career in this period, at least in his recollection?
2. What does Santa Anna's memoir reveal about the presumed indispensability of the caudillo, and the connection between his physical body and his political power?

23.2   Simón Bolívar, "The Jamaica Letter," September 6, 1815

Simón Bolívar (1783–1830), the eventual liberator of northern South America from Spanish control, was born in Venezuela but profoundly influenced by the culture of peninsular Spain and the European Enlightenment. He visited Spain in 1799, and traveled to Paris to witness Napoleon's coronation as emperor in 1804. Bolívar aspired to bring the values of the Enlightenment, and particularly the notions of liberty and popular sovereignty, to his homeland. Having declared an independent Venezuela in 1812, he was driven into exile in British Jamaica with the landing of a Spanish expeditionary force in 1815. In 1816, he returned with a military force and assumed the presidency of "Gran Colombia" in 1822. The following letter is renowned for its expression of Bolívar's ambitions, at a time when the outcome of "liberation" from Spain seemed uncertain.

Kingston, Jamaica, September 6, 1815.
My dear Sir:
I hasten to reply to the letter of the 29th ultimo which you had the honor of sending me and which I received with the greatest satisfaction.

. . .

With what a feeling of gratitude I read that passage in your letter in which you say to me: "I hope that the success which then followed Spanish arms may now turn in favor of their adversaries, the badly oppressed people of South America." I take this hope as a prediction, if it is justice that determines man's contests. Success will crown our efforts, because the destiny of America has been irrevocably decided; the tie that bound her to Spain has been severed. Only a concept maintained that tie and kept the parts of that immense monarchy together. That which formerly bound them now divides them. The hatred that the Peninsula has inspired in us is greater than the ocean between us. It would be easier to have the two continents meet than to reconcile the spirits of the two countries. The habit of obedience; a community of interest, of understanding, of religion; mutual goodwill; a tender regard for the birthplace and good name of our forefathers; in short, all that gave rise to our hopes, came to us from Spain. As a result there was a born principle of affinity that seemed eternal, notwithstanding the misbehavior of our rulers which weakened that sympathy, or, rather, that bond enforced by the domination of their rule. At present the contrary attitude persists: we are threatened with the fear of death, dishonor, and every harm; there is nothing we have not suffered at the hands of that unnatural stepmother-Spain. The veil has been torn asunder. We have already seen the light, and it is not our desire to be thrust back into darkness. The chains have been broken; we have been freed, and now our enemies seek to enslave us anew. For this reason America fights desperately, and seldom has desperation failed to achieve victory.

Because successes have been partial and spasmodic, we must not lose faith. In some regions the Independents triumph, while in others the tyrants have the advantage. What is the end result? Is not the entire New World in motion, armed for defense? We have but to look around us on this hemisphere to witness a simultaneous struggle at every point.

. . .

Source: Selected Writings of Bolívar, trans. Lewis Bertrand (New York: Colonial, 1951), as edited in: http://faculty.smu.edu/bakewell/BAKEWELL/texts/jamaica-letter.html.

This picture represents, on a military map, an area of 2,000 longitudinal and 900 latitudinal leagues at its greatest point, wherein 16,000,000 Americans either defend their rights or suffer repression at the hands of Spain, which, although once the world's greatest empire, is now too weak, with what little is left her, to rule the new hemisphere or even to maintain herself in the old. And shall Europe, the civilized, the merchant, the lover of liberty allow an aged serpent, bent only on satisfying its venomous rage, devour the fairest part of our globe? What! Is Europe deaf to the clamor of her own interests? Has she no eyes to see justice? Has she grown so hardened as to become insensible? The more I ponder these questions, the more I am confused. I am led to think that America's disappearance is desired; but this is impossible because all Europe is not Spain. What madness for our enemy to hope to reconquer America when she has no navy, no funds, and almost no soldiers! Those troops which she has are scarcely adequate to keep her own people in a state of forced obedience and to defend herself from her neighbors. On the other hand, can that nation carry on the exclusive commerce of one-half the world when it lacks manufactures, agricultural products, crafts and sciences, and even a policy? Assume that this mad venture were successful, and further assume that pacification ensued, would not the sons of the Americans of today, together with the sons of the European *reconquistadores* twenty years hence, conceive the same patriotic designs that are now being fought for?

. . .

More than anyone, I desire to see America fashioned into the greatest nation in the world, greatest not so much by virtue of her area and wealth as by her freedom and glory. Although I seek perfection for the government of my country, I cannot persuade myself that the New World can, at the moment, be organized as a great republic. Since it is impossible, I dare not desire it; yet much less do I desire to have all America a monarchy because this plan is not only impracticable but also impossible. Wrongs now existing could not be righted, and our

emancipation would be fruitless. The American states need the care of paternal governments to heal the sores and wounds of despotism and war. The parent country, for example, might be Mexico, the only country fitted for the position by her intrinsic strength, and without such power there can be no parent country. Let us assume it were to be the Isthmus of Panamá, the most central point of this vast continent. Would not all parts continue in their lethargy and even in their present disorder? For a single government to infuse life into the New World; to put into use all the resources for public prosperity; to improve, educate, and perfect the New World, that government would have to possess the authority of a god, much less the knowledge and virtues of mankind.

. . .

It is a grandiose idea to think of consolidating the New World into a single nation, united by pacts into a single bond. It is reasoned that, as these parts have a common origin, language, customs, and religion, they ought to have a single government to permit the newly formed states to unite in a confederation. But this is not possible. Actually, America is separated by climatic differences, geographic diversity, conflicting interests, and dissimilar characteristics. How beautiful it would be if the Isthmus of Panamá could be for us what the Isthmus of Corinth was for the Greeks! Would to God that some day we may have the good fortune to convene there an august assembly of representatives of republics, kingdoms, and empires to deliberate upon the high interests of peace and war with the nations of the other three-quarters of the globe. This type of organization may come to pass in some happier period of our regeneration. But any other plan, such as that of Abbé St. Pierre, who in laudable delirium conceived the idea of assembling a European congress to decide the fate and interests of those nations, would be meaningless.

Among the popular and representative systems, I do not favor the federal system. It is over-perfect, and it demands political virtues and talents far superior to our own. For the same reason I reject a monarchy that is part aristocracy and part democracy, although with such a government England has achieved much fortune and splendor. Since it is not possible for us to select the most perfect and complete form of government, let us avoid falling into demagogic anarchy or monocratic tyranny. These opposite extremes would only wreck us on similar reefs of misfortune and dishonor; hence, we must seek a mean between them. I say: Do not adopt the best system of government, but the one that is most likely to succeed.

WORKING WITH SOURCES

1. How does Bolívar's advice combine practical suggestions with idealistic principles?
2. To what extent does Bolívar believe the revolt to have been triggered by Spain's refusal to live up to its own best principles?

23.3 Domingo Faustino Sarmiento, *Travels in the United States in 1847*, 1849

The journalist and eventual Argentine president Sarmiento (1811–1888) is most famous today for his novel *Facundo: Civilization and Barbarism* (1845), a sharp and daring satire of the caudillo Juán Manuel de Rosas. His indictment of Rosas, thinly disguised as the biography of another brutal dictator (called Juán Facundo Quiroga), was written while Sarmiento was an exile from the regime. Representing the government of Chile, Sarmiento traveled throughout Europe, North Africa, and North America, observing local political and social conditions closely and comparing them with what he knew of Argentine society. The result is a fascinating travelogue of his impressions of and reactions to the people of the United States, with vivid descriptions of many of its manmade and natural wonders. Nevertheless, his hopes for his native Argentina were never very far from the foreground, as this excerpt reveals.

The fatal error of the Spanish colonization of South America, the deep wound which has condemned present generations to inertia and backwardness, was in the system of land distribution. In Chile, great concessions of land, measuring from one hill to another and from the side of a river to the banks of an arroyo, were given to the conquistadors. The captains established earldoms for themselves, while their soldiers, fathers of the sharecropper, that worker without land who multiplies without increasing the number of his buildings, sheltered themselves in the shade of their improvised roofs. The passion to occupy lands in the name of the king drove men to dominion over entire districts, which put great distances between landowners so that after three centuries the intervening land still has not been cleared. The city, for this reason, has been suppressed in this vast design, and the few villages which have been created since the conquest have been *decreed* by presidents. I know of at least five villages which were created in Chile in this official and contrived manner. But see how the American, recently called in the

Source: Michael A. Rockland. *Sarmiento's Travels in the United States in 1847.* © 1970, 1989 Princeton University Press. Reprinted by permission of Princeton University Press.

nineteenth century to conquer his piece of the world, does it. There the government has been careful to set aside land for all the coming generations. The young men aspiring to property each year crowd around the auction rooms in which public lands are sold, and, with the numbers of their lots in hand, they leave to take possession of their property, expecting to receive their titles later on from the offices in Washington. The most energetic Yankees, the misanthropes, the rustics, the SQUATTERS, in short, work in a manner which is more romantic, more poetic, and more primitive. Armed with their rifles, they immerse themselves in the virgin wilderness. For a pastime they kill the squirrels that unceasingly romp among the branches of the trees. A well-aimed bullet heads up into the sky to connect with an eagle which soars with majestic wings over the dark green surface formed by the boughs of the trees. The axe is the faithful companion of such a man, though he uses it for nothing more than to flex his muscles by throwing cedars and oaks to the ground. During his vagabond excursions this independent farmer looks for fertile land, a picturesque spot, something beside a navigable river; and when he has made up his mind, as in the most primitive times in the world's history, he says, "This is mine!" and without further ado takes possession of the land in name of the kings of the world: Work and Good Will. If one day the surveyor of the state's lands should arrive at the border of the land which he has laid out as his own, the auction will only serve to tell him what he owes for the land he has under cultivation, which will be the same sum as the adjacent uncultivated lands are going for. It is not unusual for this indomitable and unsociable character, overtaken by populations advancing through the wilderness, to sell his place and move away with his family, his oxen, and his horses searching for the desired solitude of the forests. The Yankee is a born proprietor. If he does not have anything and never has had anything he does not say that he is poor but that he is poor right now, or that he has been unlucky, or that times are bad. And then, in his imagination he sees the primitive, dark, solitary, isolated forests and in the midst of them the mansion he means to have on the bank of some unknown river, with smoke rising from the chimney and oxen returning home with slow step to his property as the sun goes down. From that moment he talks of nothing else but going out to occupy and settle new lands. His evenings are spent over the map, computing the stages of the journey, tracing a route for his wagon. And in the newspaper he does not look for anything except announcements of sales of state lands, or word of the new city that is being built on the shores of Lake Superior.

Alexander the Great, upon destroying Tyre, had to give world commerce a new distribution center for the spices of the Orient, one from which they could be sent at once to the Mediterranean coasts. The founding of Alexandria was an example of Alexander's renowned cleverness, even though the commercial routes were known and the Isthmus of Suez the indispensable trading ground between the waters of the India, Europe, and Africa of those days. This work is accomplished every day by American Alexanders, who wander through the wilds looking for points that a profound study of the future indicates will be centers of commerce.

WORKING WITH SOURCES

1. In what respects, and with what degree of conviction, does Sarmiento compare the acquisition of land in Latin America with land ownership in the United States?
2. Is Sarmiento convinced that this degree of cultivation and building of commerce cannot happen in Argentina? Why or why not?

23.4   Amulet Containing Passages from the Qur'an, Worn by Muslim Slaves Who Rioted in Bahia, Brazil, 1835

Although slavery was not abolished in Brazil until 1888, slave revolts were frequent and remarkable for their ambitions, success, and diversity of participating elements. Two urban revolts of the nineteenth century were especially significant. First, the Tailors' Rebellion of 1798, in Salvador, the capital of the Brazilian state of Bahia, drew on the assistance of freedmen, people of mixed race, and even craftspeople of Portuguese descent. The second was a Muslim-inspired and Muslim-directed uprising of slaves in Bahia in 1835, organized by African-born freedmen and slaves who had attained an Islamic education in West Africa before enslavement. This Muslim revolt is particularly fascinating because of the role of written documents, here deployed as protective amulets, among the members of the slave resistance. This excerpt from a book by a Brazilian scholar attempts to demonstrate the role of the written word in this rebellion, illustrating another, and less frequently recognized, "power" within historical documents.

The written word, which the Malês used, had a great seductive power over Africans whose roots belonged in oral cultures. The amulets consisted of pieces of paper containing passages from the *Koran* and powerful prayers. The paper was carefully folded in an operation that had its own magical dimension. It was then placed in a small leather pouch, which was sewn shut. In many cases, besides the paper, other ingredients appeared in those charms. A police scribe described the contents of one amulet as follows:

> Little bundles or leather pouches were opened at this time by cutting them at the seams with a penknife. Inside were found several pieces of insignificant things such as cotton wrapped in a little powder [*sic*], others with tiny scraps of garbage, and little sacks with some seashells inside. Inside one of the leather pouches was a piece of paper with Arabic letters written on it.

The "insignificant" substances referred to here likely included sand moistened beforehand in some sort of holy water, perhaps water used by some renowned and pious alufá or water used to wash the tablets on which Malês wrote their religious texts. In the latter case, this water could also be drunk, since the ink was made of burnt rice; such a drink was believed to seal the body against outside harm. Some of the amulets were made of West African fabric; leather was used more often, since it provided better protection for both the sacred words and the other charms. There is a remarkable similarity between the Bahian Malê talismans and those still in use in black Africa, although the Bahian amulet seems to have had more "pagan" ingredients. According to Vincent Monteil, "In general the Islamic Talisman is a leather case, sewn together and containing a piece of stiff cardboard . . . and inside this is a folded piece of paper on which are written phrases in praise of God and cabalistic symbols—that is, Arabic letters, pentacles, and the like." Kabbalistic drawings such as the ones mentioned here were found in several amulets confiscated in 1835.

The Magrebian Arabic in the Malê amulets found on the bodies of dead rebels or in Muslims' houses has been studied and translated by Vincent Monteil and Rolf Reichert. Reichert took stock of twelve amulets, some of which contained kabbalistic shapes. . . .

Source: João José Reis, *Slave Rebellion in Brazil: The Muslim Uprising of 1835 in Bahia*, trans. Arthur Brakel (Baltimore: Johns Hopkins University Press, 1993), 99–103.

The magic in the Islamic texts and drawings worked as protection against various threats. The Africans arrested in 1835 said little about their magic, and when they did say something, they avoided linking it to the revolt. However, besides their obvious political function, these amulets were especially designed to control daily life. A freedman named Silvestre José Antônio, a merchant, was arrested with five amulets in his case. He declared they "were prayers to save [him] from any unfortunate happenstance in his travels through the Recôncavo." Whether in Africa or in Brazil, a good Muslim merchant never traveled without a considerable number of protecting charms. A booklet of Islamic prayers could also work to protect its holder against evil spells. It was for that reason that a freedman named Pedro Pinto asked a literate Malê to make one for him, so he could "be free from wagging tongues." Pedro, by the way, was not a Malê.

. . .

Even so, one Malê fisherman made a good living from amulet making. According to one witness, Antônio, a Hausa slave residing in Itapagipe, "wrote prayers in his language and sold them to his partners making 4 *patacas* [1,280 réis] a day doing that." When he was arrested, a writing quill was found in his room: "Asked . . . by the justice [of the peace] why he kept such a quill, the same slave answered that he kept it so as to write things having to do with his Nation. He was then asked to write and he made a few scribbles with the phoney quill and the justice asked . . . what he had written. He answered that what he had written was the name of the 'Hail Mary.'" This Islamic-Christian melding does not seem to have impressed the justice of the peace. Antônio calmly went on telling his questioners that "when he was a young boy in his homeland, he went to school," and there he had learned Arabic so as to write "prayers according to the schism of his homeland."

WORKING WITH SOURCES

1. How did the Malês use the written word to resist authority, and why did they use the Arabic language?

2 What do the documents created by the slaveholders and their supporting institutions reveal about the power of written sources as well?

23.5   Photograph of a Chinese Coolie, Peru, 1881

Chinese migration to Latin America was a major part of the pattern of mass migration streams across the world that typified the nineteenth century. "Coolies" (from the Urdu word *kuli*, or "hireling") were indentured laborers recruited from India and China on 5- or 10-year contracts, who were forced to work to pay off the cost of their transportation. Roughly 235,000 Chinese came to Peru, Cuba, and Costa Rica, working in guano pits and silver mines, on sugar and cotton plantations, and later on railroads. Such work contracts were little better than slavery, and oftentimes were accompanied by institutions familiar from enslavement itself. This photograph, published in a Chilean army newspaper, depicts a Chinese coolie who is being liberated by an invading Chilean army in 1881.

Source: http://commons.wikimedia.org/wiki/File:Enslaved_Chinese_coolie_in_Peru_1881.jpg.

WORKING WITH SOURCES

1. Look closely at the man's feet and ankles. What might have been attached to him, and why?
2. How might this image have been deployed for propaganda purposes by the invading Chilean?

24. THE CHALLENGE OF MODERNITY: EAST ASIA, 1750–1910

24.1 Lin Zexu's Letter to Queen Victoria of Great Britain, August 27, 1839

In March 1839, the Daoguang emperor sent Lin Zexu (1785–1850), a widely respected official with a reputation for courage and honesty, to Canton as an imperial commissioner, charged with the task of cutting off the opium trade—a trade which had proved extremely lucrative to British traders in the region. Lin confiscated vast opium stocks, ordered them burned, and made merchants sign an agreement that they would no longer sell the drug, on pain of death. British merchants appealed to their government for compensation—and for military action against Lin's agents. This effort culminated in the First Opium War (1839–1842). In the midst of his anti-opium efforts, however, Lin also attempted to shame Queen Victoria (whom he believed was at the center of governmental policy in Great Britain) into cutting off the opium trade that was causing so much damage to the Chinese people, even though it generated profits for the British.

His Majesty the Emperor comforts and cherishes foreigners as well as Chinese: he loves all the people in the world without discrimination. Whenever profit is found, he wishes to share it with all men; whenever harm appears, he likewise will eliminate it on behalf of all of mankind. His heart is in fact the heart of the whole universe.

Generally speaking, the succeeding rulers of your honorable country have been respectful and obedient. Time and again they have sent petitions to China, saying: "We are grateful to His Majesty the Emperor for the impartial and favorable treatment he has granted to the citizens of my country who have come to China to trade," etc. I am pleased to learn that you, as the ruler of your honorable country, are thoroughly familiar with the principle of righteousness and are grateful for the favor that His Majesty the Emperor has bestowed upon your subjects. Because of this fact, the Celestial Empire, following its traditional policy of treating foreigners with kindness, has been doubly considerate towards the people from England. You have traded in China for almost 200 years, and as a result, your country has become wealthy and prosperous. _no moral conscience_

As this trade has lasted for a long time, there are bound to be unscrupulous as well as honest traders. Among the unscrupulous are those who bring opium to China to harm the Chinese; they succeed so well that this poison has spread far and wide in all the provinces. You, I hope, will certainly agree that people who pursue material gains to the great detriment of the welfare of others can be neither tolerated by Heaven nor endured by men. . . .

Source: *Chinese Repository*, Vol. 8 (February 1840), pp. 497–503; reprinted in William H. McNeil and Mitsuko Iriye, eds., *Modern Asia and Africa*, Readings in World History Vol. 9, (New York: Oxford University Press, 1971), pp. 111–118.

Your country is more than 60,000 *li* from China. The purpose of your ships in coming to China is to realize a large profit. Since this profit is realized in China and is in fact taken away from the Chinese people, how can foreigners return injury for the benefit they have received by sending this poison to harm their benefactors? They may not intend to harm others on purpose, but the fact remains that they are so obsessed with material gain that they have no concern whatever for the harm they can cause to others. Have they no conscience? I have heard that you strictly prohibit opium in your own country, indicating unmistakably that you know how harmful opium is. You do not wish opium to harm your own country, but you choose to bring that harm to other countries such as China. Why?

. . .

I have heard that the areas under your direct jurisdiction such as London, Scotland, and Ireland do

not produce opium; it is produced instead in your Indian possessions such as Bengal, Madras, Bombay, Patna, and Malwa. In these possessions the English people not only plant opium poppies that stretch from one mountain to another but also open factories to manufacture this terrible drug. As months accumulate and years pass by, the poison they have produced increases in its wicked intensity, and its repugnant odor reaches as high as the sky. Heaven is furious with anger, and all the gods are moaning with pain! It is hereby suggested that you destroy and plow under all of these opium plants and grow food crops instead, while issuing an order to punish severely anyone who dares to plant opium poppies again. If you adopt this policy of love so as to produce good and exterminate evil, Heaven will protect you, and gods will bring you good fortune. Moreover, you will enjoy a long life and be rewarded with a multitude of children and grandchildren! In short, by taking this one measure, you can bring great happiness to others as well as yourself. Why do you not do it?

Li: Roughly 1/3 mile.

WORKING WITH SOURCES

1. How does Lin contrast honorable with dishonorable trade? Is this "honor" bound up in the product itself?
2. What does Lin see as the responsibility of a monarch to his/her own subjects, as well as to the subjects of other monarchs?

24.2 Narrative of the British Ship *Nemesis* during the First Opium War, 1845

When hostilities broke out between China and Britain in 1839, the British fleet was the most powerful in the world and in a high state of readiness. The Chinese had no real naval forces to contest the British, but a small Chinese squadron sailed out to confront the British men-o'-war. The underfunded and frantically assembled Chinese navy could not stand up to armored steam

Source: W. H. Bernard and W. D. Hall, *Narrative of the Voyages and Services of the* Nemesis *from 1840 to 1843, and of the Combined Naval and Military Operations in China: Comprising a Complete Account of the Colony of Hong-Kong and Remarks on the Character and Habits of the Chinese,* 2nd ed. (London: Henry Colburn,1845), 149–152, available online at http://www.gutenberg.org/files/43669/43669-h/43669-h.htm.

gunboats like the *Nemesis*, whose heavy pivot gun dominated riverside batteries and allowed British expeditionary forces to land wherever they pleased. The British methodically attacked and occupied forces along the Chinese coast from Guangzhou to Shanghai, and the Treaty of Nanjing (1842) marked an end to hostilities. However, the "heroes" of the *Nemesis* continued to receive attention for their victory over the Chinese, and a book detailing the ship's voyages and military successes was rushed into print in 1845.

CHAPTER XVI

Keshen, who had spent all his life either in large provincial capitals or in the imperial city itself, could have had little opportunity of learning anything either relating to foreign trade or foreign ships, still less was he acquainted with the "outer waters" along the coast of the empire.

After describing them to his imperial master, he boldly ventures his opinion, that the reputation of the fortifications of the Bocca Tigris, as a place of defence, have been much overrated, and he goes on to say—"It is, then, clear that we have no defences worthy to be called such. It is, in truth, the local character of the country, that there is no important point of defence by which the whole may be maintained."

No wonder that such a declaration from a man who was also the third member of the imperial cabinet, taken, as it was, from personal observation, should have sounded unpalatable and even traitorous to the emperor's ear. But this was not all. Indeed, one might almost imagine that some European must have pointed out to him defects which his own unpractised and unaided eye could never have detected.

Lin [Zexu], on the other hand, had never dared to report to his master the full extent of the information which was given to him, though he was fully prepared to adopt every advice which tended to obstruct the commerce of England, and impede an amicable settlement of the difficulties.

Such truths are always hard to bear, and harder to believe, and were consequently *not* believed, *because* they were true. But Keshen did his best to improve his weapons; he sent for a founder of cannon, who gave him a new model, and undertook to make some experimental pieces. Yet it did not escape Keshen that, even if he succeeded in casting good cannon, he could only do so as a preparation *for the future.* "They could not be ready," says he, "for the business we have now in hand. These are the proofs," he adds, "of the inefficiency of our military armament, which is such *that no reliance can be placed upon it.*"

He proceeded to say that it would be necessary to employ a naval as well as a land force to defend the Bogue, but then threw out a suspicion that the seamen were not to be depended on, for that "he had heard a report that, after the battle of Chuenpee, these men all went to their commander, or Tetuh, and demanded money of him, threatening that they would otherwise disperse; and he had, therefore, personally made inquiry into the matter, and found that the report was perfectly true, and, moreover, that the Tetuh, having no other remedy, (evidently the pay was in arrear,) was obliged to *pawn his own clothes and other things*, by which means he was enabled to give each of them a bonus of two dollars, and thus only could he get them to remain for a time at their posts."

Moreover, he added, "our ships of war are not large and strong, and it is difficult to mount heavy guns upon them. Hence it is evident that our force here, (he was writing at the Bogue,) as a guard and defence against the foreigners, is insufficient."

Keshen next remarked upon the character of the people of the province. "Your slave has found them ungrateful and avaricious. Of those who are actual traitors it is unnecessary to say anything. But the rest are accustomed to see the foreigners day by day, and intimacy has grown up between them." And he proceeds to contrast them very unfavourably with the people of Chusan, "who felt at once that the foreigners were of *another race.*"

. . .

The memorial containing Captain Elliot's demands was sent up to Pekin, together with this report, which was founded upon personal observation; and Keshen implored the emperor to look with pity upon "his black-haired flock, the people, and that he would be graciously pleased to accede to the requests made by the foreigners, and to grant them favours beyond measure. Thus," he added, "shall we lay the foundation for victory hereafter, by binding and curbing the foreigners now, while we *prepare* the means of cutting them off at some future period."

Keshen was a true Chinaman of the new school, (for there are new schools even in antique China,) and, in most respects, the very opposite of Lin. Sensible of the weakness of his country when matched with England, conscious of his inability to fight his enemy with success, he nevertheless hazarded the chance, when the *commands* of the emperor compelled him to aim the blow. He, however, did his utmost to gain time, and even endeavoured to impose upon Captain Elliot, and to hope against hope itself. After all that Keshen had said, the defence of the Bogue was conducted, as we shall now perceive, with more energy than might have been expected, and, indeed, with considerable spirit.

. . .

The steamer immediately poured in a volley of grape and canister from her bow and stern guns, while the boats pulled away towards the shore, to carry the works by storm, opening their fire from their bow-guns as they advanced. The Chinese fled, after some resistance; and the battery, which was of very recent construction, was at once taken possession of by the crews of the boats, the colours being taken by Lieutenant Bowers. It was found to mount twenty guns of various calibre, which were immediately destroyed. There were also lying on the ground a vast number of guns dismounted, probably not less than sixty, which appeared to have been landed out of their junks, or recovered after the destruction of their fleet in the bay. These were all rendered useless, with the exception of a few brass ones, which were carried away as trophies. Their magazines and buildings were also totally destroyed. The number of killed among the Chinese were about thirty, but no wounded were found, as they had probably been carried off by their companions in arms. On our side no casualties happened.

WORKING WITH SOURCES

1. How and why do the captains attribute the failure of the Chinese to their inability to modernize their military?
2. What might have been the Chinese opinion concerning these operations?

24.3 A Boxer Rebel and a British Family Killed during the Boxer Rebellion, 1900

A new wave of antiforeign sentiment in China, triggered by a "race for concessions" among the Western powers in the late 1890s, was increasingly centered on a group called the Society of the Harmonious Fists. The foreign community referred to this organization, due to their ritual exercises and resistance to both Qing and foreign control, as the Boxers. By late 1899, the Boxers were regularly provoking the foreign and Christian communities throughout China, and the assassination

Sources: Boxer photo from National Archives photo no. 28-0547M. Farthing family photo from http://www.library.yale .edu/div/exhibits/boxers.htm.

of the German ambassador in 1900 launched a brutal civil war. Western countries united to oppose the Boxers, now allied with Empress Dowager Cixi, and the foreign diplomatic quarter in Beijing was besieged between June and August 1900. Nevertheless, the groups most frequently targeted by the Boxers were Western missionaries and Chinese people who had converted to Christianity. Among those killed was the entire family of G. B. Farthing, an English Baptist missionary in Shanxi province, who are shown in the photograph below.

WORKING WITH SOURCES

1. How does the image of the Boxer reflect his understanding of Chinese cultural traditions?
2. Why might the Farthing family have adopted "Chinese" (or what they believed was Chinese) dress?

24.4   The Meiji Constitution of the Empire of Japan, 1889

The Tokugawa were forced to capitulate to the samurai of two southern domains by the end of 1867, and the new regime moved to the Tokugawa capital of Edo, renaming it Tokyo (Eastern Capital). The new emperor, 15-year-old Mutsuhito, took the name Meiji (Enlightened Rule) and quickly moved to make good on that name. The throne issued a charter oath in April 1868 and promulgated edicts that spelled out how the new government would be set up. Throughout the 1870s and 1880s, Japan experienced a flourishing of government-managed social experimentation. The proclaimed goals of using "Western science and Eastern ethics" in the service of "civilization and enlightenment" were designed to put Japan on an equal footing with Western powers. The constitution itself, composed after a painstaking study of the constitutional governments of many Western countries, reflects this drive to "Westernize." Nonetheless, the document also contained various escape clauses, in case the power of the emperor was questioned too openly.

Imperial Oath Sworn in the Sanctuary in the Imperial Palace (Tsuge-bumi)

We, the Successor to the prosperous Throne of Our Predecessors, do humbly and solemnly swear to the Imperial Founder of Our House and to Our other Imperial Ancestors that, in pursuance of a great policy co-extensive with the Heavens and with the Earth, We shall maintain and secure from decline the ancient form of government.

In consideration of the progressive tendency of the course of human affairs and in parallel with the advance of civilization, We deem it expedient, in order to give clearness and distinctness to the instructions bequeathed by the Imperial Founder of Our House and by Our other Imperial Ancestors, to establish fundamental laws formulated into express provisions of law, so that, on the one hand, Our Imperial posterity may possess an express guide for the course they are to follow, and that, on the other, Our subjects shall thereby be enabled to enjoy a wider range of action in giving Us their support, and that the observance of Our laws shall continue to the remotest ages of time. We will thereby to give greater firmness to the stability of Our country and to promote the welfare of all the people within the boundaries of Our dominions; and We now establish the Imperial House Law and the Constitution.

. . .

CHAPTER I

THE EMPEROR

Article 1. The Empire of Japan shall be reigned over and governed by a line of Emperors unbroken for ages eternal.

Source: Hirobumi Ito, *Commentaries on the Constitution of the Empire of Japan,* trans. Miyoji Ito (Tokyo: Igirisu-horitsu gakko, 1889), available online at the Hanover Historical Texts Project, https://history.hanover.edu/texts/1889con.html.

Article 2. The Imperial Throne shall be succeeded to by Imperial male descendants, according to the provisions of the Imperial House Law.

Article 3. The Emperor is sacred and inviolable.

Article 4. The Emperor is the head of the Empire, combining in Himself the rights of sovereignty, and exercises them, according to the provisions of the present Constitution.

Article 5. The Emperor exercises the legislative power with the consent of the Imperial Diet.

Article 6. The Emperor gives sanction to laws, and orders them to be promulgated and executed.

. . .

CHAPTER II

RIGHTS AND DUTIES OF SUBJECTS

Article 18. The conditions necessary for being a Japanese subject shall be determined by law.

Article 19. Japanese subjects may, according to qualifications determined in laws or ordinances, be appointed to civil or military or any other public offices equally.

Article 20. Japanese subjects are amenable to service in the Army or Navy, according to the provisions of law.

Article 21. Japanese subjects are amenable to the duty of paying taxes, according to the provisions of law.

Article 22. Japanese subjects shall have the liberty of abode and of changing the same within the limits of the law.

Article 23. No Japanese subject shall be arrested, detained, tried or punished, unless according to law.

Article 24. No Japanese subject shall be deprived of his right of being tried by the judges determined by law.

Article 25. Except in the cases provided for in the law, the house of no Japanese subject shall be entered or searched without his consent.

Article 26. Except in the cases mentioned in the law, the secrecy of the letters of every Japanese subject shall remain inviolate.

Article 27. The right of property of every Japanese subject shall remain inviolate. (2) Measures necessary to be taken for the public benefit shall be any provided for by law.

Article 28. Japanese subjects shall, within limits not prejudicial to peace and order, and not antagonistic to their duties as subjects, enjoy freedom of religious belief.

Article 29. Japanese subjects shall, within the limits of law, enjoy the liberty of speech, writing, publication, public meetings and associations.

Article 30. Japanese subjects may present petitions, by observing the proper forms of respect, and by complying with the rules specially provided for the same.

Article 31. The provisions contained in the present Chapter shall not affect the exercises of the powers appertaining to the Emperor, in times of war or in cases of a national emergency.

WORKING WITH SOURCES

1. What was the source of the emperor's power, according to this document?
2. To what extent could military considerations limit the rights and freedoms of Japanese citizens? Were these merely potential limitations?

24.5   Natsume Soseki, *Kokoro*, 1914

Like nearly all the arts in late-nineteenth-century Japan, the novel was also heavily influenced by Western examples. The culmination of this trend, in Meiji society generally, was *Kokoro*, published by Natsume Soseki (1867–1916) in 1914. Soseki, a lecturer in English literature at the Imperial University in Tokyo, depicts the wrenching changes in Meiji Japan and their effect on traditional and generational values, leading ultimately to the tragic end of the central character in the novel. *Kokoro* (the word means, roughly, "the heart of things") was Soseki's best-known novel, and appeared two years after the death of Emperor Meiji. The excerpts below also touch on the real-life suicide of General Nogi, a hero of the Russo-Japanese War (1904–1905) who killed himself immediately after the death of the Meiji in 1912. The sense of honor that accompanied Nogi to his grave is thus at the heart of the novel, and Soseki's main theme may have been the ongoing interaction between Western-style reforms and traditional Japanese culture.

M y father was the first to see the news of General Nogi's death in the paper.

"What a terrible thing!" he said. "What a terrible thing!"

We, who had not yet read the news, were startled by these exclamations.

"I really did think he had finally gone mad," said my brother later.

"I must say I was surprised too," agreed my brother-in-law.

About that time, the papers were so full of unusual news that we in the country waited impatiently for their arrival. I would read the news by my father's bedside, taking care not to disturb him, or, if I could not do this, I would quietly retire into my own room, and there read the paper from beginning to end. For a long time, the image of General Nogi in his uniform, and that of his wife dressed like a court lady, stayed with me.

The tragic news touched us like the bitter wind which awakens the trees and the grass sleeping in the remotest corners of the countryside. The incident was still fresh in our minds when, to my surprise, a telegram arrived from Sensei. In a place where dogs barked at the sight of a Western-style suit, the arrival of a telegram was a great event. My mother, to whom the telegram had been given, seemed to think it necessary to call me to a deserted part of the house before handing it to me. Needless to say, she looked quite startled.

"What is it?" she said, standing by while I opened it.

It was a simple message, saying that he would like to see me if possible, and would I come up? I cocked my head in puzzlement. My mother offered an explanation. "I am sure he wants to see you about a job," she said.

I thought that perhaps my mother was right. On the other hand, I could not quite believe that Sensei wanted to see me for that reason. At any rate, I, who had sent for my brother and brother-in-law, could hardly abandon my sick father and go to Tokyo. My mother and I decided that I should send Sensei a telegram saying that I could not come. I explained as briefly as possible that my father's condition was becoming more and more critical. I felt, however, that I owed him a fuller explanation. That same day, I wrote him a letter giving him the details. My mother, who was firmly convinced that Sensei had some post in mind for me, said in a tone filled with regret, "What a pity that this should have happened at such a time."

. . .

My father began to talk deliriously.

"Will General Nogi ever forgive me?" he would say. "How can I ever face him without shame? Yes, General, I will be with you very soon."

When he said such things, my mother would become a little frightened, and would ask us to gather around the bed. My father too, when he came out of his delirium, seemed to want everybody by his side so as not to feel lonely. He would want my mother most of all. He would look around the room and, if she was not there, he would be sure to ask, "Where is Omitsu?" Even when he did not say so, his eyes would ask the question. Often, I had to get up and find her. She would then leave her work, and enter the sickroom saying, "Is there anything you wish?" There

---

Source: Natsume Soseki, *Kokoro*, trans. Edwin McClellan (Washington, DC: Regnery, 1957), 108–110, 117–118, 120–122.

were times when he would say nothing, and simply look at her. There were also times when he would say something quite unexpectedly gentle, such as: "I've given you a lot of trouble, haven't I, Omitsu?" And my mother's eyes would suddenly fill with tears. Afterwards, she would remember how different he used to be in the old days, and say, "Of course, he sounds rather helpless now, but he used to be quite frightening, I can tell you."

. . .

Almost violently, I tore open the tough paper which contained the letter. The letter had the appearance of a manuscript, with the characters neatly written between vertically ruled lines. I smoothed out the sheets which had been folded over twice for easier handling in the post.

I could not but wonder what it was that Sensei had written at such great length. I was, however, too much on edge to read the whole letter properly. My mind kept wandering back to the sickroom. I had the feeling that something would happen to my father before I could finish reading the letter. At least, I was sure that I would soon be called away by my brother, or my mother, or my uncle. In this unsettled state, I read the first page.

"You asked me once to tell you of my past. I did not have the courage then to do so. But now, I believe I am free of the bonds that prevented me from telling you the truth about myself. The freedom that I now have, however, is no more than an earthly, physical kind of freedom, which will not last forever. Unless I take advantage of it while I can, I shall never again have the opportunity of passing on to you what I have learned from my own experience, and my promise to you will have been broken. Circumstances having prevented me from telling you my story in person, I have decided to write it out for you."

I read thus far, and realized why it was that the letter was so long. That Sensei would not bother to write about my future career, I had more or less known from the very beginning. What really worried me was that Sensei, who hated to write at all, had taken the trouble to write such a long epistle. Why had he not waited, I asked myself, until I was once more in Tokyo?

I said to myself repeatedly, "He is free now, but he will never be free again," and tried desperately to understand what the words meant; then all of a sudden I became uneasy. I tried to read on further but, before I could do so, I heard my brother's voice calling me from the sickroom. Frightened, I stood up, and hurried along the corridor to where the others were gathered. I was prepared to learn that the end had come for my father.

WORKING WITH SOURCES

1. In what specific ways does this excerpt reflect the incorporation of Western ideas and items into traditional Japanese society?
2. How does Soseki use the dying father and the teacher as metaphors for a young man's life in the Meiji period?

25. ADAPTATION AND RESISTANCE: THE OTTOMAN AND RUSSIAN EMPIRES, 1683–1908

25.1 Lady Mary Wortley Montagu, *Letters from the Levant*, April 1, 1717

Mary Wortley Montagu (1689–1762), who was born into the British aristocracy, sought out an acquaintance with the leading literary and scientific figures of her day and traveled with her husband to Constantinople while he was ambassador to the Ottoman emperor. Although her husband was recalled to England within a year, Lady Mary had endeavored to learn as much as possible about Turkish customs and behavior, especially those concerning women and children. She frequently had paintings made of herself (and her son) dressed in Turkish costume, and she considered it patriotic to import Turkish customs that she thought could benefit her fellow Englishmen. Her introduction of the Turkish practice of inoculation against smallpox drew the great admiration of Voltaire, who praised her intelligence and her willingness to learn from others in his *Letters Concerning the English Nation* (1733).

To the Countess of Mar [her sister], Adrianople, April 1, 1717.

. . .

Pray let me into more particulars, and I will try to awaken your gratitude, by giving you a full and true relation of the novelties of this place, none of which would surprise you more than a sight of my person, as I am now in my Turkish habit, though I believe you would be of my opinion, that it is admirably becoming. I intend to send you my picture; in the mean time accept of it here.

The first part of my dress is a pair of drawers, very full, that reach to my shoes, and conceal the legs more modestly than your petticoats. They are of a thin rose-coloured damask, brocaded with silver flowers. My shoes are of white kid leather, embroidered with gold. Over this hangs my smock, of a fine white silk gauze, edged with embroidery. This smock has wide sleeves, hanging half-way down the arm, and is closed at the neck with a diamond button; but the shape and colour of the bosom are very well to be distinguished through it.

. . .

Upon the whole, I look upon the Turkish women as the only free people in the empire; the very divan pays respect to them, and the grand signior himself, when a pasha is executed, never violates the privileges of the *harém*, (or women's apartment,) which remains untouched and entire to the widow. They are queens of their slaves, whom the husband has no permission so much as to look upon, except it be an old woman or two that his lady chooses. It is true their law permits them four wives; but there is no instance of a man of quality that makes use of this liberty, or of a woman of rank that would suffer it. When a husband happens to be inconstant, (as those things

Source: Mary Wortley Montagu, *Letters from the Levant during the Embassy to Constantinople, 1716–18* (New York: Arno, 1971), 124, 128–129, 146–148.

will happen,) he keeps his mistress in a house apart, and visits her as privately as he can, just as it is with you. Amongst all the great men here, I only know the *tefterdar*, (i.e. treasurer) that keeps a number of she slaves for his own use (that is, on his own side of the house; for a slave once given to serve a lady is entirely at her disposal,) and he is spoken of as a libertine, or what we should call a rake, and his wife will not see him, though she continues to live in his house.

Thus you see, dear sister, the manners of mankind do not differ so widely as our voyage writers would make us believe. Perhaps it would be more entertaining to add a few surprising customs of my own invention; but nothing seems to me so agreeable as truth, and I believe nothing so acceptable to you.

. . .

Letter to Mrs. S. C——[Sarah Chiswell], Adrianople, April 1 [1717].

. . .

A propos of distempers: I am going to tell you a thing that will make you wish yourself here. The small-pox, so fatal and so general amongst us, is here entirely harmless by the invention of *ingrafting*, which is the term they give it. There is a set of old women who make it their business to perform the operation every autumn, in the month of September, when the great heat is abated. People send to one another to know if any of their family has a mind to have the small-pox: they make parties for this purpose, and when they are met (commonly fifteen or sixteen together,) the old woman comes with a nutshell full of the matter of the best sort of small-pox, and asks what vein you please to have opened. She immediately rips open that you offer to her with a large needle (which gives you no more pain than a common

scratch,) and puts into the vein as much matter as can lie upon the head of her needle, and after that binds up the little wound with a hollow bit of shell; and in this manner opens four or five veins. The Grecians have commonly the superstition of opening one in the middle of the forehead, one in each arm and one on the breast, to mark the sign of the cross; but this has a very ill effect, all these wounds leaving little scars, and is not done by those that are not superstitious, who choose to have them in the legs, or that part of the arm that is concealed. The children or young patients play together all the rest of the day, and are in perfect health to the eighth. Then the fever begins to seize them, and they keep their beds two days, very seldom three. They have very rarely above twenty or thirty in their faces, which never mark; and in eight days' time they are as well as before their illness. Where they are wounded, there remain running sores during the distemper, which I do not doubt is a great relief to it. Every year thousands undergo this operation; and the French ambassador says pleasantly, that they take the small-pox here by way of diversion, as they take the waters in other countries. There is no example of any one that has died in it; and you may believe I am well satisfied of the safety of this experiment, since I intend to try it on my dear little son.

I am patriot enough to take pains to bring this useful invention into fashion in England; and I should not fail to write to some of our doctors very particularly about it, if I knew any one of them that I thought had virtue enough to destroy such a considerable branch of their revenue for the good of mankind. But that distemper is too beneficial to them, not to expose to all their resentment the hardy wight that should undertake to put an end to it.

WORKING WITH SOURCES

1. Was Montagu naïve about the role of women in Turkish society? Is she using the experiences of Turkish women principally as a foil for those of English women?
2. How does Montagu contrast "superstition" with "reasonable" behavior, and why?

25.2   *Imperial Edict of the Rose Garden, November 3, 1839*

With a change of Ottoman sultans in 1839, the government issued the Rose Garden Edict, the first of three reform edicts which are collectively known as the Tanzimat (reorganizations). With this edict, the government bound itself to basic principles with respect to relations between it and its subjects, and it carefully avoided a definition of the position of religious minorities in the empire. The document also enumerates basic human rights, drawing on ideas from the American and French revolutionary declarations of the eighteenth century. Accordingly, it reflects the adaptability of the Ottoman Empire to Western ideas, at least in the general context of the Tanzimat reforms.

The Hatti-Sherif of Gülhane

All the world knows that in the first days of the Ottoman monarchy, the glorious precepts of the Qur'an and the laws of the Empire were always honored.

The Empire in consequence increased in strength and greatness, and all its subjects, without exception, had acquired the highest degree of ease and prosperity. In the last one hundred and fifty years a succession of accidents and divers causes have brought about a disregard for the sacred code of laws and the regulations flowing therefrom, and the former strength and prosperity have changed into weakness and poverty; an empire in fact loses all its stability as soon as it ceases to observe its laws.

These considerations are ever present in our mind and, from the day of our advent to the throne the thought of the public weal, of the improvement of the state of the provinces, and of relief to the [subject] peoples has not ceased wholly to engage it. If, therefore, the geographical position of the Ottoman provinces, the fertility of the soil, the aptitude and intelligence of the inhabitants are considered, the conviction will remain that by striving to find efficacious means, the result, which with the help of God we hope to attain, can be obtained within a few years. Full of confidence, therefore, in the help of the Most High and supported by the intercession of our Prophet, we deem it right to seek through new institutions to provide the provinces composing the Ottoman Empire with the benefit of a good administration.

These institutions must be principally carried out under three heads which are:

1. Guarantees insuring to our subjects perfect security of life, honor, and fortune.
2. A regular system of assessing and levying taxes.
3. An equally regular system for the levying of troops and the duration of their service.

. . .

From henceforth, therefore, the cause of every accused person shall be judged publicly, as our divine law requires, after inquiry and examination, and so long as a regular judgment shall not have been pronounced, no one can secretly or publicly put another to death by poison or in any other manner.

No one shall be allowed to attack the honor of any person whatever.

Each person shall possess his property of every kind and shall dispose of it in all freedom, without let or hindrance from any person whatever; thus, for example, the innocent heirs of a criminal shall not be deprived of their legal rights, and the property of the criminal shall not be confiscated. These imperial grants shall extend to all our subjects, of whatever religion or sect they may be; they shall enjoy them without exception. Perfect security is thus given to the inhabitants of our Empire in their lives, their honor, and their fortunes, as they are secured to them by the sacred text of our law.

As for the other points, as they must be settled with the assistance of enlightened opinions, our council of justice (increased by new members as shall be found necessary), to whom shall be joined, on certain days which we shall determine, our ministers and the notables of the Empire, shall assemble in order to frame laws regulating these matters concerning the security of life and fortune and the assessment of taxes. Each one in these assemblies shall freely express his ideas and give his advice.

. . .

As the object of these institutions is solely to revivify religion, government, the nation, and the Empire, we engage not to do anything which is contrary thereto.

In testimony of our promise we will, after having deposited these presents in the hall containing the glorious mantle of the Prophet, in the presence of all the *"ulama"* and the grandees of the Empire, make oath thereto in the name of God, and shall afterwards cause the oath to be taken by the *"ulama"* and grandees of the Empire.

WORKING WITH SOURCES

1. How are Islamic religious principles used to substantiate and reinforce the force of law in the Tanzimat era? Would this be applied to the adherents of *all* religions in the empire?
2. Were the declarations in this edict too vague to be workable? Are they deliberately vague?

25.3   Writings of Bahá'u'lláh, ca. 1880s

In 1844 a young merchant from Shiraz in Persia began to teach a new faith, and he was given the title of the Báb ("the Gate"). Preaching against the hypocrisy of Muslim religious leaders, he proclaimed the beginning of a new spiritual era. When he was arrested and executed in 1850, his work was continued by Mirza Husayn Ali, who was given the title Bahá'u'lláh ("the glory of God"). Despite arrest, exile, and other forms of persecution from governmental authorities, Bahá'u'lláh composed a series of revelations and meditations. He sent letters of proclamation (generally following the same template) to a host of Western leaders, including Queen Victoria, Pope Pius IX, and even American presidents. The Bahá'í faith that resulted from his teachings was organized around the central principle that the human race is one and whole, and should be united in brotherhood. Needless to say, this message did not appeal to everyone in the nineteenth century.

XXX. God witnesseth that there is no God but Him, the Gracious, the Best-Beloved. All grace and bounty are His. To whomsoever He will He giveth whatsoever is His wish. He, verily, is the All-Powerful, the Almighty, the Help in Peril, the Self-Subsisting. We, verily, believe in Him Who, in the person of the Báb, hath been sent down by the Will of the one true God, the King of Kings, the All-Praised. We, moreover, swear

Source: Gleanings from the Writings of Bahá'u'lláh, trans. Shoghi Effendi (Wilmette, IL: Bahá'í Publishing Trust, 1952), 73–76, 79.

fealty to the One Who, in the time of Mustagháth, is destined to be made manifest, as well as to those Who shall come after Him till the end that hath no end. We recognize in the manifestation of each one of them, whether outwardly or inwardly, the manifestation of none but God Himself, if ye be of those that comprehend. Every one of them is a mirror of God, reflecting naught else but His Self, His Beauty, His Might and Glory, if ye will understand.

. . .

XXXI. Contemplate with thine inward eye the chain of successive Revelations that hath linked the Manifestations of Adam with that of the Báb. I testify before God that each one of these Manifestations hath been sent down through the operation of the Divine Will and Purpose, that each hath been the bearer of a specific Message, that each hath been entrusted with a divinely-revealed Book and been commissioned to unravel the mysteries of a mighty Tablet. The measure of the Revelation with which every one of them hath been identified had been definitely fore-ordained.

. . .

XXXII. That which thou hast heard concerning Abraham, the Friend of the All-Merciful, is the truth, and no doubt is there about it. The Voice of God commanded Him to offer up Ishmael as a sacrifice, so that His steadfastness in the Faith of God and His detachment from all else but Him may be demonstrated unto men. The purpose of God, moreover, was to sacrifice him as a ransom for the sins and iniquities of all the peoples of the earth. This same honor, Jesus, the Son of Mary, besought the one true God, exalted be His name and glory, to confer upon Him. For the same reason was Husayn offered up as a sacrifice by Muhammad, the Apostle of God.

No man can ever claim to have comprehended the nature of the hidden and manifold grace of God; none can fathom His all-embracing mercy. Such hath been the perversity of men and their transgressions, so grievous have been the trials that have afflicted the Prophets of God and their chosen ones, that all mankind deserveth to be tormented and to perish. God's hidden and most loving providence, however, hath, through both visible and invisible agencies, protected and will continue to protect it from the penalty of its wickedness. Ponder this in thine heart, that the truth may be revealed unto thee, and be thou steadfast in His path.

. . .

The measure of the revelation of the Prophets of God in this world, however, must differ. Each and every one of them hath been the Bearer of a distinct Message, and hath been commissioned to reveal Himself through specific acts. It is for this reason that they appear to vary in their greatness. Their Revelation may be likened unto the light of the moon that sheddeth its radiance upon the earth. Though every time it appeareth, it revealeth a fresh measure of its brightness, yet its inherent splendor can never diminish, nor can its light suffer extinction.

It is clear and evident, therefore, that any apparent variation in the intensity of their light is not inherent in the light itself, but should rather be attributed to the varying receptivity of an ever-changing world. Every Prophet Whom the Almighty and Peerless Creator hath purposed to send to the peoples of the earth hath been entrusted with a Message, and charged to act in a manner that would best meet the requirements of the age in which He appeared.

WORKING WITH SOURCES

1. To what extent do documents like this reflect an ecumenical, all-embracing spirit among the Bahá'í?
2. Who would have found this attempt at religious synthesis worthy of suppression, and why?

25.4   Tsar Alexander II's Abolition of Serfdom, February 19, 1861

The defeat of Russia in the Crimean War (1853–1856) convinced the newly enthroned Alexander II (r. 1855–1881) of the need for fundamental reforms in his country. The first institution he tackled was serfdom, and his Emancipation Edict (1861) ostensibly freed peasants from their bondage to the landowning aristocracy. Although the edict affected some 50 million serfs, it was not fully implemented. Peasants were not given land titles per se; the land was turned over to the control of local communities (*mirs*), which then allocated parcels to individual serfs. Moreover, they were forced to make annual payments to the government in the form of loans that would compensate the former landowners; the loan amounts were often higher than the dues aristocrats had demanded before emancipation.

By the Grace of God WE, Alexander II, Emperor and Autocrat of All Russia, King of Poland, Grand Duke of Finland, etc., make known to all OUR faithful subjects: Called by Divine Providence and by the sacred right of inheritance to the Russian throne of OUR ancestors, WE vowed in OUR heart to respond to the mission which is entrusted to Us and to surround with OUR affection and OUR Imperial solicitude all OUR faithful subjects of every rank and condition, from the soldier who nobly defends the country to the humble artisan who works in industry; from the career official of the state to the plowman who tills the soil.

Examining the condition of classes and professions comprising the state, WE became convinced that the present state legislation favors the upper and middle classes, defines their obligations, rights, and privileges, but does not equally favor the serfs, so designated because in part from old laws and in part from custom they have been hereditarily subjected to the authority of landowners, who in turn were obligated to provide for their well being. Rights of nobles have been hitherto very broad and legally ill defined, because they stem from tradition, custom, and the good will of the noblemen. In most cases this has led to the establishment of good patriarchal relations based on the sincere, just concern and benevolence on the part of the nobles, and on affectionate submission on the part of the peasants. Because of the decline of the simplicity of morals, because of the diversity of relations, because of the weakening of the direct paternal relationship of nobles toward the peasants, and because noble rights fell sometimes into the hands of people exclusively concerned with their personal interests, good relations weakened. The way was opened for an arbitrariness burdensome for the peasants and detrimental to their welfare, causing them to be indifferent to the improvement of their own existence.

. . .

Having invoked Divine assistance, WE have resolved to execute this task.

On the basis of the above-mentioned new arrangements, the serfs will receive in time the full rights of free rural inhabitants.

The nobles, while retaining their property rights to all the lands belonging to them, grant the peasants perpetual use of their household plots in return for a specified obligation; and, to assure their livelihood as well as to guarantee fulfillment of their obligations toward the government, [the nobles] grant them a portion of arable land fixed by the said arrangements as well as other property.

While enjoying these land allotments, the peasants are obliged, in return, to fulfill obligations to

Source: http://academic.shu.edu/russianhistory/index.php/Alexander_II,_Emancipation_Manifesto,_1861.

the noblemen fixed by the same arrangements. In this status, which is temporary, the peasants are temporarily bound.

At the same time, they are granted the right to purchase their household plots, and, with the consent of the nobles, they may acquire in full ownership the arable lands and other properties which are allotted them for permanent use. Following such acquisition of full ownership of land, the peasants will be freed from their obligations to the nobles for the land thus purchased and will become free peasant landowners.

. . .

WE also rely upon the zealous devotion of OUR nobility, to whom WE express OUR gratitude and that of the entire country as well, for the unselfish support it has given to the realization of OUR designs. Russia will not forget that the nobility, motivated by its respect for the dignity of man and its Christian love of its neighbor, has voluntarily renounced serfdom, and has laid the foundation of a new economic future for the peasants. WE also expect that it will continue to express further concern for the realization of the new arrangement in a spirit of peace and benevolence, and that each nobleman will bring to fruition on his estate the great civic act of the entire group by organizing the lives of his peasants and his household serfs on mutually advantageous terms, thereby setting for the rural population a good example of a punctual and conscientious execution of the state's requirements.

The examples of the generous concern of the nobles for the welfare of peasants, amid the gratitude of the latter for that concern, give Us the hope that a mutual understanding will solve most of the difficulties, which in some cases will be inevitable during the application of general rules to the diverse conditions on some estates, and that thereby the transition from the old order to time new will be facilitated, and that in the future mutual confidence will be strengthened, and a good understanding and a unanimous tendency towards the general good will evolve.

. . .

And now WE confidently expect that the freed serfs, on the eve of a new future which is opening to them, will appreciate and recognize the considerable sacrifices which the nobility has made on their behalf.

They should understand that by acquiring property and greater freedom to dispose of their possessions, they have an obligation to society and to themselves to live up to the letter of the new law by a loyal and judicious use of the rights which are now granted to them. However beneficial a law may be, it cannot make people happy if they do not themselves organize their happiness under protection of the law. Abundance is acquired only through hard work, wise use of strength and resources, strict economy, and above all, through an honest God-fearing life.

WORKING WITH SOURCES

1. How does the "Tsar Liberator" attempt to use religion and morality to persuade nobles to benefit their peasants?
2. To what extent does the document limit peasants' rights? Why?

25.5 Nikolai Chernyshevsky, *What Is to Be Done?*, 1863

The novelist Nikolai Chernyshevsky (1828–1889) believed that even the emancipation of serfs was insufficient to reform Russian society, since its authoritarian and patriarchal institutions had rendered it unequal and backward by every measure. An educated elite had emerged in Russia in the mid-nineteenth century, and this group felt alienated both from the larger culture and the traditions of Russian society. Chernyshevsky advocated a top-to-bottom restructuring of Russia, and he was particularly drawn to the idea of liberating women from their subordination within the Russian family. Arrested on largely fabricated charges in 1862 and awaiting trial in St. Petersburg, Chernyshevsky produced his last significant and most influential work, the novel *What Is to Be Done?* In early 1864, he was convicted of subversion, and he spent the next eighteen years in prison or in exile in eastern Siberia. *What Is to Be Done?* offers a fascinating portrait of intelligent young people attempting to reform a society that seemed in desperate need of change.

When Rakhmetov came to Petersburg at the age of sixteen, he was an ordinary youth of somewhat above-average height and strength, but by no means remarkable. Out of any ten of his peers, two could probably have gotten the better of him. But in the middle of his seventeenth year he decided to acquire physical prowess and began to work hard at it. He took up gymnastics with considerable dedication. That was all right, but gymnastics can improve only the material available; one has to provide oneself with such material. And so, for a while, he spent several hours every day, twice as long as he practiced gymnastics, working at common labor that required physical strength. He carried water, chopped and hauled firewood, felled trees, cut stone, dug earth, and forged iron. He tried many different kinds of work and changed jobs frequently because with each job and every change, different muscles were being developed. He put himself on a boxer's diet. He began to nourish himself (precisely!) only on those things reputed to build physical strength—beefsteak most of all, almost raw; since that time he's continued on this regimen. About a year after adopting this program, he set off on his travels and had even greater opportunities to devote himself to building physical strength. He worked as a plowman, carpenter, ferryman, and laborer at all sorts of healthful trades. Once he even worked as a barge hauler along the whole length of the Volga, from Dubovka to Rybinsk. If he'd told the captain of the barge and the crew that he wanted to work as a barge hauler, they'd have considered it the height of stupidity and would never have accepted him. So he went aboard as a passenger and became friendly with the crew and began to help them tow the boat. In a week he buckled himself into a harness, just like a real barge hauler. Soon they realized his strength and put him to the test: he outpulled three or four men, the sturdiest of his comrades. He was only twenty years old at the time, and his comrades on the barge christened him Nikitushka Lomov, in memory of their hero, who'd already departed the scene. The next summer he was traveling on a steamer. One of the many common folk on deck turned out to be one of his fellow workers from the barge the year before; that was how some students, his fellow travelers, learned about his nickname, Nikitushka Lomov. In fact he had acquired and, without skimping on time, had maintained enormous strength. "It's necessary," he used to say. "It inspires respect and love of the common people. It's useful and may come in handy someday."

. . .

However, in the making of such an extraordinary man, of course the principal element had to have been nature. For some time before he'd left the university and had set off for his own estate, and later on his journey through Russia, he'd already adopted a set of original principles to govern his material, moral, and spiritual life. When he returned to Petersburg, these principles had already developed into a complete system, which he followed faithfully. He said to himself, "I shall not drink one drop of wine. I shall not touch any women." But he was so passionate by nature! "Why on earth? Such extreme measures are unnecessary!" "They are necessary. We demand complete enjoyment of life for all people.

Source: Nikolai Chernyshevsky, *What Is to Be Done?*, trans. Michael R. Katz (Ithaca, NY: Cornell University Press, 1989), 278–279, 280–281, 283–284.

Therefore, in our own lives we must demonstrate that we demand this not to satisfy our own passions, not for ourselves alone, but for man in general. We must show that we're speaking according to principles and not passions, according to convictions and not personal desires."

. . .

Gymnastics, physical labor to develop his strength, and reading were Rakhmetov's personal pursuits. Upon his return to Petersburg these activities occupied only about a quarter of his time. The remainder he devoted to matters of concern to others or to no one in particular, constantly maintaining the same rule he had for his reading: not to waste time over secondary matters or subsidiary people, to occupy himself only with things of fundamental importance, those that shape secondary matters and second rate people without their participation. For example, outside his circle he made the acquaintance only of those people who had some influence over others. Someone who wasn't an authority for other people couldn't even enter into conversation with Rakhmetov. He would say, "You'll excuse me, but I don't have the time," and would walk away. By the same token, no one could avoid becoming acquainted with Rakhmetov if the latter wanted it to happen. He simply appeared and declared what it was he required with the following prelude: "I wish to become acquainted with you. It's essential. If this isn't a good time, set another." He paid no attention whatever to your petty concerns, even if you were his closest acquaintance and were begging him to become involved in your predicament. "I haven't time," he would say and turn aside. But he did get involved in important matters, when in his own opinion it was necessary, even though no one desired it. "I must," he would say. The things he used to say and do on such occasions are beyond comprehension.

WORKING WITH SOURCES

1. How does Rakhmetov connect revolutionary activity with a direct and physical identification with the common people of Russia?
2. Is Rakhmetov's self-disciplined, ascetic lifestyle comparable to that of a medieval monk? Why might this have been the case?

26. INDUSTRIALIZATION AND ITS DISCONTENTS, 1750–1914

26.1   Charles Dickens, *Hard Times*, 1854

Although his novels are beloved as works of fiction today, Charles Dickens (1812–1870) was also an acute observer of the ways in which industrialization fundamentally transformed economic conditions in England. Fully aware of the costs of economic dislocation (as a boy, Dickens had been confined in a debtors' prison with his family), the novelist described the residents of a fictional "Coketown" in one of his lesser-known works, *Hard Times*, published in 1854. The main industry in this town is a factory, owned and operated by the blowhard (and, it is ultimately revealed, self-created) Josiah Bounderby, and the people who work in the "manufactory" are the "Hands." The novel opens in a schoolroom, where children are being drilled, literally, in the acquisition of "facts, facts, facts." Their teacher is Mr. "M'Choakumchild" (Dickens was never very subtle in his nomenclature), and the director of the school is Mr. Gradgrind. The Gradgrind method will ultimately be proved a failure within Gradgrind's own family, but *Hard Times* reveals the actual "hardness" of conditions for so many in industrial Britain.

Chapter 5: The Key-note

Coketown, to which Messrs Bounderby and Gradgrind now walked, was a triumph of fact; it had no greater taint of fancy in it than Mrs Gradgrind herself. Let us strike the key-note, Coketown, before pursuing our tune.

It was a town of red brick, or of brick that would have been red if the smoke and ashes had allowed it; but, as matters stood it was a town of unnatural red and black like the painted face of a savage. It was a town of machinery and tall chimneys, out of which interminable serpents of smoke trailed themselves for ever and ever, and never got uncoiled. It had a black canal in it, and a river that ran purple with ill-smelling dye, and vast piles of building full of windows where there was a rattling and a trembling all day long, and where the piston of the steam-engine worked monotonously up and down, like the head of an elephant in a state of melancholy madness. It contained several large streets all very like one another, and many small streets still more like one another, inhabited by people equally like one another, who all went in and out at the same hours, with the same sound upon the same pavements, to do the same work, and to whom every day was the same as yesterday and tomorrow, and every year the counterpart of the last and the next.

These attributes of Coketown were in the main inseparable from the work by which it was sustained; against them were to be set off, comforts of life which found their way all over the world, and elegancies of life which made, we will not ask how much of the fine lady, who could scarcely bear to hear the place mentioned. The rest of its features were voluntary, and they were these.

You saw nothing in Coketown but what was severely workful. If the members of a religious persuasion built a chapel there - as the members of eighteen religious persuasions had done - they made it a pious

Source: Charles Dickens, *Hard Times, for These Times*, ed. David Craig (New York: Penguin, 1969), 65–66.

warehouse of red brick, with sometimes (but this is only in highly ornamented examples) a bell in a bird-cage on the top of it. The solitary exception was the New Church; a stuccoed edifice with a square steeple over the door, terminating in four short pinnacles like florid wooden legs. All the public inscriptions in the town were painted alike, in severe characters of black and white. The jail might have been the infirmary, the infirmary might have been the jail, the town-hall might have been either, or both, or anything else, for anything that appeared to the contrary in the graces of their construction. Fact, fact, fact, everywhere in the material aspect of the town; fact, fact, fact, everywhere in the immaterial. The M'Choakumchild school was all fact, and the school of design was all fact, and the relations between master and man were all fact, and everything was fact between the lying-in hospital and the cemetery, and what you couldn't state in figures, or show to be purchaseable in the cheapest market and saleable in the dearest, was not, and never should be, world without end, Amen.

WORKING WITH SOURCES

1. How does Dickens deploy imagery from the natural world to describe something as "unnatural" as Coketown?
2. In what specific ways is Coketown a "triumph of fact" over "fancy," and does he paint a convincing portrait of a typical town in a rapidly industrializing Britain?

26.2   The Death of William Huskisson, First Casualty of a Railroad Accident, September 15, 1830

Although William Huskisson (1770–1830) was a prominent member of the British Parliament and a cabinet member in several governments, he is more famous for the circumstances of his death in a rapidly industrializing Great Britain. While attending the opening of the Liverpool and Manchester Railway in northern England, on September 15, 1830, Huskisson rode in a carriage with the Duke of Wellington, a political figure and venerated hero of the Napoleonic Wars. Exiting the train during a stop, he was attempting to shake hands with the duke when he failed to notice another locomotive, George Stephenson's *Rocket*, traveling down an adjacent track. Huskisson attempted to swing into the carriage but fell on the tracks in front of the *Rocket*. With his leg horribly mangled by the train, Huskisson was rushed to a hospital (in a train driven by George Stephenson), but he died of his injuries a few hours later. He is, therefore, the world's first reported railway casualty.

Bangor, 19 September 1830

Jack Calcraft has been at the opening of the Liverpool rail road, and was an eye witness of Huskisson's horrible death. About nine or ten of the passengers in the Duke's car had got out to look about them, whilst the car stopt. Calcraft was one, Huskisson another, Esterhazy, Bill Holmes, Birch and others. When the other locomotive was seen coming up to

Source: Letter from Thomas Creevey to Miss Ord., available online at http://www.victorianweb.org/history/accident.html.

pass them, there was a general shout from those within the Duke's car to those without it, to get in. Both Holmes and Birch were unable to get up in time, but they stuck fast to its sides, and the other engine did not touch them. Esterhazy being light, was pulled in by force. Huskisson was feeble in his legs, and appears to have lost his head, as he did his life. Calcraft tells me that Huskisson's long confinement in St George's Chapel at the king's funeral brought on a complaint that Taylor is so afraid of, and that made some severe surgical operation necessary, the effect of which had been, according to what he told Calcraft, to paralyse, as it were one leg and thigh. This, no doubt, must have increased, if it did not create, his danger and [caused him to] lose his life. He had written to say his health would not let him come, and his arrival was unexpected. Calcraft saw the meeting between him and the Duke, and saw them shake hands a very short time before Huskisson's death. The latter event must be followed by important political consequences. The Canning faction has lost its corner stone and the Duke's government one of its most formidable opponents. Huskisson, too, once out of the way, Palmerston, Melbourne, the Grants & Co. may make it up with the Beau [Wellington].

WORKING WITH SOURCES

1. What kind of commentary does Huskisson's death offer on the consequences of industrialization? Does this incident reveal another side of the history of industrialization?
2. Why does Creevey seem more interested in the political rather than the socioeconomic consequences of Huskisson's death?

26.3   Young Miners Testify to the Ashley Commission, 1842

The British Parliament took on a series of initiatives to investigate the lives of women and children in the mid-nineteenth century, and the resulting testimonies, presented by workers to the various parliamentary commissions make for fascinating—and uniquely visceral—reading. The lives of working children are rarely detailed in historical sources from any era, but these testimonies had a direct impact, if not a fully humane one, on the lives of British laborers. These documents were collected for Lord Ashley's Mines Commission of 1842, and the shocking testimony resulted in the Mines Act of 1842, which prohibited the employment in the mines of all females and of boys under 13 years of age.

Source: http://www.victorianweb.org/history/ashley.html, from *Readings in European History Since 1814*, ed. Jonathan F. Scott and Alexander Baltzly (New York: Appleton-Century-Crofts, 1930), drawing on *Parliamentary Papers*, 1842, vols. 25–27, Appendix 1, 252, 258, 439, 461; Appendix 2, 107, 122, 205.

No. 116.—Sarah Gooder, aged 8 years.

I'm a trapper in the Gawber pit. It does not tire me, but I have to trap without a light and I'm scared. I go at four and sometimes half past three in the morning, and come out at five and half past. I never go to sleep. Sometimes I sing when I've light, but not in the dark; I dare not sing then. I don't like being in the pit. I am very sleepy when I go sometimes in the morning. I go to Sunday-schools and read Reading made Easy. She knows her letters, and can read little words. They teach me to pray. She repeated the Lord's Prayer, not very perfectly, and ran on with the following addition:—"God bless my father and mother, and sister and brother, uncles and aunts and cousins, and everybody else, and God bless me and make me a good servant. Amen." I have heard tell of Jesus many a time. I don't know why he came on earth, I'm sure, and I don't know why he died, but he had stones for his head to rest on. I would like to be at school far better than in the pit.

No. 14—Isabella Read, 12 years old, coal-bearer

Works on mother's account, as father has been dead two years. Mother bides at home, she is troubled with bad breath, and is sair weak in her body from early labour. I am wrought with sister and brother, it is very sore work; cannot say how many rakes or journeys I make from pit's bottom to wall face and back, thinks about 30 or 25 on the average; the distance varies from 100 to 250 fathom.

I carry about 1 cwt. and a quarter on my back; have to stoop much and creep through water, which is frequently up to the calves of my legs. When first down fell frequently asleep while waiting for coal from heat and fatigue.

I do not like the work, nor do the lassies, but they are made to like it. When the weather is warm there is difficulty in breathing, and frequently the lights go out.

No. 26.—Patience Kershaw, aged 17, May 15.

My father has been dead about a year; my mother is living and has ten children, five lads and five lasses; the oldest is about thirty, the youngest is four; three lasses go to mill; all the lads are colliers, two getters and three hurriers; one lives at home and does nothing; mother does nought but look after home.

All my sisters have been hurriers, but three went to the mill. Alice went because her legs swelled from hurrying in cold water when she was hot. I never went to day-school; I go to Sunday-school, but I cannot read or write; I go to pit at five o'clock in the morning and come out at five in the evening; I get my breakfast of porridge and milk first; I take my dinner with me, a cake, and eat it as I go; I do not stop or rest any time for the purpose; I get nothing else until I get home, and then have potatoes and meat, not every day meat. I hurry in the clothes I have now got on, trousers and ragged jacket; the bald place upon my head is made by thrusting the corves; my legs have never swelled, but sisters' did when they went to mill; I hurry the corves a mile and more under ground and back; they weigh 300 cwt.; I hurry 11 a-day; I wear a belt and chain at the workings, to get the corves out; the getters that I work for are naked except their caps; they pull off all their clothes; I see them at work when I go up; sometimes they beat me, if I am not quick enough, with their hands; they strike me upon my back; the boys take liberties with me sometimes they pull me about; I am the only girl in the pit; there are about 20 boys and 15 men; all the men are naked; I would rather work in mill than in coal-pit.

This girl is an ignorant, filthy, ragged, and deplorable-looking object, and such an one as the uncivilized natives of the prairies would be shocked to look upon.

No. 72—Mary Barrett, aged 14. June 15.

I have worked down in pit five years; father is working in next pit; I have 12 brothers and sisters—all of them but one live at home; they weave, and wind, and hurry, and one is a counter, one of them can read, none of the rest can, or write; they never went to day-school, but three of them go to Sunday-school; I hurry for my brother John, and come down at seven o'clock about; I go up at six, sometimes seven; I do not like working in pit, but I am obliged to get a living; I work always without stockings, or shoes, or trousers; I wear nothing but my chemise; I have to go up to the headings with the men; they are all naked there; I am got well used to that, and don't care now much about it; I was afraid at first, and did not like it; they never behave rudely to me; I cannot read or write.

WORKING WITH SOURCES

1. Do the employers of these workers seem to have taken into account the unique conditions of their age and gender?
2. How does the recorder of these interviews interject his own reactions to these narratives? Why does he do this?

26.4   Karl Marx, "Wage Labour and Capital," 1847

Karl Marx (1818–1883) and Friedrich Engels (1820–1895) are best known for their collaborative work *The Communist Manifesto* (1848). However, the two had been observing the real consequences of industrialization for factory workers, particularly in Manchester, England, for many years before this. Working in his father's cotton factory in England, Engels had witnessed the inequities imposed by industrial systems, and he composed a scathing attack on these systems in his *Condition of the Working-Class in England* (1845). When Marx befriended Engels in Manchester, he too came to see how local conditions could lead to wide-ranging theories about labor, wages, and the measurement of "costs." In this lecture, delivered in December 1847, Marx took his audience through the most basic elements of the philosophy that would culminate in *Das Kapital* (vol. 1, 1867).

If several workmen were to be asked: "How much wages do you get?", one would reply, "I get two shillings a day," and so on. According to the different branches of industry in which they are employed, they would mention different sums of money that they receive from their respective employers for the completion of a certain task; for example, for weaving a yard of linen, or for setting a page of type. Despite the variety of their statements, they would all agree upon one point: that wages are the amount of money which the capitalist pays for a certain period of work or for a certain amount of work.

Consequently, it appears that the capitalist buys their labour with money, and that for money they sell him their labour. But this is merely an illusion. What they actually sell to the capitalist for money is their labour-power. This labour-power the capitalist buys for a day, a week, a month, etc. And after he has bought it, he uses it up by letting the worker labour during the stipulated time. With the same amount of money with which the capitalist has bought their labour-power (for example, with two shillings) he could have bought a certain amount of sugar or of any other commodity. The two shillings with which he bought 20 pounds of sugar is the price of the 20 pounds of sugar. The two shillings with which he bought 12 hours' use of labour-power, is the price of 12 hours' labour. Labour-power, then, is a commodity, no more, no less so than is the sugar. The first is measured by the clock, the other by the scales.

Their commodity, labour-power, the workers exchange for the commodity of the capitalist, for money, and, moreover, this exchange takes place at a certain ratio. So much money for so long a use of labour-power.

Source: http://www.marxists.org/archive/marx/works/1847/wage-labour/, first published in German in the *Neue Rheinische Zeitung* (April 5–8, 11, 1849), and edited and translated by Friedrich Engels for an 1891 pamphlet.

For 12 hours' weaving, two shillings. And these two shillings, do they not represent all the other commodities which I can buy for two shillings? Therefore, actually, the worker has exchanged his commodity, labour-power, for commodities of all kinds, and, moreover, at a certain ratio. By giving him two shillings, the capitalist has given him so much meat, so much clothing, so much wood, light, etc., in exchange for his day's work. The two shillings therefore express the relation in which labour-power is exchanged for other commodities, the exchange-value of labour-power.

The exchange value of a commodity estimated in money is called its price. Wages therefore are only a special name for the price of labour-power, and are usually called the price of labour; it is the special name for the price of this peculiar commodity, which has no other repository than human flesh and blood.

Let us take any worker; for example, a weaver. The capitalist supplies him with the loom and yarn. The weaver applies himself to work, and the yarn is turned into cloth. The capitalist takes possession of the cloth and sells it for 20 shillings, for example. Now are the wages of the weaver a share of the cloth, of the 20 shillings, of the product of the work? By no means. Long before the cloth is sold, perhaps long before it is fully woven, the weaver has received his wages. The capitalist, then, does not pay his wages out of the money which he will obtain from the cloth, but out of money already on hand. Just as little as loom and yarn are the product of the weaver to whom they are supplied by the employer, just so little are the commodities which he receives in exchange for his commodity—labour-power—his product. It is possible that the employer found no purchasers at all for the cloth. It is possible that he did not get even the amount of the wages by its sale. It is possible that he sells it very profitably in proportion to the weaver's wages. But all that does not concern the weaver. With a part of his existing wealth, of his capital, the capitalist buys the labour-power of the weaver in exactly the same manner as, with another part of his wealth, he has bought the raw material—the yarn—and the instrument of labour—the loom. After he has made these purchases, and among them belongs the labour-power necessary to the production of the cloth he produces only with raw materials and instruments of labour belonging to him. For our good weaver, too, is one of the instruments of labour, and being in this respect on a par with the loom, he has no more share in the product (the cloth), or in the price of the product, than the loom itself has.

Wages, therefore, are not a share of the worker in the commodities produced by himself. Wages are that part of already existing commodities with which the capitalist buys a certain amount of productive labour-power.

. . .

The free labourer, on the other hand, sells his very self, and that by fractions. He auctions off eight, 10, 12, 15 hours of his life, one day like the next, to the highest bidder, to the owner of raw materials, tools, and the means of life—i.e., to the capitalist. The labourer belongs neither to an owner nor to the soil, but eight, 10, 12, 15 hours of his daily life belong to whomsoever buys them. The worker leaves the capitalist, to whom he has sold himself, as often as he chooses, and the capitalist discharges him as often as he sees fit, as soon as he no longer gets any use, or not the required use, out of him. But the worker, whose only source of income is the sale of his labour-power, cannot leave the whole class of buyers, i.e., the capitalist class, unless he gives up his own existence. He does not belong to this or that capitalist, but to the capitalist class; and it is for him to find his man—i.e., to find a buyer in this capitalist class.

WORKING WITH SOURCES

1. How does Marx describe wages as a commodity price, equivalent to other sorts of "prices" in the marketplace?
2. How does he contrast larger economic forces with the lived realities of workers in a factory?

26.5   Charles Darwin, *The Origin of Species*, 1859

The name of Charles Darwin (1809–1882) is inextricably linked to the earth-shattering and (even today) controversial theory he proposed in 1859. However, it is also important to remember that he was a writer of exceptional skill and a best-selling author—even though many of his observations and conclusions were certainly too difficult for nonspecialists to appreciate. The 200th anniversary of his birth—and the 150th anniversary of the appearance of *The Origin of Species*—in 2009 resulted in a series of commemorative events around the world, a brief sample of which can be viewed online at http://darwin-online.org.uk/2009.html. Among the most famous elements of the book is the tangled-riverbank image introduced in the long book's final paragraph, and Darwin's stimulating view of the "grandeur in this view of life."

As this whole volume is one long argument, it may be convenient to the reader to have the leading facts and inferences briefly recapitulated.

That many and serious objections may be advanced against the theory of descent with modification through variation and natural selection, I do not deny. I have endeavoured to give to them their full force. Nothing at first can appear more difficult to believe than that the more complex organs and instincts have been perfected, not by means superior to, though analogous with, human reason, but by the accumulation of innumerable slight variations, each good for the individual possessor. Nevertheless, this difficulty, though appearing to our imagination insuperably great, cannot be considered real if we admit the following propositions, namely, that all parts of the organisation and instincts offer, at least individual differences—that there is a struggle for existence leading to the preservation of profitable deviations of structure or instinct—and, lastly, that gradations in the state of perfection of each organ may have existed, each good of its kind. The truth of these propositions cannot, I think, be disputed.

It is, no doubt, extremely difficult even to conjecture by what gradations many structures have been perfected, more especially among broken and failing groups of organic beings, which have suffered much extinction; but we see so many strange gradations in nature, that we ought to be extremely cautious in saying that any organ or instinct, or any whole structure, could not have arrived at its present state by many graduated steps. There are, it must be admitted, cases of special difficulty opposed to the theory of natural selection; and one of the most curious of these is the existence in the same community of two or three defined castes of workers or sterile female ants; but I have attempted to show how these difficulties can be mastered.

. . .

A grand and almost untrodden field of inquiry will be opened, on the causes and laws of variation, on correlation, on the effects of use and disuse, on the direct action of external conditions, and so forth. The study of domestic productions will rise immensely in value. A new variety raised by man will be a far more important and interesting subject for study than one more species added to the infinitude of already recorded species. Our classifications will come to be, as far as they can be so made, genealogies; and will then truly give what may be called the plan of creation. The rules for classifying will no doubt become simpler when we have a definite object in view. We possess no pedigrees or armorial bearings; and

Source: Charles Darwin, *The Origin of Species by Means of Natural Selection, or the Preservation of Favored Races in the Struggle for Life and The Descent of Man, and Selection in Relation to Sex* (New York: Modern Library, 1936), 353, 372, 373–374.

we have to discover and trace the many diverging lines of descent in our natural genealogies, by characters of any kind which have long been inherited. Rudimentary organs will speak infallibly with respect to the nature of long-lost structures. Species and groups of species which are called aberrant, and which may fancifully be called living fossils, will aid us in forming a picture of the ancient forms of life. Embryology will often reveal to us the structure, in some degree obscured, of the prototypes of each great class.

When we feel assured that all the individuals of the same species, and all the closely allied species of most genera, have, within a not very remote period descended from one parent, and have migrated from some one birth-place; and when we better know the many means of migration, then, by the light which geology now throws, and will continue to throw, on former changes of climate and of the level of the land, we shall surely be enabled to trace in an admirable manner the former migrations of the inhabitants of the whole world. Even at present, by comparing the differences between the inhabitants of the sea on the opposite sides of a continent, and the nature of the various inhabitants of that continent in relation to their apparent means of immigration, some light can be thrown on ancient geography.

. . .

It is interesting to contemplate a tangled bank, clothed with many plants of many kinds, with birds singing on the bushes, with various insects flitting about, and with worms crawling through the damp earth, and to reflect that these elaborately constructed forms, so different from each other, and dependent upon each other in so complex a manner, have all been produced by laws acting around us. These laws, taken in the largest sense, being Growth with Reproduction; Inheritance which is almost implied by reproduction; Variability from the indirect and direct action of the conditions of life, and from use and disuse; a Ratio of Increase so high as to lead to a Struggle for Life, and as a consequence to Natural Selection, entailing Divergence of Character and the Extinction of less-improved forms. Thus, from the war of nature, from famine and death, the most exalted object which we are capable of conceiving, namely, the production of the higher animals, directly follows. There is grandeur in this view of life, with its several powers, having been originally breathed by the Creator into a few forms or into one; and that, whilst this planet has gone cycling on according to the fixed law of gravity, from so simple a beginning endless forms most beautiful and most wonderful have been, and are being evolved.

WORKING WITH SOURCES

1. How does Darwin manage to convey the excitement that he feels for this new scientific field and the possibilities for applying his theory to other disciplines?
2. How does his quest for common ancestors underscore the interconnected nature of all species on our planet?

27. THE NEW IMPERIALISM IN THE NINETEENTH CENTURY, 1750–1914

27.1 The Azamgarh Proclamation, September 29, 1857

This proclamation was published in the *Delhi Gazette* in the midst of the "Great Mutiny" of 1857. The author was most probably Firoz Shah, a grandson of the Mughal emperor Bahadur Shah Zafar (r. 1837–1857), whose restoration to full power was a main aim of the rebels. General disillusionment with the pace of change and the fear that British missionaries were, with government connivance, attempting to Christianize India came to a head among the British East India Company's sepoy troops. A rumor started that the grease used in the paper cartridges of the Enfield rifle contained both cow and pig fat, an affront to the sensibilities of both Hindus and Muslims. The resulting mutiny (known to Indians as the Great Rebellion or the First War of Independence) resulted in a war dominated by mass atrocities—and ultimately in the imposition of the British "Raj," or direct rule.

It is well known to all, that in this age the people of Hindustan, both Hindoos and Mahommedans, are being ruined under the tyranny and oppression of the infidel and treacherous English. It is therefore the bounden duty of all the wealthy people of India, especially of those who have any sort of connexion with any of the Mohammedan royal families, and are considered the pastors and masters of their people, to stake their lives and property for the well-being of the public. With the view of effecting this general good, several princes belonging to the royal family of Delhi, have dispersed themselves in the different parts of India, Iran, Turan, and Afghanistan, and have been long since taking measures to compass their favourite end; and it is to accomplish this charitable object that one of the aforesaid princes has, at the head of an army of Afghanistan, &c., made his appearance in India—and I, who am the grandson of Abul Muzuffer Sarajuddin Bahadur Shah Ghazee, king of India, having in the course of circuit come here to extirpate the infidels residing in the eastern part of the country, and to liberate and protect the poor helpless people now groaning under their iron rule, have, by the aid

of the Majahdeens, or religious fanatics, erected the standard of Mohammed, and persuaded the orthodox Hindoos who had been subject to my ancestors, and have been and are still accessories in the destruction of the English, to raise the standard of Mahavir.

Several of the Hindoo and Mussulman chiefs who . . . have been trying their best to root out the English in India, have presented themselves to me, and taken part in the reigning Indian crusade, and it is more than probable that I shall very shortly receive succours from the west. Therefore, for the information of the public, the present Ishtahar, consisting of several sections, is put in circulation, and it is the imperative duty of all to take it into their careful consideration and abide by it. Parties anxious to participate in this common cause, but having no means to provide for themselves, shall receive their daily subsistence from me; and be it known to all, that the ancient works both of the Hindoos and the Mohammedans, the writings of the miracle-workers, and the calculations of the astrologers, pundits and rammals, all agree asserting that the English will no longer have any footing in India or elsewhere. Therefore it

Source: http://www.csas.ed.ac.uk/mutiny/Texts-Part2.html.

is incumbent on all to give up the hope of the continuation of the British sway, side with me, and deserve the consideration of the Badshahi, or imperial government by their individual exertion in promoting the common good and thus attain their respective ends.

. . .

Section II.—Regarding Merchants.—It is plain that the infidel and treacherous British government have monopolised the trade of all the fine and valuable merchandise, such as indigo, cloth, and other articles of shipping, leaving only the trade of trifles to the people, and even in this they are not without their share of the profits, which they secure by means of customs and stamp fees, &c., in money suits, so that the people have merely a trade in name. Besides this, the profits of the traders are taxed with postages, tolls, and subscriptions for schools, &c. Notwithstanding all these concessions, the merchants are liable to imprisonment and disgrace at the instance or complaint of a worthless man. When the Badshahi government is established, all these aforesaid fraudulent practices shall be dispensed with, and the trade of every article, without exception both by land end water, shall be open to the native merchants of India, who will have the benefit of the government steam-vessels and

steam carriages for the conveyance of their merchandise gratis; and merchants having no capital of their own shall be assisted from the public treasury. It is therefore the duty of every merchant to take part in the war, and aid the Badshahi government with his men and money, either secretly or openly, as may be consistent with his position or interest, and forswear his allegiance to the British government.

. . .

Section V.—Regarding Pundits, Fakirs, and other learned persons.—The pundits and fakirs being the guardians of the Hindoo and Mohammedan religions respectively, and the European being the enemies of both the religions, and as at present a war is raging against the English on account of religion, the pundits and fakirs are bound to present themselves to me, and take their share in the holy war, otherwise they will stand condemned according to the tenor of the Shurrah and the Shasters ; but if they come, they will, when the Badshahi government is well established, receive rent-free lands.

Lastly, be it known to all, that whoever, out of the above-named classes, shall, after the circulation of this Ishtahar, still cling to the British government, all his estates shall be confiscated, and his property plundered, and he himself, with his whole family, shall he imprisoned, and ultimately put to death.'

WORKING WITH SOURCES

1. Why does the author think Muslims and Hindus can find a common cause in resistance to the British? Is he fully representing both religious traditions?
2. How does he connect British trade interests and religious goals? Is he misstating or misunderstanding British intentions?

27.2 Ismail ibn 'Abd al-Qadir, *The Life of the Sudanese Mahdi*, ca. 1884

The religiously inspired uprising against the British in Sudan during the 1880s is associated with the figure of the self-styled "Mahdi." However, the primary motivation of Muhammad Ahmad Ibn Abdallah (1844–1885), who took on the title Mahdi ("rightly guided" or "messiah")

Source: Haim Shaked, *The Life of the Sudanese Mahdi: A Historical Study of 'Kitab Sa'adat al-Mustahdi bi-Sirat al-Imam al-Mahdi'* (*The Book of the Bliss of Him Who Seeks Guidance by the Life of the Imam al-Mahdi*) (New Brunswick, NJ: Transaction, 1978), 66–68.

was to reform Islam from within. Similar to other early modern Islamic reformers, beginning with 'Abd al-Wahhab in eighteenth-century Arabia, the Mahdi aimed to eliminate Sufi brotherhoods and remove the (to his mind) abominable medieval aberrations from Islam. The Mahdi's anti-imperialist stance against the British was thus incidental: the British happened to occupy Egypt and to be moving on the Sudan in the midst of his anti-Sufism campaigns. The British focused on the siege of Khartoum in 1883, but this contemporary biographer of the Mahdi focuses on the renovation of Islam.

---

1 The Mahdi's Propaganda (*Di'aya*)

When God bestowed the Mahdiship on the Mahdi, he secretly commenced to call the people to God. He called them to arise and save Islam and to abandon the innovations and the reprehensible characteristics of the people of the time particularly those who belonged to Sufi *tariqas* (*al-muntamun ila al-diyana*). Such characteristics are the love of honour, authority, flattery and the use, as hunters' nets for ensnaring the temporal world, of the ways which would lead to God. The Mahdi also urged them to the *jihad* and to make the *hijra* to him. He persistently called on the people, despite the troubles inflicted by some people on him and on his veteran Companions. These he bore with patience and perseverance, since the Mahdiship involves burdens which only one endowed by God with the Prophetic heritage can bear.

When the Mahdi was ordered to manifest his call (*da'wa*) and announce his Mahdiship he arose publicly, calling the people to God, to revive the religion, rectify the Custom of the Prophet, support the Truth, resist the innovators and make them repent. This is the pure religion of the Prophet and all his Companions, and it is in accordance with the Book and the Custom. The Mahdi proceeded with his call to the people until God guided the Community through him, and his Companions attained closeness to the Companions of the Prophet. The author remarks that is impossible to give an exhaustive account of the Mahdi's propaganda.

2 The Mahdi's Correspondence

Since communication by correspondence was a custom of the Prophet and as the Mahdi was his representative (*khalifa*) and followed in his footsteps, he dispatched letters to the people of Islam, in which he called them to God and to revive the Custom of the Prophet. These letters are numerous and some of them will be mentioned in the Sira so as to enjoy a blessing ('*ala wajh al-tabarruk*).

. . .

The Mahdi's correspondence can be studied by reference to the collection of proclamations (*Jami al-manshurat*). His correspondence to the Community—thereby saving them from grief—derives from the Custom of God with the essence of His creation. Its source is the announcement of good tidings (*tabshir*), warning (*indhar*), and a call for the revival of the principles of the Community which God enacted. All the Mahdi's actions and utterances are sustained by the Book and by the Custom, for he is infallible (*dhu al-isma*). The author remarks that he will incorporate the Mahdi's correspondence to the kings and commanders wherever it is appropriate in the course of the Sira. The Mahdi's letters, like the Prophet's, are written in a manner which would enable their recipients to understand them, for the Mahdi is the Successor of the Prophet and follows in his footsteps. An informant told the author that the Mahdi had said: "Verily, the Prophet . . . speaks with us now in the speech (*kalam*) of the people of our time." The author interprets this as the language and the terms with which people are acquainted at present, so that they would easily understand the meaning and come to God in the shortest time.

WORKING WITH SOURCES

1. How does the document reveal that the Mahdi's primary concern was the challenge posed by Sufism?
2. How and why is the Mahdi strongly identified with the Prophet Muhammad?

27.3   Edward Wilmot Blyden, Liberian Independence Day Address, July 26, 1865

A prominent Liberian, West African, and pan-African figure, Edward Wilmot Blyden advocated for the rights and abilities of Africans (and people of African descent) to govern themselves. Born in the Virgin Islands to free black parents in 1832, he lived briefly in Venezuela and the United States before emigrating to Liberia at the age of eighteen. Liberia had been founded by liberated African American slaves on the west coast of Africa in 1822, and Blyden was fully engaged in the project of establishing a Liberian identity, based on the intellectual and political development of the nation's citizens. Blyden was appointed professor of classics at Liberia College in 1862. In his quest to make the college (the first secular English-speaking institution of higher learning in sub-Saharan Africa) more relevant to Liberia, he began teaching Arabic in 1867. He was also a significant figure in Liberian politics, serving as secretary of state (1864–1866) and an advisor to the reformist President Roye after 1870. In this address, celebrating Liberian independence, Blyden compares his nation's constitution with that of the United States, promoting the benefits of reform and self-government for his fellow citizens.

Our Constitution needs various amendments. It is of very great importance that the utmost care should be exercised in interfering with the fundamental law of the land; but we must not attach to it such mysterious and unapproachable sacredness as to imagine that it must not be interfered with at all, even when circumstances plainly reveal to us the necessity of such interference. The Constitution is only a written document, and, like all written documents . . . it has many errors and omissions. It becomes us, then, who long for the prosperity of our country, calmly and deliberately to examine and consider such defects as may exist in that most important paper, and set ourselves to the work of remedying them to the best of our ability. It is the people's Constitution, and it is the work of the people to correct its deficiencies.

. . .

Another mistake in our Constitution and laws is the arrangement which causes several months to elapse between the election of the President and his inauguration—from May to January—which gives his predecessor, if he be of an opposing party, a long time during which to carry out his party's views. Our arrangement is alarmingly defective, for instead of four months as in the United States, we allow fully eight months to the dissentient minority to carry out their purposes. This is a defect that calls loudly for immediate remedy.

These changes . . . depend upon the will of the people; but we must remember that the people cannot be browbeaten into them. They have to be reasoned with and convinced by patient and persevering argument. The enterprise of persuading and convincing them deserves the utmost exertion of true patriots. The reward with which such efforts will be crowned is no less than the emancipation of the body politic from fatally injurious influences and the introduction among us of salutary conditions of national existence, under which we may go on prospering and to prosper.

. . .

Source: Black Spokesman: Selected Published Writings of Edward Wilmot Blyden, ed. Hollis R. Lynch (London: Frank Cass, 1971), 77–79.

We are engaged here on this coast in a great and noble work. We cannot easily exaggerate the magnitude of the interests involved in the enterprise to which we are committed. Not only the highest welfare of the few thousands who now compose the Republic, but the character of a whole race is implicated in what we are doing. Let us then endeavour to rise up to the "height of this great argument." . . . Something has been done; but what is the little we have achieved compared to what has still to be done! The little of the past dwindles into insignificance before the mighty work of the future.

We are more eagerly watched than we have any idea of. The nations are looking to see whether "order and law, religion and morality, the rights of conscience, the rights of persons, the rights of property, may all be secured," by a government controlled entirely and purely by Negroes. Oh, let us not by any unwise actions compel them to decide in the negative.

. . .

We have made a fair beginning. . . . Here we are, with all our unfavourable antecedents, still, after eighteen years of struggle, an independent nation. We have the germ of an African empire. Let us, fellow-citizens, guard the trust committed to our hands. The tribes in the distant interior are waiting for us. We have made some impression on the coast; . . . we shall make wider and deeper impressions. . . .

WORKING WITH SOURCES

1. What does Blyden seem to have considered the proper relationship between a government and the people it governs?
2. Was Blyden right in his observation that the Liberian experiment was "more eagerly watched than we have any idea of"? Why?

27.4   Rudyard Kipling, "The White Man's Burden," 1899

The phrase "the white man's burden" and its association with the British writer Rudyard Kipling (1865–1936) is well known today, but few realize that this exhortation was addressed to the American people, who had taken possession of the Philippines in 1899 as a result of the Spanish-American War (1898). Ignoring the independent Philippine government when signing a peace treaty with Spain, the US occupied Manila and within a year defeated the troops of that government under its elected president Emilio Aguinaldo. US troops captured Aguinaldo in 1901, but a full-scale guerilla war continued—and tactics like the "waterboarding" of captured insurgents were introduced—until 1913. Kipling, however, consistently advocated the position that, as he claimed for the British in India, "East is East and West is West, and never the twain shall meet."

Take up the White Man's burden—
Send forth the best ye breed—
Go bind your sons to exile
To serve your captives' need;
To wait in heavy harness,
On fluttered folk and wild—
Your new-caught, sullen peoples,
Half-devil and half-child.

Source: http://www.fordham.edu/halsall/mod/kipling.asp

Take up the White Man's burden—
In patience to abide,
To veil the threat of terror
And check the show of pride;
By open speech and simple,
An hundred times made plain
To seek another's profit,
And work another's gain.

Take up the White Man's burden—
The savage wars of peace—
Fill full the mouth of Famine
And bid the sickness cease;
And when your goal is nearest
The end for others sought,
Watch sloth and heathen Folly
Bring all your hopes to nought.

Take up the White Man's burden—
No tawdry rule of kings,
But toil of serf and sweeper—
The tale of common things.
The ports ye shall not enter,
The roads ye shall not tread,
Go mark them with your living,
And mark them with your dead.

Take up the White Man's burden—
And reap his old reward:
The blame of those ye better,
The hate of those ye guard—
The cry of hosts ye humour
(Ah, slowly!) toward the light:—
"Why brought he us from bondage,
Our loved Egyptian night?"

Take up the White Man's burden—
Ye dare not stoop to less—
Nor call too loud on Freedom
To cloke your weariness;
By all ye cry or whisper,
By all ye leave or do,
The silent, sullen peoples
Shall weigh your gods and you.

Take up the White Man's burden—
Have done with childish days—
The lightly proferred laurel,
The easy, ungrudged praise.
Comes now, to search your manhood
Through all the thankless years
Cold, edged with dear-bought wisdom,
The judgment of your peers!

WORKING WITH SOURCES

1. Why, in Kipling's estimation, should the Americans expect to encounter "sullen" reactions among the Filipinos if they go out of their way to provide "aid"?
2. Why does Kipling consider the "civilizing" of Filipinos to be a burden and a duty, and not merely an opportunity to exploit the native people?

27.5 Mark Twain, "To the Person Sitting in Darkness," 1901

To some extent, Kipling was wrong that "East is East and West is West, and never the twain shall meet," since the preeminent American man of letters Mark Twain (1835–1910) did meet the challenge posed by the poem "The White Man's Burden." Incensed by the blatant racism of Kipling's

Source: Mark Twain, *The Family Mark Twain* (New York: Harper & Brothers, 1935), 1390–1391, 1394–1395, 1397, 1398.

exhortation—as well as the role of racism in sparking the Civil War in his own United States—Twain lashed out with a brilliant satire of imperialist attitudes. This essay is emblematic of Twain's final years, during which he became increasingly embittered and pessimistic about the chances of "civilization" to overcome barbarism. It is posed in the form of a preacher's address to an American audience. The voice of the huckster-preacher conveys what to him seems the perfect alignment of financial and moral considerations; to his mind, it is just a matter of public relations to obtain the willing incorporation of the Filipinos into this (fraudulent) "Blessings-of-Civilization Trust."

Extending the Blessings of Civilization to our Brother who Sits in Darkness has been a good trade and has paid well, on the whole; and there is money in it yet, if carefully worked—but not enough, in my judgment, to make any considerable risk advisable. The People that Sit in Darkness are getting to be too scarce—too scarce and too shy. And such darkness as is now left is really of but an indifferent quality, and not dark enough for the game. The most of those People that Sit in Darkness have been furnished with more light than was good for them or profitable for us. We have been injudicious.

The Blessings-of-Civilization Trust, wisely and cautiously administered, is a Daisy. There is more money in it, more territory, more sovereignty, and other kinds of emolument, than there is in any other game that is played. But Christendom has been playing it badly of late years, and must certainly suffer by it, in my opinion. She has been so eager to get every stake that appeared on the green cloth, that the People who Sit in Darkness have noticed it—they have noticed it, and have begun to show alarm. They have become suspicious of the Blessings of Civilization. More—they have begun to examine them. This is not well. The Blessings of Civilization are all right, and a good commercial property; there could not be a better, in a dim light. In the right kind of a light, and at a proper distance, with the goods a little out of focus, they furnish this desirable exhibit to the Gentlemen who Sit in Darkness:

LOVE,   LAW AND ORDER,
JUSTICE,   LIBERTY,
GENTLENESS,   EQUALITY,
CHRISTIANITY,   HONORABLE DEALING,

PROTECTION TO
 THE WEAK,   MERCY,
 TEMPERANCE,   EDUCATION,
—and so on.

There. Is it good? Sir, it is pie. It will bring into camp any idiot that sits in darkness anywhere. But not if we adulterate it. It is proper to be emphatic upon that point. This brand is strictly for Export—apparently. *Apparently.* Privately and confidentially, it is nothing of the kind. Privately and confidentially, it is merely an outside cover, gay and pretty and attractive, displaying the special patterns of our Civilization which we reserve for Home Consumption, while *inside* the bale is the Actual Thing that the Customer Sitting in Darkness buys with his blood and tears and land and liberty. That Actual Thing is, indeed, Civilization, but it is only for Export. Is there a difference between the two brands? In some of the details, yes.

. . .

The more we examine the mistake, the more clearly we perceive that it is going to be bad for the Business. The Person Sitting in Darkness is almost sure to say: "There is something curious about this—curious and unaccountable. There must be two Americas: one that sets the captive free, and one that takes a once-captive's new freedom away from him, and picks a quarrel with him with nothing to found it on; then kills him to get his land."

The truth is, the Person Sitting in Darkness *is* saying things like that; and for the sake of the Business we must persuade him to look at the Philippine matter in another and healthier way. We must arrange his opinions for him. I believe it can be done; for Mr. Chamberlain has arranged England's opinion of the South African matter, and done it most cleverly and successfully. He presented the facts—some of the facts—and showed those confiding people what the facts meant. He did it statistically, which is a good way. He used the formula: "Twice 2 are 14, and 2 from 9 leaves 35." Figures are effective; figures will convince the elect.

. . .

We must bring him to, and coax him and coddle him, and assure him that the ways of Providence are best, and that it would not become us to find fault with them; and then, to show him that we are only imitators, not originators, we must read the following passage from the letter of an American soldier-lad in the Philippines to his mother, published in *Public Opinion*, of Decorah, Iowa, describing the finish of a victorious battle:

"WE NEVER LEFT ONE ALIVE. IF ONE WAS WOUNDED, WE WOULD RUN OUR BAYONETS THROUGH HIM."

. . .

Now then, that will convince the Person. You will see. It will restore the Business. Also, it will elect the Master of the Game to the vacant place in the Trinity of our national gods; and there on their high thrones the Three will sit, age after age, in the people's sight, each bearing the Emblem of his service: Washington, the Sword of the Liberator; Lincoln, the Slave's Broken Chains; the Master, the Chains Repaired.   *Trinity*

. . .

[And as for a flag for the Philippine Province], it is easily managed. We can have a special one—our states do it: we can have just our usual flag, with the white stripes painted black and the stars replaced by the skull and crossbones.

— saying America is not a savior but opp.

WORKING WITH SOURCES

1. How does Twain incorporate the language of the marketplace into this oration, and why?
2. Is Twain justified in seeing the conquest of the Philippines as a betrayal of American values and historical development?

28. WORLD WARS AND COMPETING VISIONS OF MODERNITY, 1900–1945

28.1   ANZAC Troops at Gallipoli, August 1915

In the aftermath of the Great War, the Allied nations compiled both regimental and general histories of the conflict. In these narratives, the experiences of the soldiers and their commanders are filtered through the ultimate outcomes—and attendant sufferings—inflicted by the war. The errors of judgment and planning made by commanders are preserved in these records, and are particularly significant to our understanding today of battles whose brutality and massive death tolls are still shocking. The contribution of ANZAC (the acronym for Australian and New Zealand Army Corps) troops to the campaigns at Gallipoli and the Dardanelles (April 1915–January 1916) against the Ottoman Turks is marked in the ANZAC countries as a solemn day of remembrance. In this excerpt from a multivolume narrative of the campaigns compiled by C. E. W. Bean, the casualty figures, and Bean's reactions to the deployment of soldiers and the possible waste of war, are striking.

Perceiving the difficulty of advancing under such an enfilade, Major Powles directed the next platoons to swing to the left and advance northwards or north-eastwards in order to subdue the fire from that direction. This attempt was quickly shattered. A part of the third company, under Major Lane, advancing towards Goodsell's left, succeeded in reaching the same trench and pushed along it towards the east. These later lines, however, only reached the trench in fragments, and the situation of the left flank was desperate. From a point of vantage in a cross-trench the Turks were flinging bombs with impunity among the Australians. An unauthorised order to retire had been given to some of Lane's men, and in withdrawing over the open they had lost heavily. At 7 o'clock the battalion was urged by a message from Russell to push on and seize the summit, but such an attempt would have been hopeless. Goodsell's left gradually withdrew southward along the trench. With such parts of the later lines as reached him he had extended farther to his right along the same sap and, finding there some of the Hampshire, discovered that he was actually in the trench which had been captured by the New Zealanders, and which encircled the lower slope of the hill. By 10 o'clock the remnant of Goodsell's men had retired along it until they reached the flank of the New Zealanders, where they remained, stubbornly holding fifty yards of the trench.

The attempt to round off the capture of Hill 60 by setting a raw battalion, without reconnaissance, to rush the main part of a position on which the experienced troops of Anzac had only succeeded in obtaining a slight foothold, ended in failure. Its initiation was due to the fact that Russell and his brigade-major, Powles, both careful and capable officers, lacked the realisation—which came to many commanders only

Source: C. E. W. Bean, *The Story of ANZAC from 4 May, 1915, to the Evacuation of the Gallipoli Peninsula*, 11th ed. (Sydney: Angus & Robertson, 1941), 743–745, 761–762, available online at http://www.awm.gov.au/histories/first_world_war/AWMOHWW1/AIF/Vol2/.

after sharp experience—that the attack upon such a position required minute preparation, and that the unskillfulness of raw troops, however brave, was likely to involve them in heavy losses for the sake of results too small to justify the expense. Within a few hours the 18th Battalion, which appears to have marched out 750 strong, had lost 11 officers and 372 men, of whom half had been killed. The action had been a severe one for all the troops engaged, the losses of the comparatively small force which attacked from Anzac amounting to over 1,300. The flank had been brought up to Susak Kuyu, and a lodgment had been obtained in the enemy's strongly entrenched position at Hill 60. Slight though it was, this gain was the only one achieved on the whole battle-front. In the Suvla area the position at first secured by the 29th Division on the crest of Scimitar Hill was untenable, a brave advance by the reserve—the 2nd Mounted Division—availing nothing. On the plain the 11th Division was unable to maintain its unconnected line in the first Turkish trench. A barricade built across the Asmak creek-bed was blown down by the enemy, and the British flank was forced back to Kazlar Chair, from which it had started, 1,000 yards in rear of the Gurkha post at Susak Kuyu, the Turks still intervening near the "poplars." To fill this dangerous space, the 19th Battalion of the new Australian brigade was marched to the left and stationed near the gap. Cox reported that he believed the new line could be held, although the position on Hill 60 "cannot be considered satisfactory."

If the Battle of Sari Bair was the climax of the Gallipoli campaign, that of Scimitar Hill was its anti-climax. With it the great offensive ended. In the words of Kitchener's message received by Hamilton on July 11th: " . . . When the surprise ceases to be operative, in so far that the advance is checked and the enemy begin to collect from all sides to oppose the attackers, then perseverance becomes merely a useless waste of life." The attempt to prolong the offensive by driving through the flank of the enemy's now established trench-line had utterly failed; and Hamilton had not the troops, nor had all the troops the morale, necessary for a fresh attack. Birdwood, however, in agreement with his subordinate commanders, desired to strengthen his flank by capturing the summit of Hill 60, and he obtained leave to renew this effort on August 27th.

. . .

Thus ended the action at Hill 60. Birdwood believed that the actual knoll had been captured, and so reported to Hamilton, who wrote: "Knoll 60, now ours throughout, commands the Biyuk Anafarta valley with view and fire—a big tactical scoop." As a matter of fact half the summit—or possibly rather more—was still in possession of the Turks. The fighting of August 27th, 28th, and 29th had, however, given the troops on the left of Anzac a position astride the spur from which a fairly satisfactory view could be had over the plain to the "W" Hills. The cost was over 1,100 casualties. The burden of the work had been sustained by war-worn troops. The magnificent brigade of New Zealand Mounted Rifles, which was responsible for the main advances, had been worked until it was almost entirely consumed, its four regiments at the end numbering only 365 all told. The 4th Australian Infantry Brigade which, through defective co-ordination with the artillery, had been twice thrown against a difficult objective without a chance of success, was reduced to 968. General Russell and his brigade-major, Powles, had worked untiringly, the latter personally guiding almost every attacking party to its starting point in the dangerous maze of trenches. It was not their fault that at this stage of the war both staff and commanders were only learning the science of trench-warfare. Had the experience and the instruments of later years been available, the action at Hill 60 would doubtless have been fought differently.

WORKING WITH SOURCES

1. What factors, in Bean's estimation, led to the very high casualty figures among the Allied troops in this campaign?
2. Does Bean consider the loss of these troops a "useless waste of life"? Were the leaders of the effort incompetent?

28.2 Vera Brittain, *Testament of Youth*, 1933

Born in 1893 into an upper-class family at a time when society expected neither intellectual nor professional achievement from such women, Vera Brittain obtained a scholarship to Somerville College at Oxford University in 1914. When the war began in August 1914, her brother, Edward, and his best friend, Roland Leighton, enlisted. Brittain left college the following year to study nursing, and she joined a VAD (Voluntary Aid Detachment) unit. Having become engaged to Leighton while he was home on leave in August 1915, Brittain learned in December of that year that he had been killed in action on the Western Front. Continuing her nursing work, Brittain experienced the loss of numerous other friends and relatives, including her brother, over the course of the war. After the war, she returned to Oxford and developed an important literary career in her own right, publishing her beautifully written and compelling wartime memoir *Testament of Youth* in 1933. Throughout the 1930s, she advocated international peace and women's rights, insisting that the shattering experiences of her youth should not be reinflicted on contemporary young people.

PERHAPS . . .
To R. A. L.

Perhaps some day the sun will shine again,
And I shall see that still the skies are blue,
And feel once more I do not live in vain,
Although bereft of You.

Perhaps the golden meadows at my feet
Will make the sunny hours of spring seem gay,
And I shall find the white May-blossoms sweet,
Though You have passed away.

Perhaps the summer woods will shimmer bright,
And crimson roses once again be fair,
And autumn harvest fields a rich delight,
Although You are not there.

But though kind Time may many joys renew,
There is one greatest joy I shall not know
Again, because my heart for loss of You
Was broken, long ago.

V. B. 1916.
From *Verses of a V.A.D.*

Whenever I think of the weeks that followed the news of Roland's death, a series of pictures, disconnected but crystal clear, unroll themselves like a kaleidoscope through my mind.

A solitary cup of coffee stands before me on a hotel breakfast-table; I try to drink it, but fail ignominiously.

Outside, in front of the promenade, dismal grey waves tumble angrily over one another on the windy Brighton shore, and, like a slaughtered animal that still twists after life has been extinguished, I go on mechanically worrying because his channel-crossing must have been so rough.

In an omnibus, going to Keymer, I look fixedly at the sky; suddenly the pale light of a watery sun streams out between the dark, swollen clouds, and I think for one crazy moment that I have seen the heavens opened. . . .

At Keymer a fierce gale is blowing and I am out alone on the brown winter ploughlands, where I have

Source: Vera Brittain, *Testament of Youth* (New York: Seaview, 1980), 239–241.

been driven by a desperate desire to escape from the others. Shivering violently, and convinced that I am going to be sick, I take refuge behind a wet bank of grass from the icy sea-wind that rushes, screaming, across the sodden fields.

It is late afternoon; at the organ of the small village church, Edward is improvising a haunting memorial hymn for Roland, and the words: "God walked in the garden in the cool of the evening," flash irrelevantly into my mind.

I am back on night-duty at Camberwell after my leave; in the chapel, as the evening voluntary is played, I stare with swimming eyes at the lettered wall, and remember reading the words: "I am the Resurrection and the Life," at the early morning communion service before going to Brighton.

I am buying some small accessories for my uniform in a big Victoria Street store, when I stop, petrified, before a vase of the tall pink roses that Roland gave me on the way to *David Copperfield*; in the warm room their melting sweetness brings back the memory of that New Year's Eve, and suddenly, to the perturbation of the shop-assistants, I burst into uncontrollable tears, and find myself, helpless and humiliated, unable to stop crying in the tram all the way back to the hospital.

It is Sunday, and I am out for a solitary walk through the dreary streets of Camberwell before going to bed after the night's work. In front of me on the frozen pavement a long red worm wriggles slimily. I remember that, after our death, worms destroy this body—however lovely, however beloved—and I run from the obscene thing in horror.

It is Wednesday, and I am walking up the Brixton Road on a mild, fresh morning of early spring. Half-consciously I am repeating a line from Rupert Brooke:

"The deep night, and birds singing, and clouds flying . . ."

For a moment I have become conscious of the old joy in rainwashed skies and scuttling, fleecy clouds, when suddenly I remember—Roland is dead and I am not keeping faith with him; it is mean and cruel, even for a second, to feel glad to be alive.

WORKING WITH SOURCES

1. How did Brittain cope with the grief of losing her fiancé?
2. Did the Great War impose unique burdens on women? In what respects?

28.3   Benito Mussolini and Giovanni Gentile, "Foundations and Doctrine of Fascism," 1932

Through a series of small demonstrations and gatherings in 1919, Benito Mussolini (1883–1945) created, at least in his own estimation, a completely new political ideology. He named this philosophy for a symbol used in the ancient Roman empire: the fasces, which was a bundle of rods together with an ax and carried by lictors as a representation of power. Mussolini was installed as Italy's leader, or "Duce," in October 1922. He published an explanation of what he had achieved as well as a statement of his political beliefs in the *Enciclopedia Italiana* in June 1932. Reflecting on

Source: Reprinted from *A Primer of Italian Fascism*, by Jeffrey T. Schnapp, translated by Maria G. Stampino, Olivia E. Sears, and Jeffrey T. Schnapp, by permission of the University of Nebraska Press. Copyright 2000 by the University of Nebraska Press.

the decade of rule following his seizure of "totalitarian" power (the word itself was coined by this regime, and specifically with the collaboration of Mussolini's court philosopher, Giovanni Gentile), Mussolini justified the violence inflicted by his regime and emphasized its fundamentally "moral" basis.

Anti-individualistic, the fascist conception of life stresses the importance of the state. It affirms the value of the individual only insofar as his interests coincide with those of the state, which stands for the conscience and the universal will of man in history. It opposes classical liberalism, which arose as a revolt against absolutism and exhausted its historical function when the state became the expression of the conscience and will of the people. Liberalism denied the state in the name of the individual; fascism reasserts the state as the true reality of the individual. And if liberty is to be the attribute of living men and not of the sort of abstract dummies invented by individualistic liberalism, then fascism stands for liberty. Fascism stands for the only liberty worth possessing: the liberty of the state and of the individual within the state. The fascist conception of the state is all-embracing. Outside of it no human or spiritual values can exist, much less have value. Thus understood, fascism is totalitarian, and the fascist state—in which all values are synthesized and united—interprets, develops, and heightens the life of the people.

No individuals outside the state; no groups (political parties, associations, trade unions, social classes) outside the state. This is why fascism is opposed to socialism, which sees in history nothing but class struggle and neglects the possibility of achieving unity within the state (which effects the fusion of classes into a single economic and moral reality). This is also why fascism is opposed to trade unionism as a class weapon. But when brought within the orbit of the state, fascism recognizes the real needs that gave rise to socialism and trade unionism, giving them due weight in the corporative system in which divergent interests are harmonized within the unity that is the state.

Grouped according to their interests, individuals make up classes. They make up trade unions when organized according to their economic activities. But, first and foremost, they make up the state, which is no mere matter of numbers, or simply the sum of the individuals forming the majority. Accordingly, fascism is opposed to that form of democracy that equates a nation with the majority, reducing it to the lowest common denominator. But fascism represents the purest form of democracy if the nation is considered—as it should be—from the standpoint of quality rather than quantity. This means considering the nation as an idea, the mightiest because the most ethical, the most coherent, the truest; an idea actualizing itself in a people as the conscience and will of the few, if not of One; an idea tending to actualize itself in the conscience and the will of the mass, of the collective ethnically molded by natural and historical conditions into a single nation that moves with a single conscience and will along a uniform line of development and spiritual formation. Not a race or a geographically delimited region but a people, perpetuating itself in history, a multitude unified by an idea and imbued with the will to live, with the will to power, with a self-consciousness and a personality.

To the degree that it is embodied in a state, this higher personality becomes a nation. It is not the nation that generates the state (an antiquated naturalistic concept that afforded the basis for nineteenth-century propaganda in favor of national governments); rather, it is the state that creates the nation, granting volition and therefore real existence to a people that has become aware of its moral unity.

. . .

A higher, more powerful expression of personality, the fascist state embodies a spiritual force encompassing all manifestations of the moral and intellectual life of man. Its functions cannot be limited to those of maintaining order and keeping the peace, as liberal doctrine would have it. The fascist state is no mere mechanical device for delimiting the sphere within which individuals may exercise their supposed rights. It represents an inwardly accepted standard and rule of conduct. A discipline of the whole person, it permeates the will no less than the intellect. It is the very principle, the soul of souls [*anima dell'anima*], that inspires every man who is a member of a civilized society, penetrating deep into his personality and dwelling within the heart of the man of action and the thinker, the artist, and the man of science.

Fascism, in short, is not only a law giver and a founder of institutions but also an educator and a promoter of spiritual life. It aims to refashion not only the forms of life but also their content: man, his character, his faith. To this end it champions discipline and authority; authority that infuses the soul and rules with undisputed sway. Accordingly, its chosen emblem is the lictor's fasces: symbol of unity, strength, and justice.

WORKING WITH SOURCES

1. How does Mussolini contrast fascism with "liberalism"? Is his contrast merely empty rhetoric?
2. Why does Mussolini pay so much attention to the "spiritual" elements that animate fascism? Why does he avoid attributing historical development to materialist causes?

What? Book
Where? Germany
Why? pass on ideas

28.4 *who:* Adolf Hitler, *Mein Kampf,* *when* 1925

Context: radio

As a result of the failure of his Beer Hall Putsch in Munich in November 1923, Adolf Hitler (1889–1945) was sent to a minimum security prison at Landsberg. However, he was paroled, four years before the completion of his sentence, in December 1924. Having met with the respect of his judges during his trial in February 1924 and with the approval of the Bavarian Supreme Court, although against the advice of state prosecutors, he had his sentence—after his conviction for a treasonable attempt to take over the state—commuted. Nevertheless, there were some restrictions, both in Bavaria and elsewhere in Germany, on Hitler's speaking and freedom of movement. In spite of these restrictions, he emerged from prison with the manuscript of a new political statement of his life and philosophy, a document he entitled *Mein Kampf* ("My struggle"). As recently discovered documents reveal, Hitler hoped to use the proceeds from the sale of this book for a new car as well as to fund his political movement. The party growing out of this movement would be labeled the National Socialist German Workers' Party, and he would be installed as its unquestioned *Führer* (leader) by 1925. The following excerpt from *Mein Kampf* reveals what he had learned about rhetoric and political action in his nascent career.

I have already stated in the first volume that all great, world-shaking events have been brought about, not by written matter, but by the spoken word. This led to a lengthy discussion in a part of the press, where, of course, such an assertion was sharply attacked, particularly by our bourgeois wiseacres. But the very reason why this occurred confutes the doubters. For

A know it all

the bourgeois intelligentsia protest against such a view only because they themselves obviously lack the power and ability to influence the masses by the spoken word, since they have thrown themselves more and more into purely literary activity and renounced the real agitational activity of the spoken word. Such habits necessarily lead in time to what

Source: Adolf Hitler, *Mein Kampf,* trans. Ralph Mannheim (Boston: Houghton Mifflin, 1998), 469–471.

repetition

distinguishes our bourgeoisie today; that is, to the loss of the psychological instinct for *mass effect* and *mass influence*.

While the speaker gets a continuous correction of his speech from the crowd he is addressing, since he can always see in the faces of his listeners to what extent they can follow his arguments with under-standing and whether the impression and the effect of his words lead to the desired goal—the writer does not know his readers at all. Therefore, to begin with, he will not aim at a definite mass before his eyes, but will keep his arguments entirely general. By this to a certain degree he loses psychological subtlety and in consequence suppleness. And so, by and large, a brilliant speaker will be able to write better than a brilliant writer can speak, unless he continuously practices this art. On top of this there is the fact that the mass of people as such is lazy; that they remain inertly in the spirit of their old habits and, left to themselves, will take up a piece of written matter only reluctantly if it is not in agree-ment with what they themselves believe and does not bring them what they had hoped for. Therefore, an article with a definite tendency is for the most part read only by people who can already be reck-oned to this tendency. At most a leaflet or a poster can, by its brevity, count on getting a moment's at-tention from someone who thinks differently. The picture in all its forms up to the film has greater pos-sibilities. Here a man needs to use his brains even less; it suffices to look, or at most to read extremely brief texts, and thus many will more readily accept a *pictorial presentation* than *read* an *article* of any *length*. The picture brings them in a much briefer time, I might almost say at one stroke, the enlightenment which they obtain from written matter only after arduous reading.

The essential point, however, is that a piece of lit-erature never knows into what hands it will fall, and yet must retain its definite form. In general the effect will be the greater, the more this form corresponds to the intellectual level and nature of those very people who will be its readers. A book that is destined for the broad masses must, therefore, attempt from the very begin-ning to have an effect, both in style and elevation,

different from a work intended for higher intellectual classes.

Only by this kind of adaptability does written matter approach the spoken word. To my mind, the speaker can treat the same theme as the book; he will, if he is a brilliant popular orator, not be likely to repeat the same reproach and the same substance twice in the same form. He will always let himself be borne by the great masses in such a way that instinc-tively the very words come to his lips that he needs to speak to the hearts of his audience. And if he errs, even in the slightest, he has the living correction before him. As I have said, he can read from the facial expression of his audience whether, firstly, they *understand* what he is saying, whether, secondly, they can *follow the speech as a whole*, and to what extent, thirdly, he has *convinced* them of the *soundness* of what he has said. If—firstly—he sees that they do not understand him, he will become so primitive and clear in his explanations that even the last member of his audience has to understand him; if he feels—secondly—that they cannot follow him, he will con-struct his ideas so cautiously and slowly that even the weakest member of the audience is not left behind, and he will—thirdly—if he suspects that they do not seem convinced of the soundness of his argument, repeat it over and over in constantly new examples. He himself will utter their objections, which he senses though unspoken, and go on confuting them and exploding them, until at length even the last group of an opposition, by its very bearing and facial expression, enables him to recognize its capitulation to his arguments.

Here again it is not seldom a question of over-coming prejudices which are not based on reason, but, for the most part unconsciously, are supported only by sentiment. To overcome this barrier of in-stinctive aversion, of emotional hatred, of prejudiced rejection, is a thousand times harder than to correct a faulty or erroneous scientific opinion. False concepts and poor knowledge can be eliminated by instruc-tion, the resistance of the emotions never. Here only an appeal to these mysterious powers themselves can be effective; and the writer can hardly ever accom-plish this, but almost exclusively the orator.

If you run into problems, make it hatred

WORKING WITH SOURCES

1. What advantages does the orator have over the writer, in Hitler's assessment? Is he convincing on this point?
2. How does a skillful speaker manipulate an audience? Does the substance of the speech matter at all, according to Hitler's description of the process of public speaking?

28.5   Franklin D. Roosevelt, Undelivered Address Planned for Jefferson Day, April 13, 1945

During his first inaugural address as the president of the United States in March 1933, Franklin D. Roosevelt had warned his fellow Americans, "The only thing we have to fear is fear itself." Through a series of radio broadcasts called "fireside chats," the president continued to reassure the American public during the darkest days of the Depression. He would go on, in January 1941, to enumerate the "four freedoms" to which every American, and perhaps every person around the globe, was entitled. Among these were freedom of speech, freedom of worship, freedom from want, and, perhaps most importantly, freedom from fear.

Suffering from debilitating illness in the final years of the war, Roosevelt persisted in envisioning a world in which those four freedoms could be guaranteed—and in which the unprecedented and horrific suffering of World War II could be transformed into a new period of human development. As Thomas Paine had argued about the American Revolution, there was now a chance "to begin the world over again." Roosevelt prepared an oration on the subject to be delivered on the occasion of Thomas Jefferson's birthday. The war was drawing to its close in Europe, and would end several months later in Asia—but Roosevelt did not live to see the achievement of peace. Although he died on April 12, 1945, the day before he was to deliver this address, the prepared speech demonstrates the tenor of Roosevelt's thought at this point in his life.

Today this Nation which Jefferson helped so greatly to build is playing a tremendous part in the battle for the rights of man all over the world.

Today we are part of the vast Allied force—a force composed of flesh and blood and steel and spirit—which is today destroying the makers of war, the breeders of hatred, in Europe and in Asia.

In Jefferson's time our Navy consisted of only a handful of frigates headed by the gallant U.S.S. Constitution—Old Ironsides—but that tiny Navy taught Nations across the Atlantic that piracy in the Mediterranean—acts of aggression against peaceful commerce and the enslavement of their crews—was one of those things which, among neighbors, simply was not done.

Today we have learned in the agony of war that great power involves great responsibility. Today we can no more escape the consequences of German and Japanese aggression than could we avoid the consequences of attacks by the Barbary Corsairs a century and a half before.

Source: Gerhard Peters and John T. Woolley, the American Presidency Project, http://www.presidency.ucsb.edu/ws/?pid=16602.

We, as Americans, do not choose to deny our responsibility.

Nor do we intend to abandon our determination that, within the lives of our children and our children's children, there will not be a third world war.

We seek peace—enduring peace. More than an end to war, we want an end to the beginnings of all wars—yes, an end to this brutal, inhuman, and thoroughly impractical method of settling the differences between governments.

The once powerful, malignant Nazi state is crumbling. The Japanese war lords are receiving, in their own homeland, the retribution for which they asked when they attacked Pearl Harbor.

But the mere conquest of our enemies is not enough.

We must go on to do all in our power to conquer the doubts and the fears, the ignorance and the greed, which made this horror possible.

Thomas Jefferson, himself a distinguished scientist, once spoke of "the brotherly spirit of Science, which unites into one family all its votaries of whatever grade, and however widely dispersed throughout the different quarters of the globe."

Today, science has brought all the different quarters of the globe so close together that it is impossible to isolate them one from another.

Today we are faced with the preeminent fact that, if civilization is to survive, we must cultivate the science of human relationships—the ability of all peoples, of all kinds, to live together and work together, in the same world, at peace.

Let me assure you that my hand is the steadier for the work that is to be done, that I move more firmly into the task, knowing that you—millions and millions of you—are joined with me in the resolve to make this work endure.

The work, my friends, is peace. More than an end of this war —an end to the beginnings of all wars. Yes, an end, forever, to this impractical, unrealistic settlement of the differences between governments by the mass killing of peoples.

Today, as we move against the terrible scourge of war—as we go forward toward the greatest contribution that any generation of human beings can make in this world—the contribution of lasting peace, I ask you to keep up your faith. I measure the sound, solid achievement that can be made at this time by the straight edge of your own confidence and your resolve. And to you, and to all Americans who dedicate themselves with us to the making of an abiding peace, I say:

The only limit to our realization of tomorrow will be our doubts of today. Let us move forward with strong and active faith.

WORKING WITH SOURCES

1. What did Roosevelt consider the root and ultimate causes of war?
2. How, in his belief, would a lasting peace be achieved and a "third world war" avoided?

29. RECONSTRUCTION, COLD WAR, AND DECOLONIZATION, 1945–1962

29.1 The Universal Declaration of Human Rights, December 10, 1948

The Universal Declaration of Human Rights, adopted by the United Nations General Assembly on December 10, 1948, was one of the most significant and lasting results of the World War II. The League of Nations, created after the World War I, had failed to prevent the beginning of another, even more catastrophic and costly conflict. The United Nations was planned throughout the war as a substitute mechanism for global peace and security, but world leaders also believed that a document was necessary to affirm the rights of individuals throughout the entire world. A formal drafting committee, consisting of members from eight countries, was charged with the task. The committee chair was Eleanor Roosevelt, the widow of President Roosevelt and a strong advocate for human rights in her own right. By its resolution 217 A (III), the General Assembly, meeting in Paris, adopted the Universal Declaration of Human Rights. Eight nations abstained from the vote, but none dissented.

PREAMBLE

Whereas recognition of the inherent dignity and of the equal and inalienable rights of all members of the human family is the foundation of freedom, justice and peace in the world,

Whereas disregard and contempt for human rights have resulted in barbarous acts which have outraged the conscience of mankind, and the advent of a world in which human beings shall enjoy freedom of speech and belief and freedom from fear and want has been proclaimed as the highest aspiration of the common people,

Whereas it is essential, if man is not to be compelled to have recourse, as a last resort, to rebellion against tyranny and oppression, that human rights should be protected by the rule of law,

Whereas it is essential to promote the development of friendly relations between nations,

Whereas the peoples of the United Nations have in the Charter reaffirmed their faith in fundamental human rights, in the dignity and worth of the human person and in the equal rights of men and women and have determined to promote social progress and better standards of life in larger freedom,

Whereas Member States have pledged themselves to achieve, in co-operation with the United Nations, the promotion of universal respect for and observance of human rights and fundamental freedoms,

Whereas a common understanding of these rights and freedoms is of the greatest importance for the full realization of this pledge,

Now, Therefore THE GENERAL ASSEMBLY proclaims THIS UNIVERSAL DECLARATION OF HUMAN RIGHTS as a common standard of achievement for all peoples and all nations, to the end that every individual and every organ of society, keeping

Source: http://www.un.org/en/documents/udhr/.

this Declaration constantly in mind, shall strive by teaching and education to promote respect for these rights and freedoms and by progressive measures, national and international, to secure their universal and effective recognition and observance, both among the peoples of Member States themselves and among the peoples of territories under their jurisdiction.

Article 1.
All human beings are born free and equal in dignity and rights. They are endowed with reason and conscience and should act towards one another in a spirit of brotherhood.

Article 2.
Everyone is entitled to all the rights and freedoms set forth in this Declaration, without distinction of any kind, such as race, colour, sex, language, religion, political or other opinion, national or social origin, property, birth or other status. Furthermore, no distinction shall be made on the basis of the political, jurisdictional or international status of the country or territory to which a person belongs, whether it be independent, trust, non-self-governing or under any other limitation of sovereignty.

Article 3.
Everyone has the right to life, liberty and security of person.

Article 4.
No one shall be held in slavery or servitude; slavery and the slave trade shall be prohibited in all their forms.

Article 5.
No one shall be subjected to torture or to cruel, inhuman or degrading treatment or punishment.

Article 6.
Everyone has the right to recognition everywhere as a person before the law.

. . .

Article 15.
(1) Everyone has the right to a nationality.
(2) No one shall be arbitrarily deprived of his nationality nor denied the right to change his nationality.

Article 16.
(1) Men and women of full age, without any limitation due to race, nationality or religion, have the right to marry and to found a family. They are entitled to equal rights as to marriage, during marriage and at its dissolution.
(2) Marriage shall be entered into only with the free and full consent of the intending spouses.
(3) The family is the natural and fundamental group unit of society and is entitled to protection by society and the State.

Article 17.
(1) Everyone has the right to own property alone as well as in association with others.
(2) No one shall be arbitrarily deprived of his property.

Article 18.
Everyone has the right to freedom of thought, conscience and religion; this right includes freedom to change his religion or belief, and freedom, either alone or in community with others and in public or private, to manifest his religion or belief in teaching, practice, worship and observance.

Article 19.
Everyone has the right to freedom of opinion and expression; this right includes freedom to hold opinions without interference and to seek, receive and impart information and ideas through any media and regardless of frontiers.

. . .

Article 23.
(1) Everyone has the right to work, to free choice of employment, to just and favorable conditions of work and to protection against unemployment.
(2) Everyone, without any discrimination, has the right to equal pay for equal work.
(3) Everyone who works has the right to just and favorable remuneration ensuring for himself and his family an existence worthy of human dignity, and supplemented, if necessary, by other means of social protection.
(4) Everyone has the right to form and to join trade unions for the protection of his interests.

Article 24.

Everyone has the right to rest and leisure, including reasonable limitation of working hours and periodic holidays with pay.

Article 25.

(1) Everyone has the right to a standard of living adequate for the health and well-being of himself and of his family, including food, clothing, housing and medical care and necessary social services, and the right to security in the event of unemployment, sickness, disability, widowhood, old age or other lack of livelihood in circumstances beyond his control.

(2) Motherhood and childhood are entitled to special care and assistance. All children, whether born in or out of wedlock, shall enjoy the same social protection.

Article 26.

(1) Everyone has the right to education. Education shall be free, at least in the elementary and fundamental stages. Elementary education shall be compulsory. Technical and professional education shall be made generally available and higher education shall be equally accessible to all on the basis of merit.

(2) Education shall be directed to the full development of the human personality and to the strengthening of respect for human rights and fundamental freedoms. It shall promote understanding, tolerance and friendship among all nations, racial or religious groups, and shall further the activities of the United Nations for the maintenance of peace.

(3) Parents have a prior right to choose the kind of education that shall be given to their children.

WORKING WITH SOURCES

1. According to the Universal Declaration of Human Rights, what would be the practical benefits of guaranteeing human rights for the entire human family?
2. How likely were these goals to be applied globally in 1948? Which articles remained to be fulfilled at that point—and perhaps even today?

29.2 Winston Churchill, the "Iron Curtain Speech," March 5, 1946

Throughout the 1930s, Churchill had opposed the policy of "appeasement" advocated by Prime Minister Neville Chamberlain and his allies in the British Parliament. His rise to the highest political office was facilitated by Chamberlain's failure to deliver on the "peace in our time" he had promised after the Munich Agreement in September 1938. However, it was not until May 1940 that Churchill got his chance. Having calmed, encouraged, and directed the British people—and others—throughout the war years, Churchill was himself removed from power in 1945. Nevertheless, at this famous address delivered at Westminster College in Missouri in 1946, Churchill warned of a new regime that also could not, and should not, be appeased. It is considered one of the first salvos in the developing Cold War between the West and the Soviet bloc.

Source: http://www.fordham.edu/halsall/mod/churchill-iron.asp.

The safety of the world, ladies and gentlemen, requires a unity in Europe, from which no nation should be permanently outcast. It is from the quarrels of the strong parent races in Europe that the world wars we have witnessed, or which occurred in former times, have sprung. Twice the United States has had to send several millions of its young men across the Atlantic to fight the wars. But now we all can find any nation, wherever it may dwell, between dusk and dawn. Surely we should work with conscious purpose for a grand pacification of Europe within the structure of the United Nations and in accordance with our Charter. In a great number of countries, far from the Russian frontiers and throughout the world, Communist fifth columns are established and work in complete unity and absolute obedience to the directions they receive from the Communist center. Except in the British Commonwealth and in the United States where Communism is in its infancy, the Communist parties or fifth columns constitute a growing challenge and peril to Christian civilization. The outlook is also anxious in the Far East and especially in Manchuria. The agreement which was made at Yalta, to which I was a party, was extremely favorable to Soviet Russia, but it was made at a time when no one could say that the German war might not extend all through the summer and autumn of 1945 and when the Japanese war was expected by the best judges to last for a further eighteen months from the end of the German war. I repulse the idea that a new war is inevitable—still more that it is imminent. It is because I am sure that our fortunes are still in our own hands and that we hold the power to save the future, that I feel the duty to speak out now that I have the occasion and the opportunity to do so. I do not believe that Soviet Russia desires war. What they desire is the fruits of war and the indefinite expansion of their power and doctrines. But what we have to consider here today while time remains, is the permanent prevention of war and the establishment of conditions of freedom and democracy as rapidly as possible in all countries. Our difficulties and dangers will not be removed by closing our eyes to them. They will not be removed by mere waiting to see what happens; nor will they be removed by a policy of appeasement. What is needed is a settlement, and the longer this is delayed, the more difficult it will be and the greater our dangers will become. From what I have seen of our Russian friends and allies during the war, I am convinced that there is nothing they admire so much as strength, and there is nothing for which they have less respect than for weakness, especially military weakness. For that reason the old doctrine of a balance of power is unsound. We cannot afford, if we can help it, to work on narrow margins, offering temptations to a trial of strength.

. . .

If the population of the English-speaking Commonwealth be added to that of the United States, with all that such cooperation implies in the air, on the sea, all over the globe, and in science and in industry, and in moral force, there will be no quivering, precarious balance of power to offer its temptation to ambition or adventure. On the contrary there will be an overwhelming assurance of security. If we adhere faithfully to the Charter of the United Nations and walk forward in sedate and sober strength, seeking no one's land or treasure, seeking to lay no arbitrary control upon the thoughts of men, if all British moral and material forces and convictions are joined with your own in fraternal association, the high roads of the future will be clear, not only for us but for all, not only for our time but for a century to come.

WORKING WITH SOURCES

1. What does this speech reveal about changing commitments and alliances after the end of the war in 1945? What factors caused a change in policy in Western countries toward the Soviet Union?
2. Why was Churchill commenting on the dangers of appeasement with regard to Soviet foreign policy?

29.3 Letters on the Cuban Missile Crisis between Fidel Castro and Nikita Khrushchev, October 28 and 30, 1962

The Cuban Missile Crisis of October 1962 marked the climax, and the most dangerous point, of the Cold War between the United States and the Soviet Union. When US spy planes discovered the presence of missiles and launching pads in Cuba, President John F. Kennedy demanded their immediate destruction and followed up this demand with a naval blockade of the island—and continued reconnaissance missions in Cuban airspace—to prevent the arrival of Russian reinforcements. The world held its breath for several days as Soviet ships, bearing more nuclear missiles, sailed steadily for Cuba. The globe teetered on the brink of nuclear annihilation, and this exchange of letters reveals, from the Soviet and Cuban side, how very close to that brink the world actually came.

Letter to Nikita Khrushchev from Fidel Castro regarding defending Cuban air space

October 28, 1962

Dear Comrade Khrushchev:

I have just received your letter.

The position of our Government regarding your statement can be found in the text of the declaration announced today, with which you are surely familiar.

I must clarify a point relating to the anti-aircraft measures which we adopted. You said: "Yesterday you shot down one of them, yet previously you did not when they flew over your territory."

Previously, there were isolated violations with no particular military purpose, and they did not result in real danger.

This is no longer the case. There was the danger of a surprise attack on certain military sites. We decided that we could not remain idle because of the danger of a surprise attack. With our warning radars turned off, the potential attackers could fly with impunity over the sites and totally destroy them. We did not believe that we should allow this, given the cost and effort which we have expended, and because an attack would have gravely weakened our morale and military capability. Because of this, Cuban forces mobilized fifty anti-aircraft batteries, our entire reserves, on October 24 in order to support the positions of the Soviet forces. If we wanted to prevent the risk of a surprise attack, the crews had to have orders to shoot. The Soviet Forces Command can give you further details on what happened with the plane that was shot down.

In the past, violations of our airspace were de facto and were conducted furtively. Yesterday the American Government tried to make official the privilege of violating our air space at any time, day and night. This we could not accept because it would mean renouncing our sovereign prerogative. Nevertheless, we agree to avoid an incident at this moment that could gravely harm the negotiations. We will instruct the Cuban batteries to hold their fire while the negotiations last, without reversing the decision we announced yesterday to defend our air space. We must consider the dangers of possible incidents in the present conditions of high tension.

I also wish to inform you that we are opposed, by principle, to inspections on our territory.

I appreciate the enormous efforts which you have made to maintain the peace, and we totally agree with the necessity to fight for this aim. If we achieve it in a just, solid, and permanent way it will be an enormous service to humanity.

Fraternally,

Fidel Castro

Source: http://www.cubanet.org/htdocs/ref/dis/10110201.htm.

Letter to Fidel Castro from Nikita Khrushchev stating Khrushchev will help to defend Cuba

October 30, 1962

Dear Comrade Fidel Castro:

We have received your letter of October 28, along with the reports of the conversations that you and President Dorticos had with our ambassador.

We understand your situation and are taking into account your difficulties in this first stage following the elimination of the maximum tension that resulted from the threat of an attack by American imperialists which you expected at any moment.

We understand that for you certain difficulties may have emerged as a consequence of the promises we made to the United States to withdraw the missile bases from Cuba in exchange for their promise to abandon their plans to invade Cuba and to prevent their allies in the Western hemisphere from doing so, to end their so-called "quarantine"—their blockade of Cuba. This commitment has led to an end to the conflict in the Caribbean, a conflict which implied, as you can well understand, a superpower confrontation and its transformation into a world war where the missiles and thermonuclear weapons would have been used. According to our ambassador, certain Cubans feel that the Cuban people would prefer a different kind of statement, one that would not deal with the withdrawal of the missiles. It is possible that such feelings exist among the people. But we, politicians and heads of state, are the people's leaders and the people do not know everything. This is why we must march at the head of the people. Then they will follow and respect us.

If, by giving in to popular sentiment, we had allowed ourselves to be swept up by the more inflamed sectors of the populace, and if we had refused to reach a reasonable agreement with the government of the USA, war would have probably broken out, resulting in millions of deaths. Those who survived would have blamed the leaders for not having taken the measures that would have avoided this war of extermination.

The prevention of war and of an attack on Cuba did not depend only on the measures taken by our governments, but also on the analysis and examination of the enemy's actions near your territory. In short, the situation had to be considered as a whole.

Some people say that we did not consult sufficiently with each other before taking the decision of which you know.

In fact, we consider that consultations did take place, dear Comrade Fidel Castro, since we received your cables, one more alarming than the other, and finally your cable of October 27 where you said that you were almost certain that an attack against Cuba was imminent. According to you it was only a matter of time: 24 or 72 hours.

Having received this very alarming cable from you, and knowing of your courage, we believed the alert to be totally justified.

Wasn't that consultation on our part? We interpreted that cable as a sign of maximum alert. But if we had carried on with our consultations in such conditions, knowing that the bellicose and unbridled militarists of the United States wanted to seize the occasion to attack Cuba, we would have been wasting our time and the strike could have taken place.

We think that the presence of our strategic missiles in Cuba has polarized the attention of the imperialists. They were afraid that they would be used, which is why they risked wanting to eliminate them, either by bombing them or by invading Cuba. And we must recognize that they had the capability to put them out of action. This is why, I repeat, your sense of alarm was totally justified.

In your cable of October 27 you proposed that we be the first to carry out a nuclear strike against the enemy's territory. Naturally you understand where that would lead us. It would not be a simple strike, but the start of a thermonuclear world war.

Dear Comrade Fidel Castro, I find your proposal to be wrong, even though I understand your reasons.

We have lived through a very grave moment, a global thermonuclear war could have broken out. Of course the United States would have suffered enormous losses, but the Soviet Union and the whole socialist bloc would have also suffered greatly. It is even difficult to say how things would have ended for the Cuban people. First of all, Cuba would have burned in the fires of war. Without a doubt the Cuban people would have fought courageously but, also without a doubt, the Cuban people would have perished heroically. We struggle against imperialism, not in order to die, but to draw on all of our potential, to lose as little as possible, and later to win more, so as to be a victor and make communism triumph.

The measures which we have adopted have allowed us to reach the goal which we had set when we decided to send the missiles to Cuba. We have extracted from the United States the commitment not to invade Cuba and not to allow their Latin American allies to do so. We have accomplished all of this without a nuclear war.

WORKING WITH SOURCES

1. Why was Castro so insistent in drawing Khrushchev's attention to violations of Cuba's sovereignty by the United States?
2. How did Khrushchev attempt to calm Castro down? Why did he do so, and what does the document reveal about his intentions during this crisis?

29.4 Ho Chi Minh, "The Path Which Led Me to Leninism," April 1960

On September 2, 1945, the day of Japan's surrender to the United States, the leader of the communist resistance in Indochina, Ho Chi Minh, read a Vietnamese declaration of independence to half a million people in Hanoi. Newly liberated from occupation by Nazi Germany, France hoped to reassert its power in the region it had colonized in the previous century, but the communist Vietminh refused to budge from their demands for independence. The French persuaded the United States that this colonial conflict was an outgrowth of the larger Cold War between the West and the Soviet Union, and the American administrations of Presidents Truman and Eisenhower (1945–1961) provided financial and moral support to the French as they clashed with Vietnamese insurgents. The French surrendered in 1954, but Vietnam was divided. The United States continued its involvement in South Vietnam—soon to be accelerated with the dispatch of military advisors and military personnel by Presidents Eisenhower and Kennedy (1961–1963). Published in April 1960 in a Soviet journal entitled *Problems of the East*, this statement by Ho Chi Minh encapsulates his thinking on the example of Vladimir Lenin in his own struggle against Western imperialism.

After World War I, I made my living in Paris, now as a retoucher at a photographer's, now as painter of "Chinese antiquities" (made in France!). I would distribute leaflets denouncing the crimes committed by the French colonialists in Viet Nam.

At that time, I supported the October Revolution only instinctively, not yet grasping all its historic importance. I loved and admired Lenin because he was a great patriot who liberated his compatriots; until then, I had read none of his books.

Source: Ho Chi Minh, *Selected Works*, vol. 4 (Hanoi: Foreign Languages Publishing House, 1962), available online at http://www.marxists.org/reference/archive/ho-chi-minh/works/1960/04/x01.htm

The reason for my joining the French Socialist Party was that these "ladies and gentlemen"—as I called my comrades at that moment—had shown their sympathy towards me, towards the struggle of the oppressed peoples. But I understood neither what was a party, a trade-union, nor what was socialism nor communism.

Heated discussions were then taking place in the branches of the Socialist Party, about the question whether the Socialist Party should remain in the Second International, should a Second and a half International be founded or should the Socialist Party join Lenin's Third International? I attended the meetings regularly, twice or thrice a week and attentively listened to the discussion. First, I could not understand thoroughly. Why were the discussions so heated? Either with the Second, Second and a half or Third International, the revolution could be waged. What was the use of arguing then? As for the First International, what had become of it?

What I wanted most to know—and this precisely was not debated in the meetings—was: which International sides with the peoples of colonial countries?

I raised this question—the most important in my opinion—in a meeting. Some comrades answered: It is the Third, not the Second International. And a comrade gave me Lenin's "Thesis on the national and colonial questions" published by l'Humanité to read.

There were political terms difficult to understand in this thesis. But by dint of reading it again and again, finally I could grasp the main part of it. What emotion, enthusiasm, clear-sightedness and confidence it instilled into me! I was overjoyed to tears. Though sitting alone in my room, I shouted out aloud as if addressing large crowds: "Dear martyr compatriots! This is what we need, this is the path to our liberation!"

After then, I had entire confidence in Lenin, in the Third International.

Formerly, during the meetings of the Party branch, I only listened to the discussion; I had a vague belief that all were logical, and could not differentiate as to who were right and who were wrong. But from then on, I also plunged into the debates and discussed with fervour. Though I was still lacking French words to express all my thoughts, I smashed the allegations attacking Lenin and the Third International with no less vigour. My only argument was: "If you do not condemn colonialism, if you do not side with the colonial people, what kind of revolution are you waging?"

. . .

At first, patriotism, not yet communism, led me to have confidence in Lenin, in the Third International. Step by step, along the struggle, by studying Marxism-Leninism parallel with participation in practical activities, I gradually came upon the fact that only socialism and communism can liberate the oppressed nations and the working people throughout the world from slavery.

WORKING WITH SOURCES

1. What did Ho make of the inner divisions among socialists? How did these divisions affect the interests of the Vietnamese, as he saw them?
2. In what respects did Ho see Lenin as a liberator of all "colonized" peoples? Was he justified in this conclusion?

29.5 Indira Gandhi, "What Educated Women Can Do," November 23, 1974

The only child of Jawaharlal Nehru, the first prime minister of India, Indira Gandhi served in turn as prime minister between 1966 and 1977 and again from 1980 until her assassination in 1984. She was the third of the country's prime ministers and the first female to hold the position. Gandhi pursued many of the same policies as her father, supported the Non-Aligned Movement, and was especially concerned to promote the interests of the women and girls of her nation and of the world. This speech, delivered to students in a women's college, reveals her concern to combine women's rights with India's drive for modernization.

An ancient Sanskrit saying says, woman is the home and the home is the basis of society. It is as we build our homes that we can build our country. If the home is inadequate—either inadequate in material goods and necessities or inadequate in the sort of friendly, loving atmosphere that every child needs to grow and develop—then that country cannot have harmony and no country which does not have harmony can grow in any direction at all.

That is why women's education is almost more important than the education of boys and men. We—and by "we" I do not mean only we in India but all the world—have neglected women's education. It is fairly recent. Of course, not to you but when I was a child, the story of the early days of women's education in England, for instance, was very current. Everybody remembered what had happened in the early days.

I remember what used to happen here. I still remember the days when living in old Delhi even as a small child of seven or eight. I had to go out in a **doli** if I left the house. We just did not walk. Girls did not walk in the streets. First, you had your sari with which you covered your head, then you had another shawl or something with which you covered your

hand and all the body, then you had a white shawl, with which every thing was covered again although your face was open fortunately. Then you were in the doli, which again was covered by another cloth. And this was in a family or community which did not observe **purdah** of any kind at all. In fact, all our social functions always were mixed functions but this was the atmosphere of the city and of the country.

Now, we have got education and there is a debate all over the country whether this education is adequate to the needs of society or the needs of our young people. I am one of those who always believe that education needs a thorough overhauling. But at the same time, I think that everything in our education is not bad, that even the present education has produced very fine men and women, especially scientists and experts in different fields, who are in great demand all over the world and even in the most affluent countries. Many of our young people leave us and go abroad because they get higher salaries, they get better conditions of work.

. . .

Sometimes, I am very sad that even people who do science are quite unscientific in their thinking and in their other actions—not what they are doing in the

---

Doli: A covered litter.

Purdah: Ritual seclusion of females.

Source: http://www.edchange.org/multicultural/speeches/indira_gandhi_educated.html.

laboratories but how they live at home or their attitudes towards other people. Now, for India to become what we want it to become with a modern, rational society and firmly based on what is good in our ancient tradition and in our soil, for this we have to have a thinking public, thinking young women who are not content to accept what comes from any part of the world but are willing to listen to it, to analyse it and to decide whether it is to be accepted or whether it is to be thrown out and this is the sort of education which we want, which enables our young people to adjust to this changing world and to be able to contribute to it.

Some people think that only by taking up very high jobs, you are doing something important or you are doing national service. But we all know that the most complex machinery will be ineffective if one small screw is not working as it should and that screw is just as important as any big part. It is the same in national life. There is no job that is too small; there is no person who is too small. Everybody has something to do. And if he or she does it well, then the country will run well.

In our superstition, we have thought that some work is dirty work. For instance, sweeping has been regarded as dirty. Only some people can do it; others should not do it. Now we find that manure is the most valuable thing that the world has today and many of the world's economies are shaking because there is not enough fertilizer—and not just the chemical fertilizer but the ordinary manure, night-soil and all that sort of thing, things which were considered dirty.

Now it shows how beautifully balanced the world was with everything fitted in with something else. Everything, whether dirty or small, had a purpose. We, with our science and technology, have tried to—not purposely, but somehow, we have created an imbalance and that is what is troubling, on a big scale, the economies of the world and also people and individuals. They are feeling alienated from their societies, not only in India but almost in every country in the world, except in places where the whole purpose of education and government has to be to make the people conform to just one idea. We are told that people there are very happy in whatever they are doing. If they are told to clean the streets, well, if he is a professor he has to clean the streets, if he is a scientist he has to do it, and we were told that they are happy doing it. Well, if they are happy, it is alright.

But I do not think in India we can have that kind of society where people are forced to do things because we think that they can be forced maybe for 25 years, maybe for 50 years, but sometime or the other there will be an explosion. In our society, we allow lots of smaller explosions because we think that that will guard the basic stability and progress of society and prevent it from having the kind of chaotic explosion which can retard our progress and harmony in the country.

So, I hope that all of you who have this great advantage of education will not only do whatever work you are doing keeping the national interests in view, but you will make your own contribution to creating peace and harmony, to bringing beauty in the lives of our people and our country. I think this is the special responsibility of the women of India. We want to do a great deal for our country, but we have never regarded India as isolated from the rest of the world. What we want to do is to make a better world. So, we have to see India's problems in the perspective of the larger world problems.

WORKING WITH SOURCES

1. What were the parameters of the "modern, rational society" that Gandhi envisioned?
2. In what terms did she contrast ancient superstitions and modern science, and how did she relate this dichotomy to Indian history and cultural identity?

30. THE END OF THE COLD WAR, WESTERN SOCIAL TRANSFORMATION, AND THE DEVELOPING WORLD, 1963–1991

30.1 Mikhail Gorbachev, *Perestroika: New Thinking for Our Country and the World*, 1987

Two years after becoming first secretary of the Soviet Politburo in 1985, Mikhail Gorbachev (b. 1931) launched his two trademark economic and political programs, perestroika ("restructuring") and glasnost ("openness"). Hoping to revitalize communism, he restructured and partially dismantled the command economy that had dominated the Soviet Union since the Bolshevik Revolution. While perestroika did not work out as intended, glasnost, which permitted frank commentary and the exposure of incompetence and cover-ups by the Soviet leadership, had more wide-ranging consequences for the Soviet Union, which finally collapsed in 1991. Gorbachev summarized his attitude toward domestic politics for Western readers in a book published in English in 1987. However, a significant portion of the book also deals with Cold War tensions, as he was negotiating with President Reagan (1981–1989) of the United States, especially over the destruction of nuclear weapons.

Who Needs the Arms Race and Why?

Pondering the question of what stands in the way of good Soviet-American relations, one arrives at the conclusion that, for the most part, it is the arms race. I am not going to describe its history. Let me just note once again that at almost all its stages the Soviet Union has been the party catching up. By the beginning of the seventies we had reached approximate military-strategic parity, but on a level that is really frightening. Both the Soviet Union and the United States now have the capacity to destroy each other many times over.

It would seem logical, in the face of a strategic stalemate, to halt the arms race and get down to disarmament. But the reality is different. Armories already overflowing continue to be filled with sophisticated new types of weapons, and new areas of military technology are being developed. The US sets the tone in this dangerous, if not fatal pursuit.

I shall not disclose any secret if I tell you that the Soviet Union is doing all that is necessary to maintain up-to-date and reliable defenses. This is our duty to our own people and our allies. At the same time I wish to say quite definitely that this is not our choice. It has been imposed upon us.

All kinds of doubts are being spread among Americans about Soviet intentions in the field of disarmament. But history shows that we can keep the word we gave and that we honor the obligations assumed. Unfortunately, this cannot be said of the United States. The administration is conditioning public opinion, intimidating it with a Soviet threat, and does so with particular stubbornness when a new military budget has to be passed through Congress. We have to ask ourselves why all this is being done and what aim the US pursues.

It is crystal clear that in the world we live in, the world of nuclear weapons, any attempt to use them to solve Soviet-American problems would spell suicide. This is a fact. I do not think that US politicians are unaware of it. Moreover, a truly paradoxical situation has now developed. Even if one country engages in a steady arms build up while the other does nothing, the side that arms itself will all the same gain nothing. The weak side may simply explode all its nuclear charges, even on its own territory, and that would mean suicide for it and a slow death for the enemy. This is why any striving for military superiority means chasing one's own tail. It can't be used in real politics.

Nor is the US in any hurry to part with another illusion. I mean its immoral intention to bleed the Soviet Union white economically, to prevent us from carrying out our plans of construction by dragging us ever deeper into the quagmire of the arms race.

. . .

We sincerely advise Americans: try to get rid of such an approach to our country. Hopes of using any advantages in technology or advanced equipment so as to gain superiority over our country are futile. To act on the assumption that the Soviet Union is in a "hopeless position" and that it is necessary just to press it harder to squeeze out everything the US wants is to err profoundly. Nothing will come of these plans. In real politics there can be no wishful thinking. If the Soviet Union, when it was much weaker than now, was in a position to meet all the challenges that it faced, then indeed only a blind person would be unable to see that our capacity to maintain strong defenses and

simultaneously resolve social and other tasks has enormously increased.

I shall repeat that as far as the United States foreign policy is concerned, it is based on at least two delusions. The first is the belief that the economic system of the Soviet Union is about to crumble and that the USSR will not succeed in restructuring. The second is calculated on Western superiority in equipment and technology and, eventually, in the military field. These illusions nourish a policy geared toward exhausting socialism through the arms race, so as to dictate terms later. Such is the scheme; it is naïve.

Current Western policies aren't responsible enough, and lack the new mode of thinking. I am outspoken about this. If we don't stop now and start practical disarmament, we may all find ourselves on the edge of a precipice. Today, as never before, the Soviet Union and the United States need responsible policies. Both countries have their political, social and economic problems: a vast field for activities. Meanwhile, many brain trusts work at strategic plans and juggle millions of lives. Their recommendations boil down to this: the Soviet Union is the most horrible threat for the United States and the world. I repeat: it is high time this caveman mentality was given up. Of course, many political leaders and diplomats have engaged in just such policies based on just such a mentality for decades. But their time is past. A new outlook is necessary in a nuclear age. The United States and the Soviet Union need it most in their bilateral relations.

We are realists. So we take into consideration the fact that in a foreign policy all countries, even the smallest, have their own interests. It is high time great powers realized that they can no longer reshape the world according to their own patterns. That era has receded or, at least, is receding into the past.

WORKING WITH SOURCES

1. Why does Gorbachev describe American foreign policy as being dictated by "illusions" and "delusions"? Was he being disingenuous or hypocritical in this assertion?
2. In what ways was Gorbachev advocating a global position on the problems of the world? Was he also guided by "delusions" in this advocacy?

30.2   Martin Luther King, Jr., "I Have a Dream," August 28, 1963

Under the accelerating pressure of the American civil rights movement—and with images of African Americans being attacked and beaten as they demanded equality beaming across television screens—President Kennedy introduced civil rights legislation during his administration. Realizing that advocacy of this position might endanger the position of his Democratic Party, particularly in the South, in the elections of 1964, Kennedy continued to find ways to shape American public opinion while also cajoling Congress to implement this legislation. Civil rights advocates, spearheaded by the Reverend Dr. Martin Luther King, Jr. (1929–1968), convened in a march on Washington, DC, in August 1963. Marchers explicitly demanded "jobs and freedom." While the electrifying speech King gave on that day is more remembered for its stirring conclusion about his "dream" and about letting "freedom ring," the prepared remarks at the beginning of the speech reveal even more of King's brilliance and the depth of his political thought.

I am happy to join with you today in what will go down in history as the greatest demonstration for freedom in the history of our nation.

Five score years ago, a great American, in whose symbolic shadow we stand today, signed the Emancipation Proclamation. This momentous decree came as a great beacon light of hope to millions of Negro slaves who had been seared in the flames of withering injustice. It came as a joyous daybreak to end the long night of their captivity.

But one hundred years later, the Negro still is not free. One hundred years later, the life of the Negro is still sadly crippled by the manacles of segregation and the chains of discrimination. One hundred years later, the Negro lives on a lonely island of poverty in the midst of a vast ocean of material prosperity. One hundred years later, the Negro is still languished in the corners of American society and finds himself an exile in his own land. And so we've come here today to dramatize a shameful condition.

In a sense we've come to our nation's capital to cash a check. When the architects of our republic wrote the magnificent words of the Constitution and the Declaration of Independence, they were signing a promissory note to which every American was to fall heir. This note was a promise that all men, yes, black men as well as white men, would be guaranteed the "unalienable Rights" of "Life, Liberty and the pursuit of Happiness." It is obvious today that America has defaulted on this promissory note, insofar as her citizens of color are concerned. Instead of honoring this sacred obligation, America has given the Negro people a bad check, a check which has come back marked "insufficient funds."

But we refuse to believe that the bank of justice is bankrupt. We refuse to believe that there are insufficient funds in the great vaults of opportunity of this nation. And so, we've come to cash this check, a check that will give us upon demand the riches of freedom and the security of justice.

We have also come to this hallowed spot to remind America of the fierce urgency of Now. This is no time to engage in the luxury of cooling off or to take the tranquilizing drug of gradualism. Now is the time to make real the promises of democracy. Now is the time to rise from the dark and desolate valley of segregation to the sunlit path of racial justice. Now is the time to lift our nation from the quicksands of racial injustice to the solid rock of brotherhood. Now is the time to make justice a reality for all of God's children.

It would be fatal for the nation to overlook the urgency of the moment. This sweltering summer of the Negro's legitimate discontent will not pass until there is an invigorating autumn of freedom and equality. Nineteen sixty-three is not an end, but a beginning. And those who hope that the Negro needed to blow off steam and will now be content will have a rude awakening if the nation returns to business as usual. And there will be neither rest nor tranquility in America until the Negro is granted his citizenship rights. The whirlwinds of revolt will continue to shake the foundations of our nation until the bright day of justice emerges.

But there is something that I must say to my people, who stand on the warm threshold which leads into the palace of justice: In the process of gaining our rightful place, we must not be guilty of wrongful deeds. Let us not seek to satisfy our thirst for freedom by drinking from the cup of bitterness and hatred. We must forever conduct our struggle on the high plane of dignity and discipline. We must not allow our creative protest to degenerate into physical violence. Again and again, we must rise to the majestic heights of meeting physical force with soul force.

The marvelous new militancy which has engulfed the Negro community must not lead us to a distrust of all white people, for many of our white brothers, as evidenced by their presence here today, have come to realize that their destiny is tied up with our destiny. And they have come to realize that their freedom is inextricably bound to our freedom.

We cannot walk alone.

And as we walk, we must make the pledge that we shall always march ahead.

We cannot turn back.

There are those who are asking the devotees of civil rights, "When will you be satisfied?" We can never be satisfied as long as the Negro is the victim of the unspeakable horrors of police brutality. We can never be satisfied as long as our bodies, heavy with the fatigue of travel, cannot gain lodging in the motels of the highways and the hotels of the cities. We cannot be satisfied as long as the Negro's basic mobility is from a smaller ghetto to a larger one. We can never be satisfied as long as our children are stripped of their self-hood and robbed of their dignity by signs stating: "For Whites Only." We cannot be satisfied as long as a Negro in Mississippi cannot vote and a Negro in New York believes he has nothing for which to vote. No, no, we are not satisfied, and we will not be satisfied until "justice rolls down like waters, and righteousness like a mighty stream."

WORKING WITH SOURCES

1. How and why did King use financial metaphors to describe the position of African Americans a century after their supposed "emancipation"?
2. How did he describe the rights and equality of African Americans as being in the interests of *all* Americans?

30.3 Simone de Beauvoir, *The Second Sex*, 1949

Encouraged by the successful strategy and tactics of the civil rights and antiwar movements, a new assertiveness also marked the drive for women's rights after the conclusion of the World War II. One important voice in the movement for women's freedoms was that of a leading French philosopher and intellectual, Simone de Beauvoir (1908–1986). Her lengthy, detailed, and compelling

Source: Simone de Beauvoir, *The Second Sex*, trans. and ed. H. M. Parshley (New York: Alfred A. Knopf, 1953), 334–336.

study *The Second Sex*, published in 1949, challenged women to take action on their own behalf in order to gain full equality with their male counterparts. Her analysis traced the origins of sexism and a sense of women's inferiority to the unique circumstances of girlhood and to society's instilling of "feminine" characteristics in young women. Only by breaking the barriers of societal expectations for "well-bred young girls," she argued, could women achieve the goal of true and complete equality with men.

The housekeeping chores and common drudgery, which mothers do not hesitate to impose on schoolgirls or apprentices, overwork them in the end. During the war I saw students in my classes at Sèvres overburdened with family tasks superimposed upon their schoolwork: one came down with Pott's disease, another with meningitis. The mother, as we shall see, is secretly hostile to her daughter's liberation, and she takes to bullying her more or less deliberately; but the boy's effort to become a man is respected, and he is granted much liberty. The girl is required to stay at home, her comings and goings are watched: she is in no way encouraged to take charge of her own amusements and pleasures. It is unusual to see women organize by themselves a long hike or a trip on foot or by bicycle, or devote themselves to games such as billiards or bowling.

Beyond the lack of initiative that is due to women's education, custom makes independence difficult for them. If they roam the streets, they are stared at and accosted. I know young girls who, without being at all timid, find no enjoyment in taking walks alone in Paris because, importuned incessantly, they must be always on the alert, which spoils their pleasure. If girl students run in gay groups through the streets, as boys do, they make a spectacle of themselves; to walk with long strides, sing, talk, or laugh loudly, or eat an apple, is to give provocation; those who do will be insulted or followed or spoken to. Careless gaiety is in itself bad deportment; the self-control that is imposed on women and becomes second nature in "the well-bred young girl" kills spontaneity; her lively exuberance is beaten down. The result is tension and ennui.

This ennui is catching: young girls quickly tire of one another; they do not band together in their prison for mutual benefit; and this is one of the reasons why the company of boys is necessary to them.

This incapacity to be self-sufficient engenders a timidity that extends over their entire lives and is marked even in their work. They believe that outstanding success is reserved for men; they are afraid to aim too high. We have seen that little girls of fourteen, comparing themselves with boys, declared that "the boys are better." This is a debilitating conviction. It leads to laziness and mediocrity. A young girl, who had no special deference for the stronger sex, was reproaching a man for his cowardice; it was remarked that she herself was a coward. "Oh, a woman, that's different!" declared she, complacently.

The fundamental reason for such defeatism is that the adolescent girl does not think herself responsible for her future; she sees no use in demanding much of herself since her lot in the end will not depend on her own efforts. Far from consigning herself to man because she recognizes her inferiority, it is because she is thus consigned to him that, accepting the idea of her inferiority, she establishes its truth.

And, actually, it is not by increasing her worth as a human being that she will gain value in men's eyes; it is rather by modeling herself upon their dreams. When still inexperienced, she is not always aware of this fact. She may be as aggressive as the boys; she may try to make their conquest with a rough authority, a proud frankness; but this attitude almost surely dooms her to failure. All girls, from the most servile to the haughtiest, learn in time that to please they must abdicate. Their mothers enjoin upon them to treat the boys no longer as comrades, not to make advances, to take a passive role. If they wish to start a friendship or a flirtation, they must carefully avoid seeming to take the initiative in it; men do not like *garçons manqués*, or bluestockings, or brainy women; too much daring, culture, or intelligence, too much character, will frighten them. In most novels, as George Eliot remarks, it is the blonde and silly heroine who is in the end victorious over the more mannish brunette; and in *The Mill on the Floss* Maggie tries in vain to reverse the roles; but she finally dies and the blonde Lucy marries Stephen. In *The Last of the Mohicans* the vapid Alice gains the hero's heart, not the valiant Clara; in *Little Women* the likable Jo is only a childhood playmate for Laurie; his love is reserved for the insipid Amy and her curls.

WORKING WITH SOURCES

1. How, in de Beauvoir's estimation, do young women internalize feelings of inferiority and carry these ideas with them into adulthood?
2. What role do the practical, daily experiences of women in the wider world play in the development of "feminine" expectations? Can these be overcome?

30.4 Coverage of the Tiananmen Square Protests, 1989

In May 1989, a protest movement gathered strength in Tiananmen Square in Beijing, as students convened and constructed a large statue called the Goddess of Democracy. By the beginning of June, the movement had turned into a generalized protest by workers and ordinary citizens in addition to the students. When they refused to disperse, the government sent in the army on June 4 to crush what, to many in the Communist Party, had become an incipient rebellion. The image of a lone man attempting to face down an approaching tank became the instant icon of the movement, but there are many other arresting narratives of the events that occurred during this protest. On the 15th anniversary of the suppression of these protests, the British Broadcasting Corporation interviewed survivors and eyewitnesses, gathering their testimonies into the report excerpted below.

Witnessing Tiananmen: Clearing the Square

The BBC's Chinese Service has interviewed some of those who witnessed the protests and subsequent bloodshed.

Zhang Boli was deputy director of the students' hunger strike at Tiananmen Square. He then spent two years on the run before fleeing to the United States, where he now lives.

"While we were making preparations news came from all sides saying that the troops had started to open fire.

I remember many students ran to the square with blood running down their faces.

In some places, troops were shooting and in some places there were clashes. Zhang Huajie had actually been beaten up. When he ran to the square his face was full of blood.

He grabbed the microphone and spoke into it: "Fellow students, they have really opened fire now. They are really shooting! They are using their guns and using real bullets!"

I couldn't believe it. We at the square at the time could not really believe it.

There was a speaker's platform under the statue of the Goddess of Democracy. It was at the time when Yan Jiaqi and I had just started to speak, the troops arrived. And they were moving into Tiananmen Square.

Under the floodlight I could see all those dark helmets moving like waves into the square towards us. I felt that the final moment must have come.

Source: http://news.bbc.co.uk/2/hi/asia-pacific/3775907.stm.

So I spoke to the students, telling them that we should still behave in the spirit we had adopted all along: "We will not fight back even if we are beaten up, and we will not talk back even if we are cursed upon."

We decided to retreat to the Monument of Heroes to wait there for instructions from our command centre. Finally we reached the Monument.

Later, Zhou Duo and Hou Dejian removed their white vests and, using them as white flags, they walked over to the troops to negotiate. After all, Hou Dejian was a famous singer of some influence. He couldn't be cast as an anti-revolutionary rebel.

When Zhou Duo returned he told the students: "They say over there 'We'll give you only half an hour to leave, to evacuate. If you don't, you will have to bear the consequences.'"

So a very important decision was to be made at the time. What are we going to do with the several thousand students here? To leave, to evacuate, or not? Actually it was quite obvious at the time that it was time that we should leave. So when Feng Congde took over the microphone he knew that a heavy burden of history was handed to him.

Finally, the lights (at the square) were switched off. When the lights were out the students thought the troops would start shooting. So, many students huddled together. When the lights were out the microphone was also cut off.

Feng Congde then used a loud-speaker to speak to the students: "Fellow students, we have two opinions here. One says we should leave now. Another says we should stay put. As I can't see you, please speak aloud to respond. I will first say "WE WILL NOT LEAVE." If you agree, please say aloud WE AGREE. Then I will say "WE WILL LEAVE." If you agree, please say "AGREE." I'll see which response is louder."

Actually it was not easy to tell which response from the crowd was louder.

Feng Congde quickly made a wise decision: "I am standing here. This is the highest place. I could hear the response for us TO LEAVE was louder. So the command centre have now decided WE SHOULD LEAVE."

After it was decided that we should leave, they left only a very small gap for us to leave—just about as wide as this room. But nobody dared to move first.

. . .

The guns of the People's Army were pointing at [us] and they were loaded. They were holding machine guns. With one pull of the finger they could fire on us.

Hou Dejian went over to say: "Would it be OK for you people to raise your guns a bit higher and point at the sky?"

It was quite a painful experience. But we came out of the Square. And they didn't fire on us. I think that was because they also had to consider the opinions of the people of the nation and of the whole world.

If they were rash enough to decide to finish the lot of us on the spot, they could, but it would not do them any good at all. So it was still quite peaceful when we left Tiananmen Square.

But when we reached Liulukou suddenly there was trouble.

It was already dawn. A speeding tank came upon us like a gust of wind trying to cut through the lines of people. It was not just trying to run over people, it was also throwing out tear gas.

I remember we were all choking and couldn't open our eyes. We just heard the loud rumblings of the tanks.

About a dozen metres behind me people were crying in hysteria. I think more than 12, or 20-odd people were in a mess of blood and flesh.

It was said later that 11 people were killed there.

WORKING WITH SOURCES

1. What did the Goddess of Democracy mean to the students, and how did they envision their protest?
2. What do the varying reactions of the soldiers sent to quell the protests suggest about the pro-democracy movement in China at that time?

30.5 Salvador Allende, "Last Words to the Nation," September 11, 1973

Salvador Allende led a coalition of socialists, communists, and liberal Christian Democrats to a plurality win as president of Chile in 1970. Many of his policies met opposition within Chile, while his ideology and nationalization of American interests in the country's mines prompted the administration of US President Nixon (1969–1974) to back Allende's opposition. With American blessings and CIA help, Allende was overthrown and murdered in 1973. He would be replaced with the repressive but friendlier (to the United States) regime of General Augusto Pinochet, who remained in office and repeatedly violated the human rights of Chileans until 1990. Nevertheless, the coup that toppled Allende ended with a riveting address by the deposed leader to his people.

My friends,

Surely this will be the last opportunity for me to address you. The Air Force has bombed the towers of Radio Portales and Radio Corporación.

My words do not have bitterness but disappointment. May they be a moral punishment for those who have betrayed their oath: soldiers of Chile, titular commanders in chief, Admiral Merino, who has designated himself Commander of the Navy, and Mr. Mendoza, the despicable general who only yesterday pledged his fidelity and loyalty to the Government, and who also has appointed himself Chief of the Carabineros [national police].

Given these facts, the only thing left for me is to say to workers: I am not going to resign!

Placed in a historic transition, I will pay for loyalty to the people with my life. And I say to them that I am certain that the seed which we have planted in the good conscience of thousands and thousands of Chileans will not be shriveled forever.

They have strength and will be able to dominate us, but social processes can be arrested neither by crime nor force. History is ours, and people make history.

Workers of my country: I want to thank you for the loyalty that you always had, the confidence that you deposited in a man who was only an interpreter of great yearnings for justice, who gave his word that he would respect the Constitution and the law and did just that. At this definitive moment, the last moment when I can address you, I wish you to take advantage of the lesson: foreign capital, imperialism, together with the reaction, created the climate in which the Armed Forces broke their tradition, the tradition taught by General Schneider and reaffirmed by Commander Araya, victims of the same social sector which will today be in their homes hoping, with foreign assistance, to retake power to continue defending their profits and their privileges.

I address, above all, the modest woman of our land, the *campesina* who believed in us, the worker who labored more, the mother who knew our concern for children. I address professionals of Chile, patriotic professionals, those who days ago continued working against the sedition sponsored by professional associations, class-based associations that also defended the advantages which a capitalist society grants to a few.

I address the youth, those who sang and gave us their joy and their spirit of struggle. I address the man of Chile, the worker, the farmer, the intellectual, those who will be persecuted, because in our country fascism has been already present for many hours—in terrorist attacks, blowing up the bridges, cutting the railroad tracks, destroying the oil and gas pipelines,

Source: https://www.marxists.org/archive/allende/1973/september/11.htm.

in the face of the silence of those who had the obligation to protect them. They were committed. History will judge them.

. . .

Workers of my country, I have faith in Chile and its destiny. Other men will overcome this dark and bitter moment when treason seeks to prevail. Go forward knowing that, sooner rather than later, the great avenues will open again where free men will walk to build a better society.

Long live Chile! Long live the people! Long live the workers!

These are my last words, and I am certain that my sacrifice will not be in vain, I am certain that, at the very least, it will be a moral lesson that will punish felony, cowardice, and treason.

WORKING WITH SOURCES

1. How did Allende combine the notions of "patriotism" and resistance to "foreign capital"?
2. What forces and institutions were most guilty, in his assessment, of betraying the economic and political interests of ordinary Chileans?

31. A FRAGILE CAPITALIST-DEMOCRATIC WORLD ORDER, 1991–2014

31.1 Osama bin Laden, "Declaration of War Against the Americans Occupying the Land of the Two Holy Places," August 23, 1996

In 1992, al-Qaeda ("the base") under the leadership of Osama bin Laden (1957–2011) had emerged as a significant terrorist organization operating on an international scale. Bin Laden, the multimillionaire son of a Yemeni-born Saudi Arabian contractor, had fought the Soviet occupation of Afghanistan (1979–1989). He now turned his attention to the United States (who had covertly funded the "mujahid" Afghan resistance in the interest of its own Cold War ambitions). In bin Laden's eyes, America was a godless country without moral principles, bent on a Western crusade to destroy Muslim independence. The al-Qaeda campaign of terrorism climaxed on September 11, 2001, but bin Laden had already ordered bombings and terrorist attacks in several parts of the world in the 1990s. This fatwa (an opinion or ruling based on Islamic law) was issued by bin Laden against the "Zionist-Crusader alliance" in 1996.

It should not be hidden from you that the people of Islam had suffered from aggression, iniquity and injustice imposed on them by the Zionist-Crusaders alliance and their collaborators; to the extent that the Muslims' blood became the cheapest and their wealth as loot in the hands of the enemies. Their blood was spilled in Palestine and Iraq. The horrifying pictures of the massacre of Qana, in Lebanon are still fresh in our memory. Massacres in Tajikistan, Burma, Kashmir, Assam, the Philippines, Fatani, Ogaden, Somalia, Eritrea, Chechnya and in Bosnia-Herzegovina took place, massacres that send shivers in the body and shake the conscience. All of this and the world watch and hear, and not only didn't respond to these atrocities, but also with a clear conspiracy between the USA and its allies and under the cover of the iniquitous United Nations, the dispossessed people were even prevented from obtaining arms to defend themselves.

The people of Islam awakened and realised that they are the main target for the aggression of the Zionist-Crusaders alliance. All false claims and propaganda about "Human Rights" were hammered down and exposed by the massacres that took place against the Muslims in every part of the world.

. . .

Utmost effort should be made to prepare and instigate the Ummah against the enemy, the American-Israeli alliance—occupying the country of the two Holy Places [Saudi Arabia] and the route of the Apostle (Allah's Blessings and Salutations may be on him) to the Furthest Mosque (Al-Aqsa Mosque). Also to remind the Muslims not to be engaged in an internal war among themselves, as that will have grievous consequences namely:

1-consumption of the Muslims' human resources as most casualties and fatalities will be among the Muslim people.

Source: http://www.pbs.org/newshour/updates/military-july-dec96-fatwa_1996/

2-Exhaustion of the economic and financial resources.

3-Destruction of the country infrastructures

4-Dissociation of the society

5-Destruction of the oil industries. The presence of the USA Crusader military forces on land, sea and air of the states of the Islamic Gulf is the greatest danger threatening the largest oil reserve in the world. The existence of these forces in the area will provoke the people of the country and induces aggression on their religion, feelings and pride and push them to take up armed struggle against the invaders occupying the land; therefore spread of the fighting in the region will expose the oil wealth to the danger of being burned up. The economic interests of the States of the Gulf and the land of the two Holy Places will be damaged and even greater damage will be caused to the economy of the world. I would like here to alert my brothers, the Mujahideen, the sons of the nation, to protect this (oil) wealth and not to include it in the battle as it is a great Islamic wealth and a large economic power essential for the soon to be established Islamic state, by Allah's Permission and Grace. We also warn the aggressors, the USA, against burning this Islamic wealth (a crime which they may commit in order to prevent it, at the end of the war, from falling in the hands of its legitimate owners and to cause economic damages to the competitors of the USA in Europe or the Far East, particularly Japan which is the major consumer of the oil of the region).

6-Division of the land of the two Holy Places, and annexing of the northerly part of it by Israel. Dividing the land of the two Holy Places is an essential demand of the Zionist-Crusader alliance. The existence of such a large country with its huge resources under the leadership of the forthcoming Islamic State, by Allah's Grace, represent a serious danger to the very existence of the Zionist state in Palestine. The Nobel Ka'ba,—the Qiblah of all Muslims—makes the land of the two Holy Places a symbol for the unity of the Islamic world. Moreover, the presence of the world largest oil reserve makes the land of the two Holy Places an important economical power in the Islamic world. The sons of the two Holy Places are directly related to the life style (Seerah) of their forefathers, the companions, may Allah be pleased with them. They consider the Seerah of their forefathers as a source and an example for re-establishing the greatness of this Ummah and to raise the word of Allah again. Furthermore the presence of a population of fighters in the south of Yemen, fighting in the cause of Allah, is a strategic threat to the Zionist-Crusader alliance in the area. The Prophet (ALLAH'S BLESSING AND SALUTATIONS ON HIM) said: (around twelve thousands will emerge from Aden/Abian helping—the cause of—Allah and His messenger, they are the best, in the time, between me and them) narrated by Ahmad with a correct trustworthy reference.

7-An internal war is a great mistake, no matter what reasons there are for it. The presence of the occupier—the USA—forces will control the outcome of the battle for the benefit of the international **Kufr**.

. . .

Our Lord, guide this Ummah, and make the right conditions (by which) the people of your obedience will be in dignity and the people of disobedience in humiliation, and by which the good deeds are enjoined and the bad deeds are forebode.

Our Lord, bless Muhammad, Your slave and messenger, his family and descendants, and companions and salute him with a (becoming) salutation.

And our last supplication is: All praise is due to Allah.

Kufr: Unbelievers.

WORKING WITH SOURCES

1. How did bin Laden conflate oil interests with the goals of religious regeneration?
2. How and why did he address the Israeli-Palestinian conflict in this document?

31.2   Vladimir Putin, Address to the Duma Concerning the Annexation of Crimea, March 19, 2014

Vladimir Putin, the former KGB officer who has dominated Russian political life since 2000, delivered this remarkable oration after annexing the Crimea region from the nation of Ukraine in March 2014. This move came after a protest movement had driven the pro-Russian president of Ukraine out of office, and as tensions between ethnic Ukrainians and ethnic Russians in the country had erupted into violence in several Ukrainian cities. Once a referendum was held in the Crimean Peninsula about whether to remain within Ukraine or to be united to Russia, Putin, believing that "the numbers speak for themselves," authorized the annexation of the region as Russian territory. In this speech, justifying his country's move against a fellow former Soviet Socialist Republic, Putin appealed to both recent and distant history—and, perhaps, signaled his further intentions for the future.

Dear friends, we have gathered here today in connection with an issue that is of vital, historic significance to all of us. A referendum was held in Crimea on March 16 in full compliance with democratic procedures and international norms.

More than 82 percent of the electorate took part in the vote. Over 96 percent of them spoke out in favour of reuniting with Russia. These numbers speak for themselves.

To understand the reason behind such a choice it is enough to know the history of Crimea and what Russia and Crimea have always meant for each other.

Everything in Crimea speaks of our shared history and pride. This is the location of ancient Khersones, where Prince Vladimir was baptised. His spiritual feat of adopting Orthodoxy predetermined the overall basis of the culture, civilisation and human values that unite the peoples of Russia, Ukraine and Belarus. The graves of Russian soldiers whose bravery brought Crimea into the Russian empire are also in Crimea. This is also Sevastopol—a legendary city with an outstanding history, a fortress that serves as the birthplace of Russia's Black Sea Fleet. Crimea is Balaklava and Kerch, Malakhov Kurgan and Sapun Ridge. Each one of these places is dear to our hearts, symbolising Russian military glory and outstanding valour.

Crimea is a unique blend of different peoples' cultures and traditions. This makes it similar to Russia as a whole, where not a single ethnic group has been lost over the centuries. Russians and Ukrainians, Crimean Tatars and people of other ethnic groups have lived side by side in Crimea, retaining their own identity, traditions, languages and faith.

. . .

In people's hearts and minds, Crimea has always been an inseparable part of Russia. This firm conviction is based on truth and justice and was passed from generation to generation, over time, under any circumstances, despite all the dramatic changes our country went through during the entire 20th century.

After the revolution, the Bolsheviks, for a number of reasons—may God judge them—added large sections of the historical South of Russia to the Republic of Ukraine. This was done with no consideration for the ethnic make-up of the population, and today these areas form the southeast of Ukraine. Then, in 1954, a decision was made to transfer Crimean Region to Ukraine, along with Sevastopol, despite the fact that it was a city of union subordination. This was the personal initiative of the Communist Party head Nikita Khrushchev. What stood behind this decision of his—a desire to win the support of the Ukrainian political

Source: http://rt.com/politics/official-word/vladimir-putin-crimea-address-658/

establishment or to atone for the mass repressions of the 1930's in Ukraine—is for historians to figure out.

What matters now is that this decision was made in clear violation of the constitutional norms that were in place even then. The decision was made behind the scenes. Naturally, in a totalitarian state nobody bothered to ask the citizens of Crimea and Sevastopol. They were faced with the fact. People, of course, wondered why all of a sudden Crimea became part of Ukraine. But on the whole—and we must state this clearly, we all know it—this decision was treated as a formality of sorts because the territory was transferred within the boundaries of a single state. Back then, it was impossible to imagine that Ukraine and Russia may split up and become two separate states. However, this has happened.

Unfortunately, what seemed impossible became a reality. The USSR fell apart. Things developed so swiftly that few people realised how truly dramatic those events and their consequences would be. Many people both in Russia and in Ukraine, as well as in other republics hoped that the Commonwealth of Independent States that was created at the time would become the new common form of statehood. They were told that there would be a single currency, a single economic space, joint armed forces; however, all this remained empty promises, while the big country was gone. It was only when Crimea ended up as part of a different country that Russia realised that it was not simply robbed, it was plundered.

At the same time, we have to admit that by launching the sovereignty parade Russia itself aided in the collapse of the Soviet Union. And as this collapse was legalised, everyone forgot about Crimea and Sevastopol—the main base of the Black Sea Fleet. Millions of people went to bed in one country and awoke in different ones, overnight becoming ethnic minorities in former Union republics, while the Russian nation became one of the biggest, if not the biggest ethnic group in the world to be divided by borders.

Now, many years later, I heard residents of Crimea say that back in 1991 they were handed over like a sack of potatoes. . . .

Like a mirror, the situation in Ukraine reflects what is going on and what has been happening in the world over the past several decades. After the dissolution of bipolarity on the planet, we no longer have stability. Key international institutions are not getting any stronger; on the contrary, in many cases, they are sadly degrading. Our western partners, led by the United States of America, prefer not to be guided by international law in their practical policies, but by the rule of the gun. They have come to believe in their exclusivity and exceptionalism, that they can decide the destinies of the world, that only they can ever be right. They act as they please: here and there, they use force against sovereign states, building coalitions based on the principle *"If you are not with us, you are against us."* To make this aggression look legitimate, they force the necessary resolutions from international organisations, and if for some reason this does not work, they simply ignore the UN Security Council and the UN overall.

This happened in Yugoslavia; we remember 1999 very well. It was hard to believe, even seeing it with my own eyes, that at the end of the 20th century, one of Europe's capitals, Belgrade, was under missile attack for several weeks, and then came the real intervention. Was there a UN Security Council resolution on this matter, allowing for these actions? Nothing of the sort. And then, they hit Afghanistan, Iraq, and frankly violated the UN Security Council resolution on Libya, when instead of imposing the so-called no-fly zone over it they started bombing it too.

. . .

Let me say one other thing too. Millions of Russians and Russian-speaking people live in Ukraine and will continue to do so. Russia will always defend their interests using political, diplomatic and legal means. But it should be above all in Ukraine's own interest to ensure that these people's rights and interests are fully protected. This is the guarantee of Ukraine's state stability and territorial integrity.

We want to be friends with Ukraine and we want Ukraine to be a strong, sovereign and self-sufficient country. Ukraine is one of our biggest partners after all. We have many joint projects and I believe in their success no matter what the current difficulties. Most importantly, we want peace and harmony to reign in Ukraine, and we are ready to work together with other countries to do everything possible to facilitate and support this. But as I said, only Ukraine's own people can put their own house in order.

WORKING WITH SOURCES

1. In what specific ways, and for what purpose, did Putin appeal to the historical past?
2. What does he believe will be the consequences of the end of "bipolarity" in global politics—and of the belief in American "exceptionalism" demonstrated by US military action since 1999?

31.3 Mohammed Bouazizi Triggers the Arab Spring, Tunisia, January 2011

On December 17, 2010, 26-year-old Mohammed Bouazizi set himself on fire in a spectacular act of despair that triggered the "Arab Spring," the initial results of which continue to reverberate throughout the Middle East and the wider world. His act of defiance, and the reactions to it, led to the ouster of Tunisia's dictator Zine El Abidine Ben Ali (ruled 1987–2011), and, once the revolt had spread to Egypt, of Hosni Mubarak (ruled 1981–2011). While this article profiles Bouazizi, and the confrontation with a policewoman that led to his action, at greater length than most portraits, it also connects the street vendor with the media-savvy young leaders of the revolt in Tahrir Square that brought down Mubarak.

On the evening before Mohammed Bouazizi lit a fire that would burn across the Arab world, the young fruit vendor told his mother that the oranges, dates and apples he had to sell were the best he'd ever seen. "With this fruit," he said, "I can buy some gifts for you. Tomorrow will be a good day."

For years, Bouazizi had told his mother stories of corruption at the fruit market, where vendors gathered under a cluster of ficus trees on the main street of this scruffy town, not far from Tunisia's Mediterranean beaches. Arrogant police officers treated the market as their personal picnic grounds, taking bagfuls of fruit without so much as a nod toward payment. The cops took visible pleasure in subjecting the vendors to one indignity after another—fining them, confiscating their scales, even ordering them to carry their stolen fruit to the cops' cars.

Before dawn on Friday, Dec. 17, as Bouazizi pulled his cart along the narrow, rutted stone road toward the market, two police officers blocked his path and tried to take his fruit. Bouazizi's uncle rushed to help his 26-year-old nephew, persuading the officers to let the rugged-looking young man complete his one-mile trek.

The uncle visited the chief of police and asked him for help. The chief called in a policewoman who had stopped Bouazizi, Fedya Hamdi, and told her to let the boy work.

Hamdi, outraged by the appeal to her boss, returned to the market. She took a basket of Bouazizi's apples and put it in her car. Then she started loading a second basket. This time, according to Alladin Badri, who worked the next cart over, Bouazizi tried to block the officer.

"She pushed Mohammed and hit him with her baton," Badri said.

Hamdi reached for Bouazizi's scale, and again he tried to stop her.

Source: Marc Fisher, "In Tunisia, Act of One Fruit Vendor Unleashes Wave of Revolution through Arab World," *Washington Post*, March 26, 2011, available online at http://www.washingtonpost.com/world/in-tunisia-act-of-one-fruit-vendor-sparks-wave-of-revolution-through-arab-world/2011/03/16/AFjfsueB_story.html

Hamdi and two other officers pushed Bouazizi to the ground and grabbed the scale. Then she slapped Bouazizi in the face in front of about 50 witnesses.

Bouazizi wept with shame.

"Why are you doing this to me?" he cried, according to vendors and customers who were there. "I'm a simple person, and I just want to work."

Revolutions are explosions of frustration and rage that build over time, sometimes over decades. Although their political roots are deep, it is often a single spark that ignites them—an assassination, perhaps, or one selfless act of defiance.

. . .

Bouazizi returned to the market and told his fellow vendors he would let the world know how unfairly they were being treated, how corrupt the system was.

He would set himself ablaze.

"We thought he was just talking," said Hassan Tili, another vendor.

A short while later, the vendors heard shouts from a couple of blocks away. Without another word to anyone, Bouazizi had positioned himself in front of the municipal building, poured paint thinner over his body and lit himself aflame.

The fire burned and burned. People ran inside and grabbed a fire extinguisher, but it was empty. They called for police, but no one came. Only an hour and a half after Bouazizi lit the match did an ambulance arrive.

Manoubya Bouazizi said her son's decision "was spontaneous, from the humiliation." Her clear blue eyes welled as her husband placed at her feet a small clay pot filled with a few white-hot pieces of charcoal, their only defense against a cold, raw, rain-swept day. The Bouazizi family has no money, no car, no electricity, but it was not poverty that made her son sacrifice himself, she said. It was his quest for dignity.

. . .

In the days after the revolution in Tunisia, Egypt's state security agents were on high alert. They knew whom to watch. They'd been onto Ahmed Maher for a long time. They'd tapped his phones, recruited informants among his friends, plugged into his e-mail. They knew he was planning something far bigger

than the marches of a few dozen people he'd organized in recent years.

But Maher, 30, was smarter this time. He stayed off e-mail and his cellphone so the authorities couldn't track him. And he worked through Facebook, a phenomenon that seemed to mystify the secret police. (The last time they took him into custody, they asked Maher questions about people who had commented on his Facebook page, apparently thinking he must know every random person who had left a posting.)

In the past, Maher, a soft-spoken civil engineer who looks as if he'd be more at home in a design studio than a demonstration, had spent much of his energy persuading Egyptians that they could speak out against Hosni Mubarak without sacrificing their careers. This time, he had Tunisia on his side.

"Everybody said, 'How come we're not like them?'" Maher said. "We'd just been waiting for something to trigger us."

The contagion of revolution has a way of wiping away differences that usually divide people. History has provided evidence of the phenomenon again and again, in years that became shorthand for waves of change—1848, 1989, and now, in the Arab world, 2011. In each case, corrupt regimes fell to people who suddenly felt free to push back. Stifling job markets, near-absolute political power and a frustrated middle class combined to create a perfect storm in which formerly divided classes joined to rise up against their rulers.

In many revolutions, the tools of oppression seem to crumble in an instant. But no one can be sure in the moment. In Egypt, the security service had foiled Maher before. Back in 2008, they'd read his blog every day as he planned a general strike to protest Mubarak's regime.

On the morning of the strike, "the security apparatus arrested everyone I knew," Maher said, erasing the protest before it could start. The authorities caught up with Maher one morning soon thereafter. Unmarked cars surrounded him. Agents blindfolded Maher, tied his hands and beat him with fists and batons.

"You think you can hide from us?" an agent said. "We can make you disappear."

Before they let him go two days later, Maher had suffered electric shock and beatings—and then the agents pivoted. "You can be head of a small political party," a "good cop" promised. "We can be friends."

Maher instead announced his ordeal to the world. He resumed blogging, writing about educated Egyptians who couldn't get work because they lacked connections, about censorship, about corruption such as that which initially drove him to activism: At his first job, he was crushed to learn that his design firm's plans for modern roads would be ignored because public contracts went to the president's cronies.

Now, Maher watched the news from Tunisia as it hopped across hundreds of Facebook pages. He decided to capitalize on the moment, recruiting friends to help plan the first big protests in Tahrir Square, the sprawling traffic circle between Cairo's colonial-era downtown and the banks of the Nile. They used Facebook to consult with Tunisians, learning how to defend themselves against tear gas (vinegar and Pepsi, applied to the eyes).

It was all about momentum, Maher believed. If the crowds kept growing, the pressure on the regime would become unbearable. They picked a day to strike—Jan. 28. To disperse the police, he devised a plan to enter the square from a dozen directions.

WORKING WITH SOURCES

1. How do the author of the article and the people he interviewed connect Bouazizi's personal humiliation with his resistance to the regime?
2. To what extent was the fall of Mubarak the result of the inability of the regime to react to emerging technologies and to counter resistance fostered by Facebook?

31.4   Arundhati Roy, "Capitalism: A Ghost Story," March 26, 2012

Indian writer Arundhati Roy (b. 1961) won the Man Booker Prize for her brilliant novel *The God of Small Things* (1997), but she is better known today for her speaking and writing on political causes. A strong advocate for the rights of lower-caste people in Indian society, she has extended her concern to matters of Indian domestic and foreign policy, protesting in particular the speed and direction of globalization in her own and in other countries. In the aftermath of the 2008 financial crisis, Roy has continued her criticism of global capitalism and has often come into conflict with the Indian government and leading figures in the Indian business world.

Indian poverty, after a brief period in the wilderness while India "shone," has made a comeback as an exotic identity in the Arts, led from the front by films like *Slumdog Millionaire*. These stories about the poor, their amazing spirit and resilience, have no villains—except the small ones who provide narrative tension and local colour. The authors of these works are the contemporary world's equivalent of the early anthropologists, lauded and honoured for working on "the ground," for their brave journeys into the unknown. You rarely see the rich being examined in these ways.

Source: Arundhati Roy, "Capitalism: A Ghost Story," *Outlook India*, March 26, 2012, available online at http://www.outlookindia.com/article.aspx?280234.

Having worked out how to manage governments, political parties, elections, courts, the media and liberal opinion, there was one more challenge for the neo-liberal establishment: how to deal with growing unrest, the threat of "people's power." How do you domesticate it? How do you turn protesters into pets? How do you vacuum up people's fury and redirect it into blind alleys?

Here too, foundations and their allied organisations have a long and illustrious history. A revealing example is their role in defusing and deradicalising the Black Civil Rights movement in the US in the 1960s and the successful transformation of Black Power into Black Capitalism.

The Rockefeller Foundation, in keeping with J.D. Rockefeller's ideals, had worked closely with Martin Luther King Sr (father of Martin Luther King Jr). But his influence waned with the rise of the more militant organisations—the Student Non-violent Coordinating Committee (SNCC) and the Black Panthers. The Ford and Rockefeller Foundations moved in. In 1970, they donated $15 million to "moderate" black organisations, giving people grants, fellowships, scholarships, job training programmes for dropouts and seed money for black-owned businesses. Repression, infighting and the honey trap of funding led to the gradual atrophying of the radical black organisations.

Martin Luther King Jr made the forbidden connections between Capitalism, Imperialism, Racism and the Vietnam War. As a result, after he was assassinated, even his memory became a toxic threat to public order. Foundations and Corporations worked hard to remodel his legacy to fit a market-friendly format. The Martin Luther King Junior Centre for Non-Violent Social Change, with an operational grant of $2 million, was set up by, among others, the Ford Motor Company, General Motors, Mobil, Western Electric, Procter & Gamble, US Steel and Monsanto. The Center maintains the King Library and Archives of the Civil Rights Movement. Among the many programmes the King Center runs have been projects that "work closely with the United States Department of Defense, the Armed Forces Chaplains Board and others." It co-sponsored the Martin Luther King Jr Lecture Series called 'The Free Enterprise System: An Agent for Non-violent Social Change'. Amen.

. . .

In the United States, as we have seen, corporate-endowed foundations spawned the culture of NGOs. In India, targeted corporate philanthropy began in earnest in the 1990s, the era of the New Economic Policies. Membership to the Star Chamber doesn't come cheap. The Tata Group donated $50 million to that needy institution, the Harvard Business School, and another $50 million to Cornell University. Nandan Nilekani of Infosys and his wife Rohini donated $5 million as a start-up endowment for the India Initiative at Yale. The Harvard Humanities Centre is now the Mahindra Humanities Centre after it received its largest-ever donation of $10 million from Anand Mahindra of the Mahindra Group.

At home, the Jindal Group, with a major stake in mining, metals and power, runs the Jindal Global Law School and will soon open the Jindal School of Government and Public Policy. (The Ford Foundation runs a law school in the Congo.) The New India Foundation funded by Nandan Nilekani, financed by profits from Infosys, gives prizes and fellowships to social scientists. The Sitaram Jindal Foundation endowed by Jindal Aluminium has announced five cash prizes of Rs 1 crore each to be given to those working in rural development, poverty alleviation, environment education and moral upliftment. The Reliance Group's Observer Research Foundation (ORF), currently endowed by Mukesh Ambani, is cast in the mould of the Rockefeller Foundation. It has retired intelligence agents, strategic analysts, politicians (who pretend to rail against each other in Parliament), journalists and policymakers as its research "fellows" and advisors.

ORF's objectives seem straightforward enough: "To help develop a consensus in favour of economic reforms." And to shape and influence public opinion, creating "viable, alternative policy options in areas as divergent as employment generation in backward districts and real-time strategies to counter nuclear, biological and chemical threats."

I was initially puzzled by the preoccupation with "nuclear, biological and chemical war" in ORF's stated objectives. But less so when, in the long list of its 'institutional partners', I found the names of Raytheon and Lockheed Martin, two of the world's leading weapons manufacturers. In 2007, Raytheon announced it was turning its attention to India. Could it be that at least part of India's $32 billion defence budget will be spent on weapons, guided missiles, aircraft, warships and surveillance equipment made by Raytheon and Lockheed Martin?

Do we need weapons to fight wars? Or do we need wars to create a market for weapons? After all, the economies of Europe, US and Israel depend hugely on their weapons industry. It's the one thing they haven't outsourced to China.

In the new Cold War between US and China, India is being groomed to play the role Pakistan played as a US ally in the cold war with Russia. (And look what happened to Pakistan.) Many of those columnists and "strategic analysts" who are playing up the hostilities between India and China, you'll see, can be traced back directly or indirectly to the Indo-American think-tanks and foundations. Being a "strategic partner" of the US does not mean that the Heads of State make friendly phone calls to each other every now and then. It means collaboration (interference) at every level. It means hosting US Special Forces on Indian soil (a Pentagon Commander recently confirmed this to the BBC). It means sharing intelligence, altering agriculture and energy policies, opening up the health and education sectors to global investment. It means opening up retail. It means an unequal partnership in which India is being held close in a bear hug and waltzed around

the floor by a partner who will incinerate her the moment she refuses to dance.

In the list of ORF's 'institutional partners', you will also find the RAND Corporation, Ford Foundation, the World Bank, the Brookings Institution (whose stated mission is to "provide innovative and practical recommendations that advance three broad goals: to strengthen American democracy; to foster the economic and social welfare, security and opportunity of all Americans; and to secure a more open, safe, prosperous and cooperative international system.") You will also find the Rosa Luxemburg Foundation of Germany. (Poor Rosa, who died for the cause of Communism, to find her name on a list such as this one!)

Though capitalism is meant to be based on competition, those at the top of the food chain have also shown themselves to be capable of inclusiveness and solidarity. The great Western Capitalists have done business with fascists, socialists, despots and military dictators. They can adapt and constantly innovate. They are capable of quick thinking and immense tactical cunning.

But despite having successfully powered through economic reforms, despite having waged wars and militarily occupied countries in order to put in place free market "democracies," Capitalism is going through a crisis whose gravity has not revealed itself completely yet. Marx said, "What the bourgeoisie therefore produces, above all, are its own grave-diggers. Its fall and the victory of the proletariat are equally inevitable."

WORKING WITH SOURCES

1. What does Roy assert that the Western and Indian foundations and think tanks are gaining from the money they spend?
2. What does she believe will ultimately result from the global financial crisis that began in 2008?

31.5   United Nations Framework Convention on Climate Change, Copenhagen, 2009

While there has been considerable debate over the last several decades on the nature and degree of global warming, there is general scientific consensus that greenhouse gases are the main contributors to temperature increases on earth. Scientists generally assume that at current rates of greenhouse gas production the earth will reach a "tipping point" of 450 parts per million, with catastrophic consequences for the planet's climate, before the middle of this century. Although 169 nations joined the 2005 Kyoto Protocol to reduce greenhouse emissions, the United States refused to sign the agreement. However, the United States did eventually sign on to an international agreement regarding climate change and the reduction of its global threat under President Barack Obama. This framework document, resulting from a conference held in Copenhagen in 2009, pledges the international community to action on the environment, in both specific and principled terms.

[*The signatory nations*] *have agreed* on this Copenhagen Accord which is operational immediately.

1. We underline that climate change is one of the greatest challenges of our time. We emphasise our strong political will to urgently combat climate change in accordance with the principle of common but differentiated responsibilities and respective capabilities. To achieve the ultimate objective of the Convention to stabilize greenhouse gas concentration in the atmosphere at a level that would prevent dangerous anthropogenic interference with the climate system, we shall, recognizing the scientific view that the increase in global temperature should be below 2 degrees Celsius, on the basis of equity and in the context of sustainable development, enhance our long-term cooperative action to combat climate change. We recognize the critical impacts of climate change and the potential impacts of response measures on countries particularly vulnerable to its adverse effects and stress the need to establish a comprehensive adaptation programme including international support.

2. We agree that deep cuts in global emissions are required according to science, and as documented by the IPCC Fourth Assessment Report with a view to reduce global emissions so as to hold the increase in global temperature below 2 degrees Celsius, and take action to meet this objective consistent with science and on the basis of equity. We should cooperate in achieving the peaking of global and national emissions as soon as possible, recognizing that the time frame for peaking will be longer in developing countries and bearing in mind that social and economic development and poverty eradication are the first and overriding priorities of developing countries and that a low-emission development strategy is indispensable to sustainable development.

3. Adaptation to the adverse effects of climate change and the potential impacts of response measures is a challenge faced by all countries. Enhanced action and international cooperation on adaptation is urgently required to ensure the implementation of the Convention by enabling and supporting the implementation of adaptation actions aimed at

Source: http://unfccc.int/resource/docs/2009/cop15/eng/11a01.pdf.

reducing vulnerability and building resilience in developing countries, especially in those that are particularly vulnerable, especially least developed countries, small island developing States and Africa. We agree that developed countries shall provide adequate, predictable and sustainable financial resources, technology and capacity-building to support the implementation of adaptation action in developing countries.

4. Annex I Parties commit to implement individually or jointly the quantified economy-wide emissions targets for 2020, to be submitted in the format given in Appendix I by Annex I Parties to the secretariat by 31 January 2010 for compilation in an INF document. Annex I Parties that are Party to the Kyoto Protocol will thereby further strengthen the emissions reductions initiated by the Kyoto Protocol. Delivery of reductions and financing by developed countries will be measured, reported and verified in accordance with existing and any further guidelines adopted by the Conference of the Parties, and will ensure that accounting of such targets and finance is rigorous, robust and transparent.

5. Non-Annex I Parties to the Convention will implement mitigation actions, including those to be submitted to the secretariat by non-Annex I Parties in the format given in Appendix II by 31 January 2010, for compilation in an INF document, consistent with Article 4.1 and Article 4.7 and in the context of sustainable development. Least developed countries and small island developing States may undertake actions voluntarily and on the basis of support. Mitigation actions subsequently taken and envisaged by Non-Annex I Parties, including national inventory reports, shall be communicated through national communications consistent with Article 12.1(b) every two years on the basis of guidelines

to be adopted by the Conference of the Parties. Those mitigation actions in national communications or otherwise communicated to the Secretariat will be added to the list in appendix II. Mitigation actions taken by Non-Annex I Parties will be subject to their domestic measurement, reporting and verification the result of which will be reported through their national communications every two years. Non-Annex I Parties will communicate information on the implementation of their actions through National Communications, with provisions for international consultations and analysis under clearly defined guidelines that will ensure that national sovereignty is respected. Nationally appropriate mitigation actions seeking international support will be recorded in a registry along with relevant technology, finance and capacity building support. Those actions supported will be added to the list in appendix II. These supported nationally appropriate mitigation actions will be subject to international measurement, reporting and verification in accordance with guidelines adopted by the Conference of the Parties.

6. We recognize the crucial role of reducing emission from deforestation and forest degradation and the need to enhance removals of greenhouse gas emission by forests and agree on the need to provide positive incentives to such actions through the immediate establishment of a mechanism including REDD-plus, to enable the mobilization of financial resources from developed countries.

7. We decide to pursue various approaches, including opportunities to use markets, to enhance the cost-effectiveness of, and to promote mitigation actions. Developing countries, especially those with low emitting economies should be provided incentives to continue to develop on a low emission pathway.

WORKING WITH SOURCES

1. In what terms does the document attempt to reconcile national policies with international environmental goals?
2. How does the document recognize, and try to account for, the differences in economic development among the world's countries?